Performed Culture

Means: Primacy of spoken language – pedagogical transcription.

Performance rehearsal – FACT & ACT ratio / situated interaction

Learner-centered: learning by experiencing / learning through modification

(NOT used to teach pronunciation

, 拼音 ?

textbook

materials

Lg program:
courses belongs to a program
* Goals: states and shared
Means (curriculum)
Assessment
Defined time frame
Participants

(子): (一)、(二)、(三).
丁(子): (四)、(子)、(一)、(二)、(三).

A publication of The Ohio State University
National East Asian Languages Resource Center

Funded by

The. U.S. Department of Education

Pathways to Advanced Skills series, Volume XI
Series General Editor: Galal Walker

Distributed by Foreign Language Publications
The Ohio State University
198 Hagerty Hall
1775 S. College Road
Columbus, OH 43210-1340

614-292-3838 • 1-800-678-6999 • Fax: 614-688-3355
flpubs.osu.edu

Executive Editor: Galal Walker
Managing Editor: Minru Li
Copy Editor: Melissa Gruzs
Production & Design: Brix Garcia
Distribution Manager: Lauren Barrett

Performed Culture

AN APPROACH TO EAST ASIAN LANGUAGE PEDAGOGY

Matthew B. Christensen

J. Paul Warnick

©National East Asian Languages Resource Center
The Ohio State University

Galal Walker
Executive Editor

This volume prepared and published by

National East Asian Languages Resource Center
The Ohio State University
100 Hagerty Hall
1775 S. College Road
Columbus, OH 43210-1340

614-292-4361 • fax: 614-688-3355
nealrc.osu.edu

Library of Congress Cataloging-in-Publication Data:

Christensen, Matthew B.
Performed culture : an approach to East Asian language pedagogy /
Matthew B. Christensen, J. Paul Warnick.
p. cm. -- (Pathways to advanced skills series ; xi)
Includes bibliographical references and index.
ISBN-13: 978-0-87415-307-1 (alk. paper)
1. East Asia--Languages--Study and teaching--United States. 2.
Chinese language--Study and teaching--United States. 3. Japanese
language--Study and teaching--United States. 4. Korean language--
Study and teaching--United States. I. Warnick, J. Paul, 1959- II.
Title.
PL493.C487 2006
495'.071073--dc22

                                        2006031781

Manufactured in the United States of America

2014 reprinted and bound by
OSU UniPrint, Columbus, OH

ISBN 978-0-87415-307-1

Table of Contents

Chapter Five

A PERFORMATIVE APPROACH TO GRAMMAR, VOCABULARY,

Chapter Six

EVALUATING AND DEVELOPING MATERIALS

Acknowledgments

As graduate students, we had the good fortune and pleasure of studying with Professors Galal Walker and Mari Noda at The Ohio State University. They contributed to our intellectual training there and have been influential in our careers since then. We appreciate their confidence in us, their mentoring, and their friendship.

We would like to thank other mentors who have been particularly influential: Charles Quinn, James Tai, Marjorie Chan, Kirk Denton, Timothy Wong, Robert Sanders, Frank Hsueh, Mineharu Nakayama, and Shelley Quinn.

We have benefited greatly from participating over the years in the Ohio State University SPEAC (Summer Programs East Asian Concentration) programs. As visiting lecturers, we have had the privilege of working with fine students and colleagues and have had the chance to teach and receive feedback on many of the principles presented in this book. During the past several summers, we have spent hours discussing many of the issues in this book with colleagues and students in the SPEAC programs. In particular, we would like to thank Yuko Kuwai, Li Yi, Yu Li, Pat McAloon, Ginger Marcus, Misako Suzuki, and Masayuki Itomitsu for their valuable insights and feedback. We would also like to thank our colleagues Xiaobin Jian and Lindsay Amthor Yotsukura for helping us better understand many language-related issues.

We are also indebted to colleagues at Brigham Young University who have shared ideas about pedagogical issues, including Dana Bourgerie, Masakazu Watabe, and Robert Russell.

An early draft of this book was reviewed and critiqued by graduate students of East Asian pedagogy at The Ohio State University. We thank them for their time and valuable comments; their insights motivated some much-needed revisions.

We are indebted to Konchol Lee, who provided the Korean restaurant script, and to Bruce Grant, who was a valuable resource concerning pedagogical issues in the Korean language and culture. We express appreciation to Aki Shirai for assistance in checking references. We also thank Keiko Moriyama Barney for help with the Japanese restaurant script.

Without the support, in terms of time and financial assistance, that we have received from our college and department at Brigham Young University, this project would not have come to fruition. We especially appreciate the encouragement and support of our former department chair, Dilworth Parkinson, and our current chair, Robert Russell.

Li Minru at the National East Asian Languages Resource Center has been very helpful during the final stages of this project. We appreciate his guidance and editorial oversight. We also express our sincere gratitude to Melissa Gruzs for her invaluable assistance in the editing process, and to Mari Noda and Ooyoung Pyun for help in reviewing the Japanese and Korean data, respectively.

We are grateful for the influence of mentors and colleagues, but we alone are responsible for the content of this book.

Finally, we are profoundly grateful to our wives, Sharon and Mimi, and our children, for their constant support and patience.

Preface

We became acquainted with the notion of *performed culture* as graduate students at The Ohio State University under the tutelage of Professors Galal Walker and Mari Noda. Little did we realize the extent of the influence that this would have on us as teachers of East Asian languages. During the years since graduate school, we have thought at length about the idea of performed culture and its implications for the language-learning process, and we have had the opportunity to apply our ideas in the classroom. We have refined our thinking and practices over the years, and we expect there will be further refinement in the future.

This book is a general summary of our experience and is intended for anyone who is involved in or interested in teaching Chinese, Japanese, or Korean as a foreign language. This includes students in graduate programs for East Asian languages as well as those who are currently teaching these languages at the secondary or postsecondary level. For this reason, we have tried to avoid specialized jargon. We feel that all teachers, even those with considerable experience, can benefit from the information in this book. We hope it will spark ideas and discussions about the pedagogical practices in these languages. At the very least, it can serve as a reminder of what is entailed in teaching and learning an East Asian language. Though we feel that this *performed culture* approach is timely and valuable as a whole, we recognize that some may wish to adopt only certain aspects of this research. However, even small changes can have positive effects.

Learning a foreign language goes far beyond linguistics. The linguistic code is only part of the puzzle, and without appropriate context and training in how and when to use the elements of the linguistic code, language learning becomes far more frustrating than it should be. We have a responsibility as teachers of East Asian Languages to train our students not only in what to say, but also in how to express themselves the way native speakers of the target culture expect people to express themselves in a given situation, whether it be orally or in writing. Furthermore, we need to train our students to interpret and make sense of the target language in a variety of social and cultural contexts. If students leave our programs with only an understanding of grammar and some vocabulary, but without an understanding of how, when, and with whom to use them, then we have done them a disservice. Students might develop excellent linguistic skills, but without the cultural and social skills to support them, they will have a difficult time adapting to life in an East Asian language environment.

Performance is the key to building foreign language competence. Learners must not only understand how to do things in the target language, but they must also have practice and coaching in actually doing it. In this way, they begin to build a memory of how to get things done in the target language in authentic, accurate, and appropriate ways.

For some readers, the ideas presented in this book may seem straightforward, even to the point of being a matter of common sense. However, in our observations and discussions with colleagues around the country and abroad, we have come to realize that this kind of approach is rare. We acknowledge that the performed culture approach may require some rethinking of what it means to learn a foreign language; it also requires quite a bit more planning, preparation time, and effort to implement successfully. However, we feel that the extra time and effort are well spent and that in the long run, our students will be better prepared to survive and thrive in East Asian language communities.

Though the book is written specifically for East Asian languages, we feel that much of the information herein is applicable to other less commonly taught languages as well.

Provo, Utah
Spring 2006

Introduction

THE NEED FOR A NEW APPROACH

In the past two or three decades, there has been a significant increase in cross-cultural communication between the countries of North America and Pacific Rim countries, particularly China (including Taiwan and Hong Kong), Japan, and Korea. This increase in communication has been spurred by increasingly open foreign policies, expanding economic interests, and heightened awareness of and interest in Asian cultures. In an article urging foreign language departments to broaden the range of major world languages offered, Garcia (1998, 10) says, "The increased global awareness of Americans has rendered the literature and other manifestations of the world's major languages and cultures more interesting than before. Students aware of the economic and technological significance of the Asian Rim countries often have a strong motivation to understand Japanese and Chinese culture in depth." The number of Asian Americans living in the United States and Canada and the number of students going to these countries to study have also increased dramatically. For example, there are approximately 47,000 Chinese students studying at American universities and 2,000 Americans studying in China. (Brod and Welles 2000). This has all amounted to an increase in exposure to the peoples and cultures of East Asia. Rising enrollments in Chinese, Japanese, and Korean language courses at colleges and universities are also a result of these recent changes. According to a Modern Language Association (MLA) survey conducted in 2002 (Welles 2004), Japanese enrollments at institutes of higher learning in the United States totaled 52,238,

Chinese enrollments were 34,153, and Korean enrollments were 5,211. These figures reflected a 21.1% increase in Japanese students since 1998, a 20.0% increase in those studying Chinese, and a 16.3% increase in Korean students. According to these statistics, Japanese is the sixth most-commonly studied language, Chinese is seventh, and Korean is fifteenth. Although Japanese ranks sixth in enrollment, students of Japanese comprise only 3.7% of the total number of language learners, because of the large number studying Spanish, French, and German. The rise in enrollments in East Asian languages (EALs) has increased the need for qualified and effective teachers to meet the demands associated with this increase in students. There is a need for "culturally literate" advanced speakers of East Asian languages.

The problem facing the field of East Asian language pedagogy is that the foreign language education tradition in North America has depended heavily on Western European language and ESL pedagogies. There are many areas in which the pedagogical foundation and tradition in teaching Western European languages are insufficient or even misleading when it comes to East Asian languages (specifically, Chinese, Japanese, and Korean). Although there are many published works treating foreign language education, including some that focus on a communicative framework and the importance of culturally contextualized activities, there is still a lack of materials that treat specific linguistic and cultural challenges for native English speakers in approaching foreign languages such as Chinese, Japanese, and Korean from a holistic, culturally centered approach. In addition to the Eurocentric body of published works on the topic, the institution of teaching foreign languages at the postsecondary level is based almost entirely on the learning of Western European languages.

The School of Languages at the Foreign Service Institute (FSI), a U.S. government school for teaching foreign languages to diplomats, categorizes foreign languages into four groups, based on

the amount of time it takes for a learner to reach a specified level of proficiency (Omaggio Hadley 2001). Group One languages in the FSI categorization include French, Spanish, Italian, Norwegian, and Portuguese. Group Two includes Bulgarian, German, Greek, Indonesian, and Hindi. Group Three languages include Czech, Hebrew, Finnish, Polish, Russian, and Turkish. Finally, Group Four is composed only of Arabic, Chinese, Japanese, and Korean. √

The FSI scale ranges from 0, indicating a novice with no functional ability, to 5, suggesting proficiency at the level of an educated native speaker. Level 2 on this scale is equivalent to the Advanced level on the ACTFL (American Council on the Teaching of Foreign Languages) Proficiency Scale. An Advanced learner is said to be one who can handle the following communicative activities:

- describe and narrate in major time or aspect frames;
- deal with most formal and some informal settings;
- discuss concrete and factual topics of personal and public interest;
- be understood without difficulty by speakers unaccustomed to nonnative speakers;
- communicate using paragraph-length discourse (Omaggio Hadley 2001).

According to FSI research, it takes approximately 480 hours of training for the average native English-speaking learner to reach level 2 proficiency in Group One languages. To reach the same level of proficiency for the languages in Group Two, it takes 720 hours, on average, compared to the 480 hours for Group One languages. For Group Three languages, 720 hours also are required to reach a level 2 proficiency; however, other levels of proficiency, both lower and higher, take longer to attain than for Group Two languages. As for Group Four, which includes the three East Asian languages we are concerned with here, to reach a level 2 proficiency requires 1,320 hours of training, nearly triple the time required for Group One languages!

In a typical university setting, 1 year of instruction consists of 30 weeks. Because most foreign language skill classes are held for one hour per day, 1 year of instruction totals 150 hours. Given such an arrangement, to reach level 2 proficiency in Spanish would require 3.2 years of university instruction, on average, and achieving the same level of proficiency in German or Russian would require 4.8 years, based on the FSI figures. To become similarly proficient in Chinese, Japanese, or Korean would require an astonishing 8.8 years! It is obvious that teachers have a responsibility to maximize the efficiency and the effectiveness of instruction.

Why is so much more time required for native English speakers to learn East Asian languages? Is it because they are so different from Western languages? Is it because the methodologies commonly used to teach these languages are somehow lacking? In other words, does the way these languages are taught have any bearing on how long it takes to master them? From the perspective of native English speakers, East Asian languages are vastly different from Indo-European languages. The greater time required to learn EALs may also be due to the common use of methodologies that are based on teaching Indo-European languages to native speakers of other Indo-European languages. In Chapter One, we discuss in detail what makes the development of proficiency in East Asian languages more time-consuming and labor intensive and why existing methodologies fall short, and we introduce a new methodology that is more effective when dealing with these languages.

Truly Foreign Languages

Jorden and Walton (1987, 111) have proposed that languages that are "linguistically unrelated to English—that is, they are non-Indo-European—and spoken within societies that are *culturally in marked contrast* to our own" (emphasis added) may be called *truly foreign languages* (TFLs). They suggest that when the language and culture being studied are in sharp contrast to the learner's native language and culture, the challenges become enormous because the learner's base (native) culture "automatically and unconsciously" influences how the foreign language and culture are perceived. Furthermore, to base one's judgment of the foreign language and culture on one's native culture is both naive and potentially dangerous. Schumann (1976) suggests that the greater the social distance between two cultures, the more difficult it is to learn the second language; conversely, the smaller the social distance (the greater the social solidarity between two cultures), the easier it is to learn the second language. Schumann specifies congruence as a factor in determining social distance: "Congruence or similarity between the culture of the TL (target language) group and that of the 2LL (second language learning) group also affects social distance. If the two cultures are similar, then integration is facilitated and social distance is reduced" (1976, 137). He argues convincingly that societies with very different cultures (he uses the examples of Americans learning Arabic in Saudi Arabia) will have greater social distance, resulting in greater difficulties in learning those languages. Incongruent features include different religions and social customs. Among European languages and cultures, the rift between target and base is not as substantial or as imposing to an eager learner. The social distance between native English speakers and Western European cultures is much smaller than that between English-speaking and East Asian cultures. In short, the primary challenges between the native base and the target may not be linguistic in nature, as might be assumed. We suggest that the more complex part of learning to participate in a truly foreign society lies with the cultural code (Jorden and Walton 1987; Walker 2000; Walker and Noda 2000). The cultural code includes not only the linguistic code (at every level—phonological, morphological, syntactic, discourse, pragmatic) but also many nonlinguistic issues such as body language, gestures, proxemics, 空間關係学 kinesics, and other aspects of behavior. In other words, the cultural code also includes a sense of time and space. Given that behavioral culture in East Asian societies is so different from Western norms, it is no wonder that Chinese, Japanese, and Korean are classified as Group Four languages, those taking the longest time to learn. Complexities in the cultural code as well as differences in the linguistic code raise significant challenges for the Western learner.

Current pedagogical practices seem to fall short in addressing the many unique issues presented by truly foreign languages such as Chinese, Japanese, and Korean. These East Asian languages use orthographies that are very different from the Roman alphabet, which makes progress for learners from Western language backgrounds much slower. Progress can be very uneven because the written language is much more complex and time-consuming to learn than the oral language. It is not as simple as using the written orthography to represent speech, as can be done effectively in Western European languages. Besides this, native speaker language paradigms (traditional views of natives concerning teaching and learning; see Chapter Six) in teaching methodology and materials have also prevented East Asian language programs from reaching their potential. By relying on Western European language or traditional East Asian teaching practices, we fail to prepare our students as well as we can to participate successfully in East Asian language-speaking societies.

The Scope of This Book

This book has two purposes: 1) propose a new approach for dealing with truly foreign languages such as Chinese, Japanese, and Korean based on the idea that becoming proficient in a foreign language is really a matter of *performing culture*, and 2) provide research-based systematic means for teaching East Asian languages within our *performed culture* approach. Though we specifically treat Chinese, Japanese, and Korean and provide examples from these languages, many issues and ideas are applicable and can be adapted to other foreign languages.

This approach has been developed based on research in cultural anthropology, cultural psychology, anthropological linguistics, foreign language pedagogy and performance theory. The term *performed culture* (from Walker 2000) well reflects the issues at stake when teaching and learning a language and culture in marked contrast to one's own. The first half of the term, *performed,* reflects our belief that performance is an essential part of learning how to successfully integrate oneself in the culture and societies of the target language; the second part, *culture,* reflects our belief that language and communication cannot be divorced from the cultural context in which they occur. Consequently, our approach has a strong cultural component with an emphasis on the performative aspect of language learning. We stress the importance of cultural contextualization and authenticity and focus on scripts and stories as an approach to learning. As will be seen, this approach shares some characteristics with the communicative approach and the task-based approach to language teaching and learning.

The ideas we discuss also draw on specific research in the teaching and learning of East Asian languages. We have observed that pedagogical decisions often seem to be based on intuition or philosophy arising from one's own experience as a learner, rather than on empirical data, resulting in less than optimum results.

The first chapter of this book discusses our performed culture approach, which provides a foundation and a rationale for the material presented in subsequent chapters. Chapter Two addresses practical issues related to this approach and emphasizes the primacy of the spoken language. Chapter Three discusses issues in developing listening and speaking skills, and the cultural and social importance of pronunciation and intonation. Chapter Four discusses orthography and developing reading and writing skills. Emphasis is placed on the social role of reading and writing. Grammar, context, and discourse strategies are addressed in Chapter Five. The emphasis in this chapter is on the importance of developing nativelike discourse strategies. Chapter Six addresses authentic materials, with an emphasis on the effective use of video materials in the classroom. The review and development of materials for East Asian languages are the focus of Chapter Seven. The conclusion summarizes our performed culture approach and lists recommendations for using the material in each chapter in the classroom.

*Culture: The shared pattern of behavior and interactions,
cognitive ~~constructs~~ constructions, and affective understanding that
are learned through a process a socialization.*

• A patterned way of being and behaving w/ other ppl in a shared world.

Chapter One

PERFORMED CULTURE

• Based on the idea that language cannot be ~~seperated~~ separated from culture.

Inasmuch as the complexity of the cultural code may be the most difficult aspect of learning East Asian languages, a pedagogical approach that places an emphasis on cultural behavior is desirable. This chapter outlines how this can be done. We begin with a discussion of the importance of culture in the foreign language studies curriculum. To more fully articulate the nature of culture and its relationship to language, we define culture to show how it can be categorized and how certain aspects of culture are more applicable to foreign language studies. We follow this with a description of performance and how performance provides the key to culturally appropriate behavior, both in word and action. We also discuss the concept of script and how learning the expectations and accompanying behavior of specific communicative functions and situations facilitates successful interaction in the target community. Genres and styles of communication are addressed as they relate to learning a foreign language. This chapter ends with a description of the notion of *performed culture* and suggestions for applying the foregoing ideas in functional classroom practice.

THE PRIMACY OF CULTURE

As Walker and Noda (2000) have pointed out, professionals in the field of foreign language pedagogy have recognized the importance of the relationship between language and culture since the early 1950s; the theme of a 1953 seminar held at the University of Michigan, "Developing Cultural Understanding Through Foreign Language Study," bears this out. Many language teaching professionals agree that culture should be a part of the language classroom, and abundant literature from diverse fields suggests that when language is used for communication, it is inextricably connected to a specified cultural context that provides the meaning and enables understanding of the situation.

Walker and Noda have further suggested that learning to speak an East Asian language is really a process of learning how to behave in the corresponding culture. Based on this premise, teaching a foreign language is synonymous with teaching culture. They go on to say, "The implication of this concept of performed culture for language study is that no one really learns a foreign language. Rather we learn how to do particular things in a foreign language; and the more things we learn to do, the more expert we are in that language"(2000, 190).

Although there has been a great deal of research dealing with the importance of culture in language studies, the majority of teachers still seem to consider the teaching of culture separate from language skills. A fairly recent publication, *Pathways to Culture* (Heusinkveld 1997), contains twenty-nine articles on the teaching of culture, the majority of which treat culture as a skill separate from, though related to, language learning. Those that do treat culture as part of the language-learning process relate culture to learning in context, hardly a new concept, though it is a step in the right direction.

Omaggio Hadley (2001) suggests that there are at least three reasons why teachers are reluctant to teach culture in a foreign language class. First, many teachers do not think they have time to teach it; with approximately five hours per week in the classroom for most language classes, no one will deny that time is severely limited. Second, many teachers do not feel comfortable or familiar enough with the target culture to incorporate it into the curriculum. Third, discussing cultural issues in the classroom deals with student attitudes; because cultural issues are not as quantifiable and clear-cut as linguistic information, many teachers consider it a difficult topic to easily integrate into the classroom.

We believe the biggest issue is that most teachers seem to be missing the point. Even though teachers of foreign languages generally agree that culture is inextricably connected to language, most still opt for a linguistic-only focus in the curriculum. In other words, they say one thing and do another, primarily for the reasons just mentioned. It seems to be ingrained in the North American tradition of foreign language teaching that culture is treated as the

10

fifth skill along with listening, speaking, reading, and writing. We see a need to retrain our collective thinking to reflect the idea that the four skills are integrally and inseparably connected with cultural context. Even the study of grammar, as quantifiable and scientific as we can make it, can and should be viewed as a cultural phenomenon. For example, there are many cases where Chinese grammar reflects how the Chinese view the world and world events. For instance, Chinese word order follows a predictable pattern of temporal sequence. Tai (1985) proposes the Principle of Temporal Sequence, or PTS, which captures the fact that Chinese word order follows the real-life ordering of events. In English, we might say, "I read a book at the library today." In Chinese, this sentence would be ordered as, "I today at the library read a book (*wǒ jīntiān zài túshūguǎn kàn shū*)." In other words, to the Chinese, one must be at the library before any reading can take place. Other grammatical factors are discussed in Chapter Four.

Brooks (1997, 13) identifies the need for a solution to this problem when he says,

> The desire for a cultural accompaniment to language acquisition has long been felt though only vaguely understood by the great majority of language teachers. There is little need to exhort them to teach culture; their willingness is already manifest. But there is a need to help them understand what meaning they should assign to the word *culture* and how it can become significant and fruitful in a sequence of years of language study.

We agree with this statement in that how we define culture and how we treat it in the classroom are essential. Too often, at the mention of culture, many automatically think of art, literature, history, and so on. Brooks goes on to say, "Up to now there have not been very serious attempts to deal with the subject of culture in language instruction at a professional level and in a systematic way" (1997, 16).

Before we deal specifically with our performed culture approach, it is important to understand what we mean by *culture*, what issues it entails, and how it relates to learning a foreign language.

DEFINING CULTURE

There are as many definitions of *culture* as there are people who have tried to define this elusive term. It has been defined most broadly as everything in human life and the best of human life, which fits closely with the well-documented distinction of Olympian, or big "C," culture, as opposed to hearthstone, or little "c," culture. Big "C" culture is what we usually refer to as high-brow culture, such as classical music, architecture, literature, and art. Little "c" culture consists of the everyday, common things that make up a society, including food and eating practices, transportation, fashions, and the general behavioral norms of a society. This distinction is widely used, but it is very broad and provides few details about cultural authenticity and how culture is best taught and learned. Hammerly (1985) describes culture in three useful categories or divisions: achievement culture, informational culture, and behavioral culture.

Achievement culture represents the great achievements of a society, corresponding to big "C" culture. For East Asian cultures, this includes philosophical traditions such as Taoism, Confucianism, and Buddhism (Zen and other schools); Beijing opera, *p'ansori* folk songs, *Kabuki*, *Noh*, and *Bunraku* and other music and drama; *sijo*, *waka*, and *haiku* poetry and other literary traditions; *minhwa* and other painting and calligraphy traditions, architectural traditions, and funerary traditions. This is the type of culture that is most often taught in a "culture" class and usually involves what some might call ancient or traditional culture. Basically, it deals with old things, ideas, and performances, or at least those things that can be traced back to premodern times. This type of cultural information is most often introduced in the language classroom by means of a variety of activities, such as the "culture capsule," the "culture cluster," the "culture assimilator" (which are basically minilessons or activities on some aspect of culture), the minidrama, video presentations, and lectures.

Informational culture deals with the kinds of information that a society values, as well as historical and other facts and figures about the society, including information about political systems, geography, population, and industry and resources. For China, this includes the dynastic cycle, the civil service examination system, and the current socialist form of government. In Japan, it includes the

12

samurai ethic, the Meiji Restoration, and economic structures. For Korea, informational culture includes relations with North Korea, marriage customs, and the role of the *yangban* in history, the development of the *ondol* heating system, and the unique nature of the development of *Han'gul*. ③ comfortable distance between ppl,

Hammerly's third category, *behavioral culture*, refers to the common daily practices and beliefs that define an individual and dictate behavior in a specific society; this has also been referred to as "functional culture" (Spinelli 1997, 213–224) and includes such common things as eating habits and manners, the manner of greeting, the protocols of traveling by public transportation, how to conduct a transaction at a bank, how to order a meal in a restaurant, how one treats siblings, parent-child relationships, teacher-student relationships, how emotions are displayed, and how gifts are exchanged. This is usually the type of cultural behavior people speak of when they naively say things such as "that's just the way the Japanese (or Chinese or Korean) are." It is the way people behave within their own group (in-group) and in interactions with others (out-group). It also includes the things that a person does on a daily basis to negotiate various events and situations in society.

Cultural ideals are typically viewed differently by natives of a culture than they are by outsiders: Natives seem to be more anxious to share some aspects of their culture than others. Native attitudes toward the sharing of culture can be characterized by three distinctions: revealed culture, ignored culture, and suppressed culture (Walker 2000). *Revealed culture* refers to those aspects of culture that natives are anxious to share with others; these are the aspects of their lives, traditions, and country that they are proud of and wish others to know about. They include the types of things you might read about in travel brochures or in books about a particular country or people, typically written from a native perspective and presented in a positive, sometimes biased viewpoint. Organized tours to foreign countries focus on this type of culture. Revealed culture includes many of the elements of achievement culture and informational culture discussed here. It also includes what natives perceive as good or desirable traits, practices, and behaviors. For example, Koreans are proud of the importance that is placed on family and clan in their society; the Japanese are proud of their work ethic, the politeness and respect that are displayed in everyday interactions, the education system, and the high rate of literacy; the Chinese are eager to tell about their long and enduring history, about the variety and uniqueness of Chinese cuisine, of the virtues of traditional Chinese medicine and exercise, and so on.

Ignored culture refers to behavior, practices, or customs that native members of a culture may believe are universal until they encounter someone from another culture behaving contrary to expectations. Edward Hall (1959, 1966, 1976) has referred to this type of culture as "hidden" or "covert" culture. For East Asian cultures, this includes such things as toilet and bathing practices (bathing in the evening before bed, public baths), bowing as opposed to shaking hands, and taking shoes off before entering a home; Koreans ask many questions as part of normal interaction that most Westerners would consider far too private for public discussion; natives think little of the crowded and cramped conditions of public transportation in East Asia, though the average American is usually quite alarmed by them; the lack of queuing or forming lines in China is probably taken for granted, as is dinner-table etiquette such as slurping, burping, or spitting bones on the table.

Suppressed culture refers to characteristics that natives are not eager for foreigners to know about; behavior or conditions they are typically defensive about and feel they have to justify. In China, this includes the anonymous vigorous shoving (and even elbowing) to board public transportation, the lack of sanitary bathroom facilities (from an American viewpoint), and the common practice of spitting in public. In Korea, it includes public spitting and people bumping into others on the sidewalk. In Japan, it may be the prevalence of vending machines, which offer convenience but also make it possible for underage purchases of tobacco or alcohol.

Revealed culture is by far the most commonly taught cultural content in textbooks and classroom lectures. However, it is the ignored or hidden culture that is of the most value to learners of a foreign language, because these issues or situations are most likely to cause confusion and/or misunderstanding for learners of Chinese, Japanese, or Korean. Behavioral culture, as already discussed, provides the most applicable and immediate knowledge and skills necessary for language learners to be familiar with because language use is so dependent on behavior, linguistic as well as nonlinguistic. Behavioral culture also has the most similarities with ignored culture. Though behavioral culture has some similarities with suppressed culture, it is the cultural behavior that is so common in life that natives usually regard it as universal behavior. Behavioral culture is most important for learners of these languages to know in order to develop and maintain relationships with natives of that culture. Without a knowledge of behavioral culture, learners are likely to offend those whom they are trying to befriend. Though a knowledge of the linguistic code (vocabulary, grammar, sound system) is essential, it is only a part of the communication process.

To be equipped with the linguistic code is not enough. Simply knowing how to phrase one's thoughts using the vocabulary and grammar of the second language may cause more harm than good when it comes to communication in the target culture. Agar (1994, 29) goes as far as saying, "You can master grammar and the dictionary, but *without* culture you won't communicate. With culture, you can communicate *with* rocky grammar and a limited vocabulary." We should also keep in mind that we are training our students not just to communicate, but to be able to develop and maintain long-term relationships with individuals in the target cultural environment. Morain (1986, 64) says,

> Those who interact with members of a different culture know that a knowledge of the sounds, the grammar, and the vocabulary of the foreign tongue is indispensable when it comes to sharing information. But being able to read and speak another language does not guarantee that *understanding* will take place. Words in themselves are too limited a dimension. The critical factor in understanding has to do with cultural aspects that exist beyond the lexical— aspects that include the many dimensions of nonverbal communication.

A colleague is fond of telling beginning language students that the goal is not to help them become comfortable speaking Japanese; rather, the goal is to have the Japanese feel comfortable with the students when they speak in Japanese. A story illustrates this point: A student several years ago had excellent Chinese skills. He had great command of the linguistic code. His pronunciation was precise, his fluency nearly nativelike, and his command of the lexicon impressive. Despite these important skills he had worked hard to acquire, the cultural component was lacking. He had never spent any time abroad, though he had considerable experience in North American Chinese-speaking communities. We might describe him as "+linguistic code, –cultural code," that is, having good linguistic skills but insufficient cultural skills. This student went to China for an internship where he was placed in a Chinese company in which he was the only foreigner. His time there did not last long: His linguistic skills were so impressive to the Chinese that when the inevitable offenses came as a result of his weakness in cultural skills, they thought his rudeness was intentional. The sad part of this story was that he was not aware that he was giving offense, nor did he feel a need to change or alter his behavior. He could not understand why his colleagues were having such a hard time getting along with him. He was merely playing the part of the American, except that he was speaking Chinese. He eventually was placed in an American company in China where he fit in much better. Another young American man also participated in the same internship program. We might characterize him as +cultural code, and –linguistic code: His language skills were average, but what he lacked in linguistic skills, he more than made up for in cultural savvy. He understood where the Chinese were coming from, and more important, he was a keen observer of the behavior around him and had a strong desire to learn as much as he could about how the Chinese did things. He also was placed in a Chinese company where he was the only foreigner. Because of his attitude, he got along well with his Chinese colleagues, and as a result, his language skills improved dramatically. Incidentally, he was offered full-time, permanent employment at the conclusion of the internship. This is a clear case where one learner knew how to develop and maintain relationships in a Chinese-speaking context, and another did not. There are many other stories like this that illustrate the importance of being conversant in behavioral culture as an integral part of well-developed language skills.

Cultural behavior is an essential part of speaking a foreign language in the target environment. How to teach these skills in the classroom is the essence of this book.

PERFORMANCE: TO KNOW IS TO DO

For learners to fully grasp and understand the concept of behavioral culture, they must understand that it involves performing. Walker's (2000) notion of performed culture reflects the idea that culture is the basis of meaning and that language not only transmits, but also creates or constitutes knowledge or reality (Bruner 1986).

　　According to Victor Turner (1987, 81–82) performance is what human beings are about every day of their lives:

° Learning to perform a

foreign culture entails

constructing a memory

* How do we [perform
　　　　　　culture]

- break culture into

[performable chunks]

* Characteristics of a

skilled player/performer

· knows the right moves

· responds quickly

· Anticipates (audience

· can be flexible

also matters)

　　The basic stuff of social life is performance, "the presentation of self in everyday life." Self is presented through performance of roles, through performance that breaks roles, and through declaring to a given public that one has undergone a transformation of state and status, been saved or damned, elevated or released. Human beings belong to a species well endowed with means of communication, both verbal and non-verbal, and, in addition, given to dramatic modes of communication, to performance of different kinds. There are various *types* of social performance, and *genres* of cultural performance, and each has its own style, goals, entelechy, rhetoric, developmental pattern, and characteristic roles. These types and genres differ in different cultures, and in terms of the scale and complexity of the sociocultural fields in which they are generated and sustained.

　　As Turner indicates, different cultures call for different styles and ways to communicate. Every morning when we walk out the door, we are acting according to the protocols that are dictated by the situation we encounter, playing the roles of student, teacher, customer, clerk, friend, business associate, and so on. When dealing with a foreign culture, it is imperative that we understand the expectations and intentions that are associated with the various roles we play as well as the roles we encounter.

　　The cultural psychologist Jerome Bruner (1996, 20) also espouses the virtue, even the necessity, of performance in the learning process.

　　It is principally through interacting with others that children find out what the culture is about and how it conceives of the world. Unlike other species, human beings deliberately teach each other in settings outside the ones in which the knowledge being taught will be used. Nowhere else in the animal kingdom is such deliberate "teaching" found—save scrappily among higher primates. To be sure, many indigenous cultures do not practice as deliberate or decontextualized a form of teaching as we do. But "telling" and "showing" are as humanly universal as speaking.

It is customary to say that this specialization rests upon the gift of language. But perhaps more to the point, it also rests upon our astonishingly well developed talent for "intersubjectivity"—the human ability to understand the minds of others, whether through language, gesture, or other means. It is not just words that make this possible, but our capacity to grasp the role of the settings in which words, acts, and gestures occur. We are the intersubjectivity species par excellence. It is this that permits us to "negotiate" meanings when words go astray.

Bruner clearly believes that there is more to communication than the linguistic code and that teaching perhaps should involve more than just telling. He suggests that teaching should also include showing. Bruner goes on to say, "Just as the omniscient narrator has disappeared from modern fiction, so will the omniscient teacher disappear from the classroom of the future" (22). He alludes to the traditional teacher who conducts a very teacher-oriented class—that is, one in which the teacher does most of the talking, often through a lecture format. This is certainly the tradition in East Asian cultures, where the teacher is regarded as the purveyor of knowledge. Questions and classroom discussion, and especially expressing one's own thoughts or opinions on a subject, are generally discouraged. The teacher "teaches" (i.e., lectures) and the students silently take notes. Bruner suggests, as do most foreign language teachers now, that more effective learning happens in a learner-oriented class where the responsibility lies primarily with the learners. The learners should do the majority of the speaking during a given class period (Lee and VanPatten 1995). Allowing learners to perform in the target language gives them the opportunity to practice in meaningful, authentic cultural contexts. When language is tied to context and the learner understands the social roles involved, the language will more likely be remembered over time. Omaggio Hadley (2001) mentions several studies that reinforce this point (e.g., Bransford and Johnson 1972; Mueller 1980; Hudson 1982). Most professional language teachers will agree that meaningful practice fosters learning more readily than practice presented out of the appropriate cultural context.

Kenneth Burke (1969) examines language as a mode of action and discusses five key aspects in understanding what people do and why they do it (xv):

- what was done   (act)
- when or where it was done   (scene)
- who did it   (agent)
- how it was done   (agency)
- why it was done   (purpose)

Carlson (1996, 36–37) discusses the influence of Burke's ideas on performance theory, given his focus on situating human action in context. These aspects of human action provide the basis for Walker's (2000) description of performance, as related to foreign language study, as "conscious repetitions of 'situated events.'" According to Walker (228), performance is characterized by the following:

- place of occurrence
- time of occurrence
- appropriate script (or program or rules)
- roles of participants
- accepting and/or accepted audience

When we are interacting in a language and culture, these elements of a performance determine not only what is said, but also how it is said and the behavior appropriate to the communicative situation. We certainly speak differently in the board room and at the street market, at a new year's celebration or on a typical day, with the manager at a bank versus the waitress at the corner noodle shop, and the task being undertaken will dictate the behavior and actions that are appropriate in that specific situation. The audience, or those passively involved in the situation, may also play a role in the speech that we decide to use and what is culturally appropriate. If the elements of a performance are not all taken into consideration when communicating in a foreign culture, learners risk misunderstanding and/or offending the interlocutor.

Behavior, both linguistic and nonlinguistic, in communicative situations or other performances is heavily influenced by the genres and styles of those situations. The genre tells what type of a performance is presented, and the style tells how to function within that performance.

GENRES AND STYLES

The concepts of *genre* and *style* are central to helping learners perform the target culture rather than just produce target language sentences. As already mentioned, meaning derives from the cultural context in which communication occurs. Native performance is *always* situated in some context, and that context involves a particular genre and style. During classroom instruction, it is important to help learners develop a sense for different genres and different styles and their applicable situations. The kinds of things that are said and the way they are said will vary depending on the specific situation. In planning the course curriculum, it is helpful to begin with those genres and styles that the learners will be most likely to encounter in interactions in the target culture, and then expand from there.

A *genre* can be thought of as a category of communicative situations that share certain purposes (Swales 1990). In other words, a genre constitutes a class of related performances. Genres in oral speech include greetings, face-to-face conversations, telephone conversations, making purchases at a store, asking directions on the street, ordering food at a restaurant, making a hotel reservation, visiting someone at the person's home, debating, and participating in a job interview (Chafe 1994).

Style refers to the way in which the communicative situation is carried out. For example, the genre of visiting someone will vary stylistically depending on the relationship with the person being visited, when the visit takes place, and the purpose of the visit; in other words, the performance will differ linguistically and behaviorally depending on these kinds of factors. Performances within the genre of greeting someone may vary dramatically depending on who is greeted, when and where the greeting takes place, and so on. Similarly, a telephone conversation will vary depending on the relationship between the caller and the receiver and the purpose of the call. These variations are referred to as the *style*.

In the written language, genres include letters, memos, essays, stories, invitations, advertisements, newspaper articles, and train or television schedules. Within each, style may vary depending on the context. The format and content of a letter will depend on the relationship between the writer and the recipient. Variations can arise based on whether it is a personal or a business letter, whether the purpose is to make a request or to inform, how long it has been since the last communication, and how much information the writer and the recipient share.

In Japanese and Korean, and to a lesser extent, Chinese, language use varies based on the social relationship between interlocutors as well as on the relationship between the interlocutors and any third parties referred to in a conversation. Because there are important differences in style, it is essential that classroom activities be contextualized so that the learners can understand how the performance will change based on the relationship between the various factors of role, time, place, script, and audience.

Scholars from a variety of fields have discussed the relationship between language use and social factors and the idea that meaning arises from contextualized use rather than being an independent, unchanging entity (Hymes 1974; Schiffrin 1994; Wardhaugh 1992; Fasold 1990; Bruner 1986). To become comfortable with a range of variations in style and genre, learners need to have exposure to such variations and guided practice in negotiating a range of contexts and situations. As humans, we are not "one-shot" learners; we generally do not learn things through a single exposure. Even in our native culture, we become familiar with cultural norms through repeated experiences as we grow up. As second-language learners experience the contextualizations provided in the curriculum and understand the role of each of the five elements of performance, they will build a repertoire that will enable them to negotiate interactions in the target culture on their own.

In summary, culture, background, and situation are not only relevant, but also essential when talking about communicating in culturally appropriate performances. For example, Hinds (1986) notes that discourse in Japanese tends to focus on the situation rather than on the people involved. It also affects the frequent omission of elements in a sentence, how people are referred to (the use of personal pronouns is rare), the use of transitive and intransitive verbs, possession marking, and so on. Jorden (1992) also notes that culture affects attitudes toward time and space, styles of interaction, and identification of self and others. In Korean as well as in Japanese, culture affects the kind of information that is shared with regard to personal feelings and how it is communicated. Culture has a profound effect on interpersonal relationships—what emotions are shown and how, how negotiations take place, what prompts apologies, and so on. In Chinese, the relationship one has with a person (an insider vs. an outsider) will determine how the interaction is carried out, both linguistically and behaviorally.

If we allow learners to simply say what they want, without acknowledging the role of situated social factors, they will tend to rely on their knowledge of their base culture without regard to how native speakers of the target culture might interpret or misinterpret their intentions. As learners become sensitive to stylistic variations within the genres of the target culture, they will be better prepared to create and maintain relationships. Natives of the target culture will become increasingly comfortable with the learners in whom they can see appropriate cultural grounding.

The role of the hearer must not be overlooked in discussions about communication. In its full sense, communication does not occur merely because the speaker says something; the interpretation of the hearer also plays a significant role. It is not unusual for the intended message to differ from the received message, even between two native speakers of a language, so it is all the more important to help learners see how cultural contexts affect meaning in the target culture.

Language is something that is *lived*. It is situated in society and culture. Learning a language can be thought of as learning a skill and therefore has many similarities with developing musical or athletic ability. When learning to play the piano, an understanding of music theory is important. However, one cannot learn to play the piano merely by listening to lectures about that theory, nor can one learn to play simply by practicing hitting the keys. The ability comes as one applies the theoretical knowledge in guided practice. Knowing the key, the time signature, and the fingering of a piece, and being able to count the music correctly are all important, but this knowledge must be *applied* repeatedly in order to gain true skill in playing the piano.

Likewise, in baseball, one cannot learn how to bat, for example, merely by watching others do it, or by listening to others tell about it. The skill comes as one actually holds the bat and experiences the swing while watching the ball come from the pitcher. The ability to play the piano or to swing a bat (and hit!) successfully requires the development of component skills. These are important building blocks: Even professional musicians and professional athletes spend time in practicing component skills.

In language learning as well, both theory and practice are important. Theory may include discussion about the language and about the culture, and the practice will include guided application of the theory in context.

Differences between two cultures might be thought of as two separate sports (Walker and Noda 2000). Certainly there are significant differences between the language and culture of Korea and those of the United States. Suppose that the United States is represented by the game of baseball, and Korea is represented by tennis. When natives of the United States are learning Korean, they will certainly recognize some things that are familiar, represented perhaps by the ball and an implement for hitting the ball (the tennis racket). It is natural that they will tend to relate these items to things they are familiar with in their own culture, namely, the baseball and something used to hit it (the bat). As a result, they may try to hit the tennis ball over the fence, which in their native experience is desirable (hitting a home run). However, in the new culture, hitting the ball beyond the boundary is something to be avoided. Learners will see similarities and differences between the native and the target culture, but they also need to know the significance of these and what the rules of the game are in the target culture.

When we speak of communication and meaning, it is important to remember that *meaning* encompasses several things. For example, *referential meaning* is what the word refers to, such as

Meaning is derived from the culture context in which communication occurs.

言外之意

pragmatic

meaning

"book" or "dog." Indexical words, such as "this" and "that," and pronouns, such as "she" and "it," depend on the context for their interpretation. There is also *pragmatic meaning*. This is also dependent on the context. The sentence "It's hot in here" could mean "Why don't you open the window?" or "Why don't you turn down the thermostat?" or "I'd like a drink," and so on. Accent and intonation can indicate sarcasm or focus or anger or exasperation. A given sentence can "mean" a variety of things based on the prosodic features as well as the pragmatic features. Meaning can be expressed in a multitude of ways by every level of language. The interpretation of certain features, however, varies between cultures. Therefore, it is essential that learners develop the appropriate L2 scripts for authentic interpretation.

These kinds of issues affect styles and genres in language use. Style varies based on the situation and the context, affected by the five elements of performance. Also, language use is affected by genres, or categories of language-use situations.

Genre and style are crucial in the teaching and learning of languages: Language is used to achieve social and cultural ends, and genres provide ways to achieve intentions through linguistic and cultural means. In order for speakers to achieve intentions, language has come to be used in conventionalized ways, organized in genres and styles. Genres and styles reflect culture. Scripts exist because members of a culture respond in similar ways to situations with similar structures and elements, having learned what is appropriate and how their actions and utterances are likely to affect others (Miller 1984). Unless the language learner understands how scripts guide expectations and interpretations, he or she will be at a serious disadvantage in operating in the target culture. Genres, styles, and scripts become keys for effective participation in a community (Miller 1984).

The L2 curriculum, the syllabi, and the materials, especially at the earlier levels, should be designed around well-established genres (e.g., telephone conversations between friends, interaction when visiting a home, and giving directions to a taxi driver). At more advanced stages, the repertoire of genres can be expanded to include contexts such as telephoning to report a problem with utilities and participating in a job interview. Because every level of language is affected by the rhetorical structure of genre, decisions regarding sentence pattern instruction, lexical instruction, and pronunciation instruction should be organized within a comprehensive outline of teaching genres. This is similar to the task-based syllabus (Nunan 1989). Because the rhetorical moves inherent in genre affect discourse, sentence structure, lexical selection, and prosody, students should be guided, even at the stage of developing component skills, with the motivation of helping them understand, recognize, and use these genres to achieve their intentions in L2. This applies to both spoken and written genres. The principle is the same: Genre provides an organizing rhetorical device that helps learners to understand the aspects of the given performance sufficiently for them to understand how the target native interprets the various cultural components of the exchange.

The development of skills within genres proceeds at different levels. To develop automaticity in lower-level skills, there is a role for more mechanical practice. Just as practice has a role in the development of music or athletic ability, working on component skills is important in language learning. To use the performing analogy, rehearsals are important, and sometimes rehearsals focus on given parts of the overall performance. Even so, the more mechanical activities that focus on component skills should be contextualized so the practice is more than just mindless repetition of sounds. Ideally, the more mechanical types of practice can be done out of class using multimedia aids that include feedback. Memorization plays an important role in helping learners understand accurate, authentic, and appropriate language in everything from pronunciation and intonation to discourse segments. Class time can be used for the more holistic practice, giving the learners opportunities to apply the component skills in contextualized, socially appropriate, authentic communicative activities. The underlying goal is to guide the learners in *performance*, as they develop a sense for the cultural aspects of language use within specified genres.

Genres become recognizable categories because of similarities in performances. These performances are culturally determined, and the time, place, roles, script, and audience determine the style and genre being performed. As learners become sensitive to the elements of performance and to the expectations for different genres and styles, they will be able to adjust their behavior in a culturally appropriate manner that will enable them to achieve their intentions in the target culture.

CULTURAL SCRIPTS

The script, one of the essential elements of a performance, will be determined by the genre of the communicative situation as well as the other elements of the performance. It plays an important role in the communication process, incorporating not only what is said, but also what behavior is expected. Roger Schank (1990, 7–8), in his work on real and artificial memory, describes the notion of *script* as follows:

> A script is a set of expectations about what will happen next in a well-understood situation. In a sense, many situations in life have the people who participate in them seemingly reading their roles in a kind of play. The waitress reads from the waitress part in the restaurant script, and the customer reads the lines of the customer. Life experience means quite often knowing how to act and how others will act in given stereotypical situations. That knowledge is called a script.
>
> Scripts are useful for a variety of reasons. They make clear what is supposed to happen and what various acts on the part of others are supposed to indicate. They make mental processing easier by allowing us to think less, in essence. You don't have to figure out every time you enter a restaurant how to convince someone to feed you. All you really have to know is the restaurant script and your part in that script....One just has to play one's part, and events usually transpire the way they are supposed to. You don't have to infer the intentions of the waitress if her intentions are already known. Why concentrate one's mental time on the obvious?

This description of a script emphasizes the importance of knowing what to expect in a given situation. For language learners, this means we need to move beyond a sole focus on the linguistic code—what one should say—to how one should *act* in order to achieve the desired results. Taking the restaurant script as an example, we see many differences in practices or unwritten rules between restaurants in the United States, China, Japan, and Korea. We outline the restaurant script here based on Walker's (2000) model.

Basic outline of restaurant script

1. **Time:** the dinner hour
2. **Place:** a small, casual (informal) restaurant
3. **Roles/actors**
   a. Customer
   b. Server
   c. Host/hostess
4. **Script**
   a. Being seated
   b. Ordering
   c. Eating etiquette
   d. Paying the bill
5. **Audience**
   a. Other diners
   b. Restaurant staff

Next, we provide excerpts of the restaurant script for the United States, China, Japan, and Korea. Our purpose is to make clear the potential complexities of a seemingly simple task, in this case, eating at a restaurant, when one is functioning in another culture. It will become clear that though one may have sophisticated linguistic skills, if the script is unfamiliar, or if one acts according to one's own native script, the simple task will take on difficult and frustrating proportions. The script excerpts described here, as well as other scripts, can be effectively simulated in the classroom. See Appendix 1 for more complete restaurant scripts for the United States, China, and Japan.

It should be noted that the descriptions that follow do not describe every dining situation that may be encountered in the target culture. Our purpose is to provide a general description of a restaurant situation that one will likely encounter in the target culture. As with most cultural scripts, there are many possible variations.

The Restaurant Script

Knowing how to behave in a dining situation is extremely important. It will put the hosts at ease, and it will allow one to feel comfortable knowing what to expect and ultimately to become a full participant in this kind of situation. Knowing what to say in these kinds of situations will give one even more confidence and the ability to participate fully with dining associates.

American Restaurant

The following excerpt describes an American cultural script for an average sit-down restaurant in urban American culture (note that even within a culture, the script will vary somewhat, particularly among different types of restaurants (fast food, fine dining, etc.). Though protocols may differ among restaurants, even within a culture (e.g. the fast-food restaurant script is different from the fine-dining script), there is a general procedure that is followed. Significant differences are pointed out in the text that follows. In this excerpt, we describe how to pay for a meal and tipping conventions.

<u>After the meal/paying the check</u>

In most American restaurants, a meal can be paid in two ways: either from the table, or directly to a cashier near the entrance to the restaurant. It is not difficult to determine which procedure should be followed: If the server brings the bill in a folder or on a small plastic tray, the money for the bill (or a charge card) and the bill are generally put in the folder or on the tray, and the server will shortly come by and pick it up. The change will then be brought back a few minutes later. In the case of a charge card, the receipt is returned to the table, and the customer will generally add a tip to the charge and sign the receipt. If the bill is presented alone, the standard procedure is to leave a tip on the table, take the bill to the cashier and pay directly. At more expensive restaurants, the bill is paid from the table; less expensive restaurants will generally require that the customer take the bill to the cashier.

Leftover food can be taken brought home to eat at a later time. This is particularly true of more expensive restaurants. If there is food remaining, it is acceptable to ask the server for a "doggie bag"; he or she will then return with a container. Sometimes the diner will transfer the food to the container, or the server may take the plates and return with the leftover food in the take-out box.

Tipping
Tips for the server are expected at nearly all sit-down restaurants in the United States. Currently, in most areas of the country the standard tip is 15% of the total cost of the meal. If it is a large party, such as eight or more, the tip will usually be included automatically in the bill. Exceptionally good service may be rewarded with a 20% tip or more. The tip may be added to the bill if the customer is paying with a credit card, or left on the table when paying with cash. It is considered rude to not leave a tip. A small tip is interpreted as an indication of dissatisfaction with the service.

Chinese Restaurant
Next, we describe the script for a typical sit-down casual restaurant in China; in more expensive formal restaurants, service and eating etiquette will differ slightly.

If one has been invited out by a Chinese friend or associate, it is important to wear nice clothes. To the Chinese, appearances are very important: Dressing up for friends or associates tells them that the relationship is valued and one is honored to be their guest. Here we describe the scene when paying the bill.

Concluding the meal and paying the check
At the conclusion of a meal, the customer must ask the server to bring the bill; it generally will not be brought unless the customer asks for it. This is usually done by saying either *suàn zhàng* or *mǎi dān*. Usually the host person will ask for the bill.

To the Chinese, eating is a very social affair, sometimes lasting for hours. Restaurants, therefore, do not presume when the customers will be finished; they wait for the customers to indicate they are ready to go. Determining who will pay the bill at a Chinese restaurant is a memorable experience. Because of the Chinese group orientation, it is considered an honor to be able to pay the bill for a group of friends. At the conclusion of a meal, it is very common for an argument to erupt concerning who will pay the bill. Typically, several in the party will offer and banter with each other for this privilege. Paying the bill brings some prestige and honor to a person.

Sometimes the arguing can get fairly vigorous, with money pushed into another's hands, then thrown back, and so forth. In the end, one person will usually pay the entire bill. Chinese friends will play this game of offering to pay the bill even if they know they will not, in the end, do so. There is an informal order that says the person who pays the bill this time will not be expected to do so the next time. Everyone usually takes even turns paying the bill. Nevertheless, it is still important to offer to pay the bill after a meal and banter with the others who will also offer to pay. Everyone in the group offers sincere thanks to the person who eventually pays the bill. Chinese will almost certainly pay for the meals of visitors, even if it is a financial burden to them. The Chinese view this as their responsibility to take care of guests. In recent years, it has become more common for groups of close friends to split the bill equally, though even these groups on occasion will banter to pay the bill.

Tipping is not required or expected at Chinese restaurants. The insistence to leave a tip will usually be met with discomfort by the Chinese. In other service industries such as hotels, service charges are usually automatically added to the price.

Japanese Restaurant

Appropriate behavior in a Japanese restaurant depends on the kind of restaurant that is being visited. Behavior at more-expensive Western-style restaurants will more closely mirror behavior at restaurants in the United States than at traditional Japanese restaurants. Likewise, fast-food establishments will also be slightly different than typical traditional Japanese restaurants. We again describe the portion of the script that deals with paying the check.

Paying the check

The bill is usually brought to the table after all the dishes have been served, and the customer goes to the payment counter near the entrance to pay the bill. At some restaurants, the customer will not receive a bill, and instead is expected to go to the cashier directly and pay there when finished eating. Generally, the person who made the invitation to dinner is expected to pay the bill for the group. Some restaurants have a display near the payment counter with items customers can purchase, such as homemade pickles, dressing, and specialty foods. If shoes were checked, the number ticket and receipt are returned and the shoes are received. After payment is made, both the customers and the restaurant personnel express thanks, and the customers leave. Tipping is not customary in Japanese restaurants.

Korean Restaurant
The following description relates to less expensive small restaurants in Korea.

<u>Paying the bill</u>
One person in the group will almost always pay for everyone else. Koreans tend to think that having a joint bill contributes to friendliness and unity. There is often a friendly argument over who will pay the bill, but usually the person with the most seniority will pay in the end. The one who pays gains the respect of the others in return, not because of the money paid but because of the kindness expressed by paying for the others in the group. If the diners are equal in age and position, one might insist on paying and ask the friend to pay the next time, whether it is immediately afterward for a cup of coffee or sometime in the future. However, the friend may insist on paying this time and have the first person who insisted pay the next time. The one who takes money out first to give to the cashier usually wins the argument. In any case, it is important that the person who does not pay this bill pays next time; to avoid taking one's turn results in a loss of respect from others.

In terms of the price, because there is no sales tax in Korea, diners always know the exact amount of the bill. Tipping is not expected.

*   *   *   *   *

Those who do not understand the appropriate cultural script or who choose not to "play by the rules" are often looked upon with suspicion. Natives of the target culture are usually fairly forgiving of inexperienced language learners and may even expect foreigners not to understand how to act in some situations. However, if one has good linguistic skills, natives of the target culture expect one also to have good cultural skills (i.e., to know the script). If an American did not make any attempt to pay the bill in a Chinese restaurant with a group of Chinese colleagues, it could be offensive to his colleagues. Using the metaphor described before, it would be akin to trying to play baseball on a tennis court. It would lead to frustration, annoyance, or even anger on the part of the tennis players.

As learners practice these kinds of scripts in the classroom, they will better understand the relationship between the language that is used and the actions and behavior that accompany the communicative situation. Integral to authentic performances is an understanding of the various genres and styles of communication. Different genres and styles of communication provide the script with the specific language and behavior necessary for effective, nativelike communication.

CONCLUSION

In this chapter, we have discussed the concepts of *culture* and *performance* and how they relate to the teaching of East Asian languages. Behavioral culture is intricately tied to language. Communication involves not only the linguistic code of the target language but also the cultural code. The cultural code includes the many kinds of nonlinguistic communication such as body language and gestures. It also entails knowing what to do, how to act, and how others respond in a given communicative situation (i.e., knowing the script). When learners encounter unfamiliar scripts, they should have the ability to improvise based on similar scripts they have practiced.

Chapter Two

PERFORMING CULTURE:
PERFORMANCE-BASED CURRICULUM

The idea of performed culture reflects the fact that learning to speak a foreign language involves learning the culture of that language, or how to behave in that culture, linguistically as well as behaviorally. The foundation of this approach is based in the principles discussed in the preceding chapter, which outlines the definitions of *culture* and how behavioral culture relates to language study, the role and importance of performance in learning to behave in culturally appropriate ways, and our discussion of genres and scripts. Language learning should be culture-bound; more specifically, it should be founded in behavioral culture. In other words, learners should understand that there is more to communicating in a foreign culture than simply learning how to say "x" in language "y." There are a multitude of behaviors that make smooth, successful communication more likely. Because performance is such a basic part of communicating, it makes sense to have learners learn by doing; that is accomplished most effectively in culturally appropriate contexts. Understanding the genres and scripts of situations enables learners to navigate smoothly through these interactions.

In this chapter, we begin by further clarifying the notion of *performed culture* and how it applies to the East Asian language classroom and curricular issues. We follow this with a discussion of the relationship between the spoken language and the written language and its implications on appropriate sequencing and balance in learning the four skills and on the role of Romanization in the learning process. Next, we describe two concrete suggestions that can be implemented in the classroom to facilitate the performed culture model. We end with a brief discussion of the roles of the teacher and the learner in the East Asian language classroom.

PERFORMANCE IN A FOREIGN CULTURE

Regarding the notion of performed culture, Walker (2000, 226) states, "Performed culture as an approach to language study starts with meaning and treats the linguistic code—and with it the concept of the sentence—as a medium for accessing and thereby more fully participating in that meaning." Typical linguistic approaches use a bottom-up strategy that builds meaning through the analysis of various parts, with the assumption that the complete, well-organized sentence is the focus of language learning; however, those who have dealt with natural, unscripted oral discourse know that people often speak in incomplete sentences. The typical foreign language textbook begins with an introduction to the vocabulary and grammar patterns, and often includes a dialogue or other type of passage; the idea is that the learners study the vocabulary and the grammar as a means of accessing the material in the dialogue. Unfortunately, dialogues generally are presented without any explanation of the genre (of language), the roles or relationships of the participants, where or when the situation takes place, or the script—in other words, the expected behavior of the participants. Similarly unfortunate is the fact that teachers seldom supply this foundational information.

Nearly every beginning Chinese language text has a lesson that introduces the greeting *nǐ hǎo*. However appropriate this may be, there is seldom any discussion about when, where, and with whom this greeting is socially and culturally appropriate. Learners are given an English equivalent such as "hello" or "hi." Without any further clarification of *how* this greeting is used among Chinese, learners are left with the assumption that they can use *nǐ hǎo* in Chinese anytime they would say "hello" or "hi" in English. However, simply learning to say *nǐ hǎo* in Chinese does not constitute knowing how Chinese greet each other; learners must understand how to greet Chinese based on the performance or communicative situation at hand. Greetings in Chinese vary considerably based on where you are, when the greeting occurs, the roles that are involved, and the audience present. Based on these conditions, the script will tell which greeting to use and what nonlinguistic behavior is appropriate.

A performed culture approach places meaning in cultural context as the focus of study. It is a top-down approach in which the learner looks at the overall context and the intentions in a given situation and learns to participate accordingly. This is not to say that linguistics is not an important part of the equation. Rather than linguistics being the sole focus, the language is viewed as a medium, along with other nonlinguistic behaviors, for participating in the situation. The language becomes one of several means to successfully present oneself in a social situation. For example, instead of simply learning the single phrase *nǐ hǎo* or *konnichi wa*, one should learn how to greet people in Chinese, Japanese, or Korean within various genres or social situations, which will inevitably involve much more than these simple phrases. For example, greetings in East Asia may vary based on the time of day and/or the relationship between the two people involved in the exchange. At the initial stages of language study, a certain amount of memorization of vocabulary and grammar is required, but the focus can still be on the intended meanings and functions of various realistic situations.

The performed culture approach is readily apparent when learning oral and aural skills, though it may be less obvious, but just as important, when dealing with reading and writing. All skills have a social and a practical application. It is these applications that are the focus of the performed culture approach. For example, when we read, not only is it for a specific purpose, but there is also a social outcome. When we read a text, we usually do something with the information gained. For example, we often talk with others about what we read. There is some social application that is at play. The performed culture approach focuses on meaning and performance as a means to learning the language and cultural behavior.

PRIMACY OF THE SPOKEN LANGUAGE

To better understand the relationship between speaking, listening, reading, and writing activities within the performed culture approach, it will be helpful to consider a fundamental question, namely: What is "language"? Although everyone has an intuitive understanding of what language is, teachers of language and culture should carefully consider how they view language so that the decisions they make are consistent with their views and not merely the result of hearing about an idea that "sounds good." Reflecting on language raises the issue of the relationship between the spoken language and the written language. This relationship has a direct bearing on language pedagogy, yet it seems that it is often overlooked or does not receive explicit attention; perhaps this is because we all feel that intuitively, we understand what *language* means. As a result, we tend to avoid the kind of careful examination that is important in guiding what we do in teaching languages.

There are several notable differences between the spoken language and the written language (Jannedy et al. 1994; Crystal 1987; Chafe 1994; Christensen 1994; National Foreign Language Center 1993; Kubler et al. 1997), and these differences show the importance of treating each mode of language separately in our pedagogy. Most cultures that have a written language have different conventions for oral speech and written text. Sometimes these differences are substantial. In some cases, the purposes for writing are different from the purposes for speaking.

Native speakers of a language often consider the written language to be *the* language, or in other words, the official language. This perception may be partly because children generally acquire speaking skills naturally. When the language is studied explicitly at school, the focus is usually on reading and writing, and this leads to associating the written language and the concept of language itself. As a result, teachers of East Asian languages, native speakers of the target language in particular, tend to give the writing system disproportionate attention in the curriculum, perhaps because it was a focal area in their own educational experience (Konomi 1997).

A review of some of the differences between the spoken language and the written language will help show the importance of treating the two differently in the foreign language curriculum. Writing is often more crafted than speech, with fewer errors, better organization, and better wording. Speech, on the other hand, is more spontaneous. This is because writing is generally the result of deliberation and revision rather than being spontaneous and simultaneous with the formulation of ideas. Writing is considered to be more stable and more permanent, whereas speech changes more rapidly over time. These facts contribute to the preferred status written language often has in the curriculum.

Writing is also associated with education and educated speech. The prescriptive tradition (see Chapter Five), which teaches what is and is not appropriate language use, is based largely on the written language, and some regard speech as an imperfect approximation of the ideals of the written language. Writing appears to be more stable because texts can transcend time and space whereas speech is transient. Also, there is less variation in spelling than in pronunciation; for example, speakers of English around the world may spell a given word the same way, but there may be several variations in pronunciation.

Despite the preferred status of the written language, a basic assumption of modern linguistics is that speech is primary and writing is secondary. Given the common perception that the written language is *the* language, what reasons are there for considering speech to be primary?

Speech, not writing, is the most immediate manifestation of language. Units of writing, regardless of the writing system used in a given language, are based on units of speech (such as words, sounds, or syllables). History shows that in any culture, writing develops *after* the spoken language. There is no culture or society that uses only a written language with no spoken form (although people with disabilities may be an exception). On the other hand, many languages have no written form at all. Even in cultures that use written language, there are many people who are illiterate but are capable in the spoken language (Fromkin and Rodman 1998; National Foreign Language Center 1993); certainly such people would not be thought of as not "knowing" their language. Regardless of its complexity, the writing system of a language is something that is always taught, yet the spoken language is acquired naturally by native speakers in a culture (Fromkin and Rodman 1998). Even those who never attend school are considered competent users of the spoken language. Neurolinguistic evidence suggests that spoken language involves distinct areas in the brain that are different from those associated with processing the writing system. Research also shows that subvocalization, a process of articulating the phonological component (which is based on the spoken language) of the text inaudibly while reading, occurs in the reading of all languages (National Foreign Language Center 1993). Interestingly, research in both Chinese and Japanese (Ke 1996; Horodeck 1987; Matsunaga 1994, 1995) has shown that native readers of these languages seem to rely more on the phonetic component of characters than on the semantic or graphemic components; this is contrary to popular intuition that it is the meaning that is most salient. (Unger [2004] and Erbaugh [2002] debunk the myth that characters reflect meaning independent of any association with a particular language. More is said about this is Chapter Four.)

Crystal (1987, 178) quotes the linguist Leonard Bloomfield as saying, "Writing is not language but merely a way of recording language by means of visible marks." In this same discussion, Crystal also cites Robert Hall: "When we think of writing as more important than speech we are putting the cart before the horse in every respect."

Although writing is used to represent sounds, it is important not to confuse orthography with the sounds of a language (Tsujimura 1996). As the following example from English shows, the same sound can be represented by different spellings. (Fromkin and Rodman 1998, 217).

Did he believe Caesar could see the people seize the seas?

Here, seven letters or letter combinations (noted in bold type) all reflect the same sound. On the other hand, the same spelling can represent different sounds, as in *dough, rough, through, bough, cough,* and *hiccough*. These examples suggest that writing is more conservative over time, with spelling no longer reflecting past pronunciation in some cases (Fromkin and Rodman 1998).

In some respects, what the written language represents is only a subset of the spoken language because there are many elements of language that cannot be expressed in natural writing, such as pause length, intonation, or stress (Crystal 1987). Crystal also notes that differences between the spoken language and the written language are evidenced in the kinds of conventions used to represent graphically some elements of speech. He also points out that a given convention may be interpreted differently in various languages, noting, for example, the graphic representation *ye-e-s* might be interpreted as representing emphasis (as in Russian) or hesitation (as in English). Crystal provides the following examples, demonstrating ways in which writers attempt to approximate the expression of some of these elements of speech (1987, 180).

Verbal description
> ...a soft, greasy voice, made up of pretence, politeness and saliva.
>> Anthony Trollope, *Ralph the Heir*

Punctuation
> These two - they're twins, Sam 'n Eric. Which is Eric - ? You? No - you're Sam -
>> William Golding, *Lord of the Flies*

Spelling
> Aw knaow you. Youre the one that took away maw girl.
>> G. B. Shaw, *Major Barbara*

Capitalization
> Heedless of grammar, they all cried, 'THAT'S HIM!'
>> R. H. Barham, *The Jackdaw of Rheims*

Type spacing and size
> Once on the bridge, every other feeling would have gone down before the necessity - the n e c e s s i t y - for making my way to your side and getting what you wanted.
>> G. B. Shaw, *The Man of Destiny*

Letter repetition
> 'Shhhhhhhhhhh! Shhhhhhhhhhhhhh!' they said.
>> William Faulkner, *Dry September*

Italics
> 'What *can* you mean by talking in this way to *me*?' thundered Heathcliffe with savage vehemence.
>> Emily Bronte, *Wuthering Heights*

Conversely, the written language can make distinctions that are not evident in speech, such as "my cousin's friends" as opposed to "my cousins' friends" and "The book was red" as opposed to "The book was read" (Fromkin and Rodman 1998). Usually such distinctions can be clarified in the spoken language by context, but the examples do point out differences between the spoken language and the written language.

Despite such written conventions that attempt to describe or otherwise express graphically certain elements of the spoken language, there are other aspects of conversation that cannot be expressed naturally in writing. Part of the environment of a conversation is how closely the people stand to each other, body language, such as facial expressions, eye movements, hand gestures, and patterns of intonation, stress, accent, and volume, to list a few.

Aside from the fact that the written language cannot adequately represent all elements of speech, the written language is more than just a written representation of speech (National Foreign Language Center 1993). Languages may have very different conventions for writing that are not applicable to speaking. For example, the spoken language often includes shorter clauses, more coordinating conjunctions, less formal vocabulary, more contractions, and more redundancy (Chafe 1994). Crystal (1987) points out, for example, that "whatchamacallit" is normally not a written form. The written language usually includes longer clauses, more subordination, more variety in vocabulary, and less common words. In both speaking and writing, the given genre and the situated performance affect how language is used.

These kinds of variations are clearly evident in Chinese, as seen in the difference between *kǒutóuyǔ (spoken language)* and *shūmiànyǔ (written language)*. For example, *rì* is used for "day" in written Chinese, and the colloquial *hào* is used in speech. Also, the colloquial *jiù*, meaning "then," is often expressed by the more literary word *biàn* in written discourse. In the case of Japanese, differences are seen in the use of *de aru* in writing and *da* in speech and in the use of *no* in writing (e.g. *...no de aru*) and the corresponding contracted form *n* in speech (e.g. *...n da*). In Korean, for example, the initial "i" in *imnida* drops in speech but not in writing. Aside from examples of lexical and grammatical forms that are not shared, the spoken language and the written language have different rhetorical conventions associated with their various genres.

Given these differences between the spoken language and the written language, it is important not to confuse the two in foreign language pedagogy by treating them as though they were one and the same. In the curriculum, it is important to treat the two styles of language independently and help learners develop facility with each as they cultivate skills in speaking, listening, reading, and writing. For learners to interact in culturally appropriate ways with both the spoken and the written language, they need to have experience with the conventions of each. Given the differences between the two modes of language, we argue for an ordered approach in the development of these four skills, rather than dealing with each of them equally from the beginning. Particularly in the case of East Asian languages, where the orthography itself presents new challenges, it is important to structure our approach to help learners to progress systematically. We therefore treat the spoken and the written language separately in order to better address issues unique to each mode of language.

For the reasons just outlined, the discussion that follows is based on the idea that *speech is primary*. Consequently, the development of speaking and listening skills should precede the development of reading and writing skills. Language is more than a collection of sounds, words, or phrases. The written language is more than a string of symbols. Language is a system, and reading and writing require knowledge of the language as a system in order for learners to effectively process units of meaning, as opposed to merely decoding strings of characters (a process of trying to determine the meaning of a word or sentence by converting individual symbols to sounds). When reading and writing are introduced prematurely into the curriculum, the learner has no choice but to resort to decoding, and the development of effective reading skills and strategies is hampered. Without a sense of the language as a system, a text cannot be processed in significant units of meaning.

This focus on the primacy of speech is reflected in the pedagogical approach outlined here. When we help learners understand the distinction between the spoken language and the written language, they can better understand how conventions differ, and the effects of those differences when using each mode of language. The appropriate use of the writing system is as important as the appropriate use of the spoken language as learners *perform* the target culture in different language modes.

Crystal (1987) reminds us that it is possible to go too far in maintaining that speech is primary, if the result is to omit the written language. Our focus on speech coming first does not diminish the importance of the written language nor does it ignore the roles each type of communication fills. Rather, we focus on speech first as the foundation for developing competency in the language generally and for developing competency in reading and writing skills later. We argue that each language medium fills an essential role and that an ordered approach that accounts for the differences between the two and that takes advantage of structured skill development is most beneficial for learners in both the short and the long term. Without an understanding of the relationship between the spoken and the written language, the visual reinforcement in the writing system can be confusing (National Foreign Language Center 1993). The discussion of reading and writing in Chapter Four shows that the ordered approach we outline for introducing the writing system does not imply a lengthy delay in reading and writing activities. The issue is not whether to teach the writing system, but when and how. Literacy is not a prerequisite for acquiring linguistic competence. Building on the foundation of the spoken language, reading and writing can focus on actual, fluent reading and writing skills, rather than simply being character-by-character decoding (or encoding) exercises (National Foreign Language Center 1993). As seen in the following section, in our approach, the relative balance in the skill mix will vary depending on the level of instruction.

THE SKILL MIX

In a language curriculum, teachers generally seek to integrate all four skills—listening, speaking, reading, and writing. Often there may even be administrative pressure to develop all four skills equally from the beginning. However, because of the differences noted here, the key issue is one of balance between the four skills and the relative weight placed on each at a given point in the curriculum. In seeking this balance, we must understand the relationships among the four skills and keep in mind a proper ratio at each level of instruction. In the following discussion, we treat the relative roles of reading and writing in comparison with speaking and listening.

Given the primacy of speech as already discussed, speaking and listening should precede reading and writing. The greater importance placed on speaking and listening in the earliest stages of language learning (in the case of these TFLs in particular) does not mean that reading and writing need to be postponed until speaking and listening have been "mastered" (in which case they would never be covered); it merely suggests that reading and writing, at each level, should be founded on language to which the learners have been exposed and have had opportunity to practice in speaking and listening activities. Reading and writing activities should be based on the domain and range of the learners' understanding of the target language system. Some activities that focus on skill and strategy development, such as hypothesis formation, may involve unknown lexical or other elements. In such cases, however, the content is carefully controlled to meet the objectives of the activity in question. Also, learners should be exposed to the relevant written conventions related to the kinds of texts being used.

When reading and writing activities are introduced immediately in the beginning course, learners are required to deal simultaneously with spoken and written conventions, the orthography itself (which is a significant issue in the case of Chinese and Japanese), as well as vocabulary, grammar, sociocultural appropriateness, and pronunciation and intonation issues. Although most programs seek to foster the development of all four skills, the particular mix should vary by level. Learners can develop skills in both the spoken language and the written language more effectively and efficiently if they are not forced to deal with the entire range of issues simultaneously. Without knowledge of the issues related to the writing system and written conventions, learners have no recourse but to resort to decoding rather than actual *reading*. Presenting the writing system as the gateway to the language can be problematic for the learner. Providing a foundation in the spoken language first is a great help in developing actual, productive reading and writing skills. The development of skills in speaking and listening should not depend on a knowledge of the writing system. If the writing system is the primary access to the language, any learners who encounter difficulties with the orthography are limited in their ability to converse, not to mention subject to problems that can arise from misunderstandings about spoken and written conventions. We discuss this issue in more detail later.

Another core principle in the performed culture approach is authenticity. When the goal is to help learners to operate in culturally appropriate ways, it becomes very important to expose them to authentic language and authentic situations and provide tasks that enable them to practice responding authentically; this applies to both the spoken and the written language. With the written language, authentic texts and authentic tasks are essential. An authentic text is often defined as one produced by native speakers for native speakers. However, this definition can be too narrow: Language used naturally by native speakers when speaking with nonnatives, as well as linguistically and pragmatically acceptable language used by nonnatives speaking with native speakers, can also legitimately be considered authentic (Noda 1994). Another way of defining *authenticity* in foreign language education is language that is "interesting and comprehensible" (Krashen 1997, 34). Beyond interest or comprehensibility, however, cultural authenticity is essential in helping learners understand the role of texts in the target culture. We adopt Noda's definition of *authenticity* in our discussion and acknowledge the role pedagogically created materials can play in authentic tasks.

A useful way of looking at the relative balance of the skill mix through the course of a program has been proposed by Walker (1989): His pedagogical model distinguishes between Learning Model Instruction (LMI) and Acquisition Model Instruction (AMI) (discussed further in Chapter Five). The LMI/AMI pattern fits well with the goals of a performed culture approach. Based on the characteristics of this model, programs should begin with LMI and proceed to AMI. Kubler et al. (1997, 117) describe these models as follows:

> The learning model is concerned with the mastering of "product" such as sounds, patterns, communicative conventions, and lexicon. In many ways, the traditional textbook embodies the Learning Model. The Acquisition Model, by contrast, focuses on the learning of processes and strategies—global abilities rather than discrete items. Strategies for improving skills receive special attention in

the Acquisition Model: artifacts and authentic materials are also introduced.

We suggest that artifacts and authentic materials can be effectively introduced even in LMI. The kinds of activities based on a given artifact will vary, however, depending on the LMI/AMI balance. In AMI, additional artifacts and materials are introduced. We discuss this in more detail later.

In terms of the balance between reading and writing activities, given the natural ratio of the four language skills for native speakers and the needs of (almost) all learners, it is appropriate to focus more on reading than on writing; most adult native speakers of any language spend more time listening than speaking and more time reading than writing. This does not suggest that writing skills are unimportant. However, given that writing is the least used of the four main skill areas, writing activities in the curriculum should not overshadow the development of other skills. Reading and writing tasks should be contextualized and should focus on the needs of the learners. For example, most learners will have little opportunity to write formal research papers in Chinese, Japanese, or Korean. Before concentrating on the development of skills in this genre, it is more useful to provide opportunities to write letters, memos, faxes, or e-mail messages in the target language. In any case, before learners are given writing tasks, they should have adequate exposure to the conventions of that genre in the target language. In other words, because of the goal of learning to *perform* in the target culture, before we ask learners to practice writing letters in the target language, they should know what conventions are applicable, including why, when, and how natives of that culture write letters. It is helpful to see many examples of the genre before producing a text; otherwise, the task will amount to little more than practice in manipulating the orthography. If the learners don't understand how target natives deal with the text, the structure, content, and rhetorical conventions will, by default, be those of the base culture. Just as cultural authenticity is essential in contextualizing conversational activities, learners benefit from exposure to authentic texts and from authentic tasks based on those texts.

The written language is not merely the spoken language in written form. It is important, therefore, to have an established understanding of the spoken language, which can then be used as the foundation for understanding issues unique to the written language. Each mode of expression has its own conventions and styles; for example, learning to read (or write) involves far more than processing written representations of the spoken language. This is certainly true of Japanese and Korean, and in Chinese in the previously noted differences between *kǒutóuyǔ (spoken language)* and *shūmiànyǔ (written language)*. Remember that the written language itself does not signify intonation or pause length, for example.

In the early stages of developing reading skills (LMI), however, there is a role for written representations of the spoken language. As always, these representations need to be presented in culturally authentic contexts. In these cases, teachers should be careful to point out differences between spoken and written representations. Walker (1984) identifies two important strategies that learners must acquire in the reading process: *literacy strategy* and *reading strategy*. The goal of *literacy* is to enable learners to read what they would be able to understand in speech. In other words, beginners first need to learn how to read and write what they have learned how to speak and understand; in Chinese, this usually correlates with the first 150 to 300 characters. *Reading strategy* is used when introducing learners to *shūmiànyǔ* elements common in literary Chinese. Texts in reading strategy–based exercises are authentic texts written in Chinese. Literacy-based activities might also include authentic texts. The purpose of reading strategy instruction is to enable learners to make the connection between *kǒutóuyǔ* elements and their *shūmiànyǔ* counterparts. In short, written representations of the spoken language may be used to foster the development of literacy skills. The development of reading skills is based on exposure to conventions of the written language.

Walker (1984) also stresses that it is not enough to know what is in the text; learners must also know what to do with a text once the content is understood. To participate in text-based activities in the target culture, learners need to know not only the conventions of written genres, but also their purposes in that culture. Texts serve a social role, and so reading is a social behavior.

Unless learners have a prior foundation in the spoken language, reading tasks will amount to little more than decoding, where the learners simply translate individual symbols to sounds. With a prior foundation in the spoken language, on the other hand, learners will be able to process a text in meaningful units and develop skills similar to those used in reading their native language.

When the written language is introduced simultaneously (i.e., with no prior foundation *in the given language of the text*), any problems a learner has with the writing system will affect the ability to speak. If materials are presented in the target orthography prematurely, the development of speaking skills becomes a function of the degree of ability in reading. The learner must be able to read to benefit from the expressed content.

When considering how to present the writing system for learners, it is important to keep in mind that the functions of the writing system do not include teaching pronunciation. The sound system of a language is independent of its orthography. The orthography can represent sounds, but does not include notations for accent, intonation, or tones (or even pronunciation in the case of Chinese characters).

Having listening and speaking activities precede reading and writing matches the natural order of acquisition: Children learn to read and write their native language after extensive experience with conversation. Certainly with a second language, the time frame is compacted, and in a university setting, the learners are adults with developed cognitive abilities, but the fact remains that learning to read and write is facilitated when the learner already has an understanding of the how the language works as a system, with structures, lexicon, and a sound system. Because it is helpful to focus on speaking and listening first, the question is not whether to introduce the writing system, but when. As reading and writing skills follow the development of speaking and listening skills, reading and writing can provide reinforcement and review of vocabulary and structures learned previously in the spoken language.

If the introduction of the writing system is delayed, what is an appropriate time lag? If the native script is not used initially, is a pedagogical transcription necessary in the meantime? What would such a transcription be like? When the writing system is introduced, how should instruction proceed? In the case of Japanese, should *kana* be used exclusively prior to the introduction of *kanji*?

Based on the foregoing discussion, we suggest that use of a pedagogical transcription has an important role when teaching East Asian languages. The purpose of a pedagogical transcription is to *remind* learners visually of sounds that they have already been exposed to in speaking and listening activities. Even in the development of conversational skills, it is useful to have access to visual reminders of what has been heard already. The point of such a transcription system is to use an orthographic system already familiar to the learners so that the development of spoken skills is not tied to a new writing system.

Theoretically, any transcription system that uses symbols already familiar to the learners should suffice. The point is that the learners need to understand the relationship between the visual representation and the actual sound in the target language. Remember that the sounds of a language are independent of any writing system, even the one used in the culture of that language. It makes sense to use a transcription already familiar to the learners in order to save time and energy. In the case of native English speakers, Romanization is a natural choice. In the discussion that follows, the term "Romanization" refers broadly to both Romanization as used in Japanese and *pīnyīn* in Chinese.

ROMANIZATION

The issue of Romanization is one where opinions seem to be more deeply held than in other areas in East Asian language pedagogy. In fact, it seems to be one of the most contentious issues among teachers. Some of the complaints apparently come from the fact that Romanization has been misused at times, and others arise from misunderstandings about the purpose of Romanization. This is, in fact, a very crucial issue because it affects in a fundamental way how the language is presented in every set of materials. The question of whether to use Romanization gets to the core of some of the most crucial issues in language pedagogy, namely: What is language? What is the relationship between the spoken and the written language? What is reading? What is the significance of authenticity and cultural appropriateness? In this section, we address some of the concerns raised about using Romanization and show why it is valuable in the early stages of learning East Asian languages.

A pedagogical transcription is a visual reminder of what the learner has heard, and it is intended as a quick reference to aid in developing conversational skills and learning grammar and vocabulary. It can give access to the spoken language in the early stages of conversational skills without requiring the learner to first master the writing system and develop reading skills. The advantage of Romanization is that the symbols are already familiar to the learners. Romanization can represent the sound system of Japanese with about twenty characters that learners already know, as opposed to the forty-six symbols in the *kana* systems. Learners thus have immediate access to the script. However, a disadvantage comes from this very reason: Because learners already know the Roman alphabet, they may rely on their knowledge of the sounds represented by a given letter in their native language. This is also the case with *pīnyīn* in Chinese. Therefore, it is essential to teach the phonology of the target language aurally and then help the learners see the relationship between the visual image and the aural image.

Even when learning another language that uses the same script, it is necessary to teach the correspondence between the sounds of the language and the visual representation. For example, when native English speakers are learning Spanish, they are taught the proper pronunciation of words such as *Mexico* or *haber* or *llamar* and learn the visual representation of these words in Roman letters, even though the pronunciation in Spanish is different from what they might expect based solely on their knowledge of English. Similarly, when Romanization is used in teaching East Asian languages, it is important to teach the relationship between the pronunciation, which is the focal point, and the way that pronunciation is represented using the Roman alphabet. This is true of any writing system: Learners need to know the relationship between the symbol and the sound, with the understanding the symbol is not the sound; it merely represents it.

We next address some of the specific arguments commonly raised concerning the use of Romanization.

#1: "I'm opposed to using Romanization because it is not an authentic script of the target language."

Using Romanization for reading and writing is certainly not a natural activity in Japanese, Chinese, or Korean. In fact, even native

Japanese and Chinese who read English very well often have some difficulty in processing Romanized representations of their native language. Remember, however, that Romanization is *not* used to teach pronunciation, nor is it used for tasks related to the development of reading and writing skills. It is intended only as a visual reminder of pronunciation for conversation-based activities. These sounds should be taught first aurally through class activities and interactions with other media, such as videos or computer software.

If we reject Romanization because it is inauthentic, what should be used in its place? For Japanese, many would say that *hiragana* is the natural choice. Certainly few, if any, would argue that learners of Japanese should be exposed to *kanji* before *kana*. However, if Japanese is presented to beginning learners by using *kana*, then the development of conversational skills using information in the text materials is limited to the ability to recognize the *kana* characters. Any students who have difficulties in this regard will be hampered in their development of conversational skills if they cannot access lexical and grammar examples that are given only in that script; activities meant as speaking exercises then become reading (or decoding) exercises. Some would then argue that there are only 46 basic *kana* characters, which is not an overwhelming burden. However, learning *kana* is a process, and it should not be assumed that learners will necessarily have no problems or concerns in that process. More is said about this later.

Although *kana* is a native script in Japanese, when a sentence or a text written for adults is represented completely in *kana*, this results in an unnatural or inauthentic use of an authentic script. Some who argue against Romanization based on the claim that it is not authentic don't seem to mind a lack of authenticity in the way *kana* is used. Texts written completely in *kana* are not intended for adults, or else they have been modified from their original representation. Writing texts completely in *kana* is not an activity Japanese adults engage in when communicating with other adults. Many adult Japanese have a difficult time processing extended texts of *kana* with no *kanji*, just as they have some difficulty with Romanization.

In short, neither Romanization nor *kana*, as used in elementary textbooks, can be considered an authentic representation of Japanese conversation. Given that in the earliest stages of the Japanese curriculum, at least, learners do not have sufficient background to read texts with *kanji*, some adaptation is required. The issue then becomes deciding which is more desirable (in other words, more effective)—an "unnatural" script as a stepping stone for legitimate pedagogical purposes in representing authentic Japanese, or an authentic script used in inauthentic ways (orthographically and socioculturally) just for the sake of using an authentic script. Why not choose the alternative that makes sense for pedagogical purposes rather than confounding the issue by introducing a new script prematurely?

Remember that authenticity is a primary principle in the performed culture approach. Although cultural authenticity is essential, as we argue throughout this book, it is important to recognize that to help learners develop skills in an authentic manner, some tools are useful, effective, and efficient for pedagogical purposes, even though native speakers may not use those tools in the same way. Such tools are limited, and must be chosen carefully. One example is repeated interaction with multimedia software in the effort to develop automaticity in listening comprehension related to a certain pattern, or repeated writing of a certain character in the process of learning the graphic form of a word.

What we are advocating is the use of Romanization as a visual reminder of spoken discourse. We are not suggesting that it is appropriate to use Romanization to teach pronunciation or as a medium for reading and writing activities. We are proposing that there is a clear distinction in function and use between Romanization and native scripts. When *hiragana* is used unnaturally, as it necessarily must be when used as the only script, it may be more misleading to learners than a pedagogical script used for a particular pedagogical (and temporary) purpose.

It should be further emphasized that Romanization systems are designed to be a bridge to the authentic language represented in the native orthography. Learners must understand that they will not find complete texts written in Romanization. On the other hand, native teachers of Chinese and Japanese must also realize that learners will use Romanization. Many learners, even those who are not exposed to Romanization in the curriculum, create their own Romanization system, such as in transcribing new aural input for future reference. Whether we like it or not, or care to admit it, Romanization is an important tool in the learning process.

Everson's (1988) study highlighted learners' reliance on Romanization systems. He found that beginners read faster and comprehend more when reading a text in *pīnyīn* versus reading the same text in characters. It is wholly likely that as learners progress, they will become more comfortable with characters. Everson's findings show that learners rely heavily on Romanization (in this case, *pīnyīn*) throughout their first year of study. These findings also indicate that learners are adapted to associating the sound with the word when reading (see also Light 1976). As learners progress, they will become familiar with the various phonological clues in characters and rely more on the native orthography. Research demonstrates that even when reading nonalphabetical orthographies such as Chinese or Japanese, native readers still rely on phonological variables when reading (Matsunaga 1994, 1995; Horodeck 1987; Ke 1996). In other words, subvocalization plays a role when native Chinese and Japanese speakers read. For nonnative readers, a foundation built on knowledge of the phonological components of words *before* starting to read will aid in the reading process.

There are other practical advantages to knowing Romanization. For example, it allows access to dictionaries, particularly in the earlier stages of learning. There are Japanese-English dictionaries with entries listed in *kana* and those with entries in Romanization. Nearly all Chinese-English and English-Chinese dictionaries use *pīnyīn*. Romanization is necessary for using word processors in Japanese. It is useful in reading maps and signs (e.g., at airports), and it is necessary when using some library catalogs. Also, it is becoming the standard method of representing some lexical items in Japanese (e.g., *OL* for "office lady"). Romanization is also useful in Japanese in that it captures morphological regularities more systematically, which in turn facilitates presenting and learning grammar points (e.g., *kak-u*, *kak-anai*, and *kak-imasu*).

#2: "Romanization fosters poor pronunciation."
Romanization is only a *printed* form! As already noted, theoretically, any written representation is as good as another in reflecting pronunciation as long as the users of the system know the "code," that is, the relationship between the written representation and the

corresponding pronunciation. Proper pronunciation is based on what the learners *hear*, not what they *see*. *Kana* has no inherent superiority when it comes to reflecting pronunciation. Remember that Romanization is not used to *teach* pronunciation. *Kana* is not a tool for *teaching* pronunciation either. Even if we grant that *kana* is better in reflecting pronunciation, what about intonation? Diacritics can be easily added to Romanization as a visual reminder of intonation contours. Markings can be added to *kana* also (Makino et al. 1998) but the result, again, is an unnatural use of the script. The purpose of any script in the beginning stages of language learning is only to *remind* the learner of what he or she has already been exposed to, whether in class, on audiotape, on videotape, or through the computer. Romanization, properly used, is never meant to *teach* pronunciation (McGinnis 1997b).

#3: "Romanization hampers reading ability."
As already noted, Romanization is meant only to remind learners of pronunciation. It is *not* intended as a means for learners to read and write. Activities for developing reading and writing skills are based on the native script and are introduced gradually based on the linguistic development of the learner. This point is discussed in more detail in Chapter Four.

Rather than hampering reading ability, the use of Romanization in fostering conversational ability prior to the development of reading and writing skills has been shown to be beneficial. Watabe (1996) reports that independent tests administered to students from a variety of Japanese programs over several years show that learners who first developed facility with the spoken language (through Romanization) performed better than learners whose experience was based on materials that introduced the native script immediately. Such results are based on appropriate use of Romanization.

Reading and writing require far more than knowing the writing system. Certainly, knowing the characters is essential, but there is much more involved in the development of true reading and writing ability. Also, remember that we are not arguing for a lengthy delay in the introduction of native scripts; we merely suggest that Romanization has value in the beginning stages for certain pedagogical purposes. It can be misused if it is meant as a tool to teach pronunciation or as a means for "reading" and "writing" texts.

#4: "The writing system is hard, and learners must get an early start in order to develop any reasonable level of proficiency."

It is true that the orthography of Chinese or Japanese (and less so for Korean) poses significant challenges to the learner whose native language uses an alphabetic script. However, length of exposure does not necessarily equate to proficiency in using a script. Starting prematurely is not "reading." When learners "read" without sufficient knowledge of the language as a system, they tend to see characters as isolated symbols, which leads to decoding from symbol to sound, rather than reading in any meaningful sense. There is no sense of the text as a text. Undue emphasis on characters alone can result in a lack of awareness of a sentence as a meaningful unit of information. Learners often focus on understanding individual characters and lose sight of what the text is saying. Although knowledge of the individual symbols is essential in reading, early exposure in and of itself does not provide meaningful assistance in the development of reading skills. In the case of English, being a good speller, for example, does not make one a good reader. When dealing with truly foreign languages, linguistic and cultural issues are no less challenging than orthographic ones. Mere exposure to the script does not automatically address linguistic, cultural, textual, or social challenges. We argue that these issues are addressed most effectively *after* the learners have a foundation in the spoken language. When learners have a solid understanding of the language as a system of meaning, learning characters is more efficient and fosters actual reading skills rather than just character recognition.

#5: "All four skills should be taught at once."

As already noted, given the primacy of spoken language, it is not unreasonable in the beginning stages of language learning to focus on speaking and listening first (Jorden and Walton 1987). Native speakers of a language do not learn to read and write before learning how to speak. There is no culture that developed a written language before a spoken language. It may be argued that there are some learners who care to develop only reading and writing skills; they may consider that speaking and listening skills are not relevant to their purposes in studying the language. However, knowledge of the spoken language has been shown to help reading and writing skills. Learners can be more effective readers or writers if they first develop a sense for the language as a system.

We suggest introducing reading and writing gradually, based on the linguistic units that the learners have encountered. Initial exercises in reading and writing can begin relatively soon in the curriculum, but they need to be geared to the learners' level of language ability.

#6: "Administrators want to see reading taught—I need to provide evidence that all four skills are being taught."

A major purpose of this book is to show that teaching languages such as Chinese, Japanese, or Korean to native English speakers requires a new paradigm. By and large, if administrators have a sense of language teaching, they have the perspective of teaching Indo-European languages. Thus it may be necessary to educate administrators about the particular challenges and issues in teaching East Asian languages. Methods and philosophies that are justified and appropriate in teaching Indo-European languages may not fit well when teaching East Asian languages (or TFLs). As shown in Chapter One, the amount of class time required to reach a particular level of proficiency will vary widely between languages. It may be necessary to explain to administrators that it takes longer for learners of Chinese, Japanese, or Korean to acquire a sufficient foundation to read literature in the original than it may take for learners of Indo-European languages. Learners of Indo-European languages often begin reading literature in the target language in the second year of study, but it is unreasonable to expect that native English-speaking learners of East Asian languages will do the same. Again, the delay in introducing reading and writing is based on the learners' foundation in the language and the types of texts and tasks used. Teachers need not wait months or years to begin any reading. The issue is the relative ratio at the given level.

#7: "The native script is exotic and therefore motivating; it gives learners the feeling that they really are learning."

The importance of motivation and affective issues must not be underestimated. However, the fact that some learners may have a greater sense that they are really learning something just because they are learning characters is again evidence of the perception that the written language *is* the language. Just as administrators sometimes need educating, we must also educate our students about what we do and why we do it. We are advocating a very different approach from the way other languages are taught. Students enroll in our courses with a perception of what language learning is and what language classes are like, which is often based on prior experience learning an Indo-European language. We often must gently instruct them about what we do and why so that they can understand (even if they may not agree). Sound pedagogy must be based on sound theory, which must be informed by solid research. The theory and pedagogy of teaching East Asian languages are informed by research beyond that arising from teaching Spanish or French to native English speakers.

The native script definitely can be exciting and motivating, but it can also be overwhelming; this is particularly true of *kanji* (as opposed to *kana*) and Chinese characters. If learners are asked to negotiate the script before they have a sufficient foundation in how the language works as a system, the very thing that is the source of excitement can quickly become one of discouragement and frustration. We stress again that it is advantageous to introduce the script using an ordered approach, geared to the linguistic level of the learners, to enable them to read and write texts naturally at the given level.

In Chinese, *Hànyǔ pīnyīn* has become the standard form of Romanization with the vast majority of textbooks, dictionaries, and other reference books using *pīnyīn*. DeFrancis (1984) has explained why the *pīnyīn* system is superior to other Romanization systems. Whether or not one agrees with DeFrancis, *pīnyīn* is likely to remain as the dominant Romanization system for pedagogical purposes as well as dictionaries. Even dictionaries and textbooks published in Taiwan use *pīnyīn*, at least as a supplementary system.

Some feel that there are better phonological representations of the Chinese sound system. The primary critics of *pīnyīn* are proponents of the Taiwan phonetic symbols, *zhùyīn fúhào* (or *bopo mofo*), and the *Gwoyeu Romatzyh* (or GR, which is a way of representing the tone of the word in the spelling). Johnson (1985), Lundelius (1992), and Bryant (1992) have argued against DeFrancis's views in favor of GR. Some of these advocates are very passionate about the benefits of the two alternative Romanization systems. They have even suggested that learners who use *zhùyīn fúhào* or GR to learn Chinese will have better pronunciation than those who use *pinyin* or some other system. We know of no empirical research data that suggests this is true. On the other hand, McGinnis (1997b) conducted a study with two control groups, one that used *pīnyīn* and the other that used *Gwoyeu Romatzyh*; his findings likewise do not suggest the superiority of one Romanization system over another. With any system, the learner must associate the graphic representation of a sound with the actual sound, regardless of the symbol used. It is important to emphasize to our students the importance of not relying too heavily on Romanization, and that Romanization is a bridge and an approximation of the actual sound. This is one of the reasons why it is so important for learners to heavily use audio and video programs when learning Chinese, Japanese, or Korean, and not rely solely on the written representation of the sounds. We do not think that one Romanization system is better than any other. Whichever system is used, learners must learn it well.

In the case of Japanese, there are two primary Romanization systems in common use; one is used often in dictionaries and on maps and signs, and the other is used by linguists. However, there are only a handful of differences between the two. Whichever one is used, the important point is to help learners understand the relationship between the sounds of the language and the visual representation in Romanization.

Next, we introduce two characteristics of the performed culture approach that can be applied in the classroom to help instill in learners an understanding of the relationship between language and culture. These have proven to be valid and effective tools in the process of learning East Asian languages. They are a distinction and balance between ACT classes and FACT classes, and the use of a daily evaluation of learner performance.

ACT AND FACT

A performed culture approach to teaching utilizes two types of classes, referred to as FACT and ACT. This model reflects the distinction between declarative and procedural knowledge. Knowledge is gained through both theory and practice. Simply put, declarative knowledge is what one knows *about* the language, and procedural knowledge is what one can *do* with the language, one's ability to perform in the language. Declarative knowledge may be thought of as the theoretical component and procedural knowledge as the practical component, or the application of theory. O'Malley and Chamot (1990) describe the difference as language as a skill (procedural—ACT) and language as an object of study (declarative—FACT). The analogy has also been made that declarative knowledge is like the data stored on a computer and procedural knowledge is like the software that makes it possible to use the data in a practical way: Both are essential and work together in a complementary manner.

With regard to teaching, declarative knowledge includes the study of language learning, that is, the research and theories of second language acquisition and how they apply to Chinese, Japanese, and Korean as foreign languages, and involves studying the processes of learning. The practical application of theory and research in the classroom is conveyed by both procedural and declarative knowledge. The presentation of practice, the methods and techniques used in effective teaching, or the explanation of how to apply the theory, is declarative, and implementation of the practice, or the physical manifestation of theory and practice, is procedural. Both declarative and procedural strategies not only provide a balanced means for learners to understand why something is said in a specific context, but also give them the practice to be able to perform confidently in the future. This FACT/ACT approach also accommodates both inductive and deductive learning styles. A purely inductive approach may leave some students feeling unfulfilled in their understanding of grammar patterns, vocabulary usage, and cultural context. Most learners will benefit from discussion and explanation of these grammar points and cultural aspects of language use, particularly when learning the target language as an adult. On the other hand, a purely deductive approach, which is the emphasis of approaches such as the grammar-translation method, seldom produces learners with actual productive communicative skills that can be applied immediately in the target culture. Learners of these types of approaches often have a firm grounding in abstract grammar principles but have difficulty applying this knowledge to real-life situations.

In summary, the FACT classes include discussion about the language and the culture, such as explanations about how to produce the sounds of the target language, grammar patterns and how they are used, when and how certain vocabulary items are used, when and how natives of the target culture make apologies, how business cards are exchanged, and what the restaurant script for the target culture is like. The ACT classes provide opportunities for learners to *perform* in the culture, in contextualized settings that allow them to make apologies or exchange business cards or enact restaurant settings. It is essential that the situations are culturally authentic and that the learners understand the genre and the style involved, including the five elements of performance—the time, the place, the roles, the script, and the audience. Ideally, FACT classes are taught by natives of the base language who have the experience of learning the target language as a foreign language. On the other hand, ACT classes are taught, ideally, by natives of the target culture because they can provide a model of language use that is culturally and linguistically accurate.   * Depends on the learner

The ratio of ACT to FACT classes is an important issue in creating an effective balance between procedural and declarative knowledge. We recommend at least four ACT sessions for every ✓ FACT session, although the ratio may vary depending on local circumstances. One session of FACT-based learning provides a solid foundation in the social and cultural implications of the language, grammar explanation and drills, and vocabulary review in order to enable learners to understand how to apply the information in meaningful and stimulating exchanges. The emphasis on procedural knowledge, or ACT-based learning, provides ample opportunities for learners to practice the material they have learned and reviewed outside the class with audio, video, multimedia, and print materials and then continue in activities giving opportunities to *apply* their developing skills. Another reason there is a greater emphasis on ACT sessions is that learning a skill through performance is a time-consuming process and requires repeated practice before automaticity is attained, just as it takes much repetition to learn any skill (such as hitting a baseball with a bat).

Declarative knowledge is important for the teacher for several reasons. First, knowing how learners learn most effectively will ultimately steer one toward more useful and effective teaching approaches. Second, sound research provides concrete data as to what theories or approaches actually work in the classroom. It teaches us which pitfalls to avoid and how to apply that which has been proven effective in the classroom. Third, most students are not satisfied with explanations such as "that's just the way it is." They benefit far more by knowing why and what kind of language is used in specific contexts, as well as the social and cultural implications of various communicative situations. Fourth, declarative knowledge reinforces the implicit or procedural knowledge. It gives learners a better overall understanding of the language and why it is used the way it is.

Theory gives teachers conceptual power and creative freedom. It provides more teaching options and possibilities, and the ability to develop a repertoire of teaching techniques based on the best aspects of a variety of research and experiments.

ACT Sessions · Exclusively in the target lg   · performances in contextualized setting   · Application of the declarative knowledge   · opportunity to apply skills

In an ACT-based class, the focus is performance, or procedural knowledge. The role of the teacher may be viewed as that of a theatrical director. The director does not stand up and "teach" by lecturing. He or she stands at the sidelines coaching, correcting, guiding the learners not only in what to say, but how to say it, and how to carry themselves in relation to others participating in the performance. As needed, the director models the desired performance. Traditional classrooms tend to be teacher oriented, that is, the teacher does most of the talking. In a true ACT class, the teacher plays a more peripheral role, guiding and directing the learners in their performances. The teacher strives to provide as much opportunity as possible for learners to apply the knowledge they have studied and prepared outside the class and in the FACT sessions. The learners do the bulk of the speaking (or reading). They are forced to take responsibility for their learning and must perform to make the grade. This is not the classroom for a passive learner who makes minimal effort to prepare, and hides in the back of the

60

Act teachers :
• To know the FACT knowledge
• attend FACT class

Chapter 2: Performing Culture

room hoping to avoid being called on by the teacher. In the ACT class, learners know that they will be expected to perform, and not just a few lines here and there, but extensively. To allow all students the opportunity to perform at length necessitates that class size be kept small. We recommend class size not to exceed fifteen students, with eight to twelve being optimum. Often administrative issues make this difficult.

ACT sessions will be far more effective if they are conducted entirely in the target language, which simulates the target speaking community as much as is possible. If teachers and students take this seriously, the rewards of better, more natural communication will result. If the base language is used, even briefly, the learners tend to speak more and more in English as time goes on, thereby diminishing the precious time that could have been spent in target language application. Situations that require use of the base language are treated out of class or in FACT class.

Anatomy of an ACT Class
Here we describe a typical ACT class. We first describe a beginning level class, then an advanced level class.

Beginning-level ACT class
A typical week might look like this:

Monday:	Dialogue performance; oral performance activities (drills and exercises)
Tuesday:	FACT class
Wednesday:	oral performance activities (drills and exercises)
Thursday:	Reading and writing exercises; orthography quiz
Friday:	improvisational dialogues; oral performance activities

1. At the start of the instructional cycle (lesson), the class will begin with a dialogue performance. Students are expected to memorize the dialogue outside class and come to class prepared to perform. The teacher will have a variety of visual aids to set up the context for the performance; for a greeting performance, this may include nametags to indicate the roles of the learners as well as other props to indicate the time, location, and so on. The teacher may spend a moment

modeling the dialogue to refresh the students' memories. Students are then called randomly to come to the front of the class to perform the dialogue. This should be done without any reference to books or notes: The emphasis is on performance. Students should understand that this is not a recitation but a performance that involves interacting with another person. It also requires nonlinguistic forms of communication, such as bowing and other body language.

2. Drills and Exercises

Drills and exercises are both important aspects of the learning process. Drills may be regarded as scaffolding activities in that they prepare the learners for more open-ended and realistic performances. Often learners can perform drills with the aid of instructional materials such as audio programs. Typical drills include substitution activities, fill-in-the-blank, and answering questions, and are characterized by having predictable, sometimes "set" answers. Some class time can (and should) be used for drills, but the bulk of time should be dedicated to exercises. Having learners practice a few drills provides a nice warm-up and review of the material needed to perform in the coming exercises. Exercises are performances where there is no "set" answer. Learners are typically free to respond in an improvisational manner. Two important principles to keep in mind are that exercises should be *authentic* and *useful* in both language and task. It makes no sense to have learners practice using language that is not authentic to the target culture. Likewise, they should be practicing language that they will likely use in the target culture. Teachers thus should design activities that require learners to perform realistic tasks. For example, students can find out from five classmates where they were born and grew up; this activity allows students to practice asking this common question a number of times with different classmates. Teachers can follow up with questions to the students about what they learned from their classmates, which teaches them the importance of accountability. It can also be used as a listening comprehension exercise.

In a typical classroom, one could start with drills to review the material that will be rehearsed in the class that day. For example, the teacher may begin with some simple questions, such as "Do you like to eat Chinese food?" "Do you like to eat American food?" "Do you like to eat Thai food?" This can then progress to calling on students to ask these questions of their fellow students (in a group setting). Finally, students can be assigned to find out the eating preferences of several classmates. They then report to the class (guided by the teacher) what they learned about their classmates.

3. Another day of the week can be devoted to reading and writing. Students are given reading and writing assignments to complete before coming to class. At the beginning level of instruction, reading aloud may be employed as a means of checking reading fluency, recognition of the orthography, and accuracy of pronunciation. However, this should not be the only reading activity used in the classroom. Other class activities may include oral questions based on a reading passage, having students write comprehension questions based on the reading passage and having other students write the answers, and sentence-writing practice using selected vocabulary items. It is more challenging at the beginning level of instruction to make all classroom activities authentic and useful. Scaffolding activities (such as writing sentences), however, build toward authentic and useful tasks. Authentic tasks at the beginning level include creating a shopping list, a short note to a friend, a simple letter, and a list of daily activities. A short quiz covering orthography (vocabulary items) can also be given on a reading and writing day.

4. Once beginning learners have established a foundation in the language, they can create their own improvisational performances based on the material presented in the current lesson; this is an ideal way to end an instructional cycle. Classmates can work together to create an authentic dialogue incorporating the context, grammar, and vocabulary items presented in the lesson. They will rehearse outside of class and come to class prepared to perform. After each performance, the teacher can ask a series of comprehension

questions, which requires students to pay attention to the performance and allows for more use of the target language, because students will discuss what they have observed.

Advanced-Level ACT Classes

At the advanced level of instruction, it is easier and more practical to integrate the four skills, specifically reading with speaking and listening. Most advanced-level classes have a significant reading and writing component. Following is a list of suggested activities for an advanced-level ACT language class. Remember that in an ACT class, the target language is used exclusively. These same suggestions could also be utilized in a literature course. A more detailed description of reading and writing activities is found in Chapter Four.

- Have students do the bulk of reading assignments outside class.
- Have a question-and-answer session on the content of the passage, which will show whether students actually did the reading.
- Have a discussion about the author's point of view, the background to the passage, the genre of writing, and so on. This could also be done in a FACT class.
- Have students express their opinions about the reading passage.
- Have students give oral summaries of the reading passage.
- Have a debate on a topic or issue addressed in the reading passage.
- Have students respond to various issues as characters or the author of the reading passage would.

FACT Sessions (To support ACT class)

Whereas an ACT session attempts to create a target language speaking environment, a FACT session focuses on talking *about* the target language and culture to help the learners develop a cognitive understanding to prepare for performance activities. In this kind of teaching session, the learners' native language may be used, and learners are encouraged to ask about grammar, vocabulary, culture, or any other related topic. In a FACT session, it is important to help learners understand the social and cultural implications of the language and not just the grammatical structures. This time can be spent in helping the learners to understand aspects of the genres and styles they are practicing in ACT classes.

Anatomy of a FACT Class
One day of the week or instructional cycle is dedicated to a FACT session. The primary purpose of this class is to support ACT performances. As already noted, FACT time focuses on declarative knowledge, the purpose of which is to provide a structure for performance. FACT classes include a range of material, such as discussions of the following.

1. grammar patterns
2. vocabulary and usage
3. social and cultural issues
4. pronunciation, accent, and intonation
5. writing system
6. reading and writing conventions
7. learning strategies
8. how the five elements of performance relate to past and future class scenarios and applications
9. the background, genre, cultural significance, author, and so on of a reading passage.

This class allows the teacher to monitor student learning, follow up on previous ACT performances, and help set the stage for future performances. It is a time when learners can ask questions freely and provides the teacher with a good opportunity to motivate and encourage.

FACT class might include short quizzes covering any of the items just listed. The teacher may choose to conduct short rehearsal activities to help prepare for the ACT performances to follow. He or she may discuss the various meanings and connotations of vocabulary items that are not fully treated in textbooks. For example, the Japanese word *sumimasen* has a variety of meanings depending on the context in which it is used; these variations should be pointed out, together with an explanation of how changes in the five elements of performance account for the different uses. The teacher may also discuss other behavioral cultural items related to the lesson content.

The FACT teacher may also act as a coach, helping the learners to discover the relevant information rather than presenting everything in a lecture format. In FACT class as well as in ACT class, the learners should be held accountable for their preparation and their performance.

As a general principle, it is helpful when introducing grammar structures to present the common before the rare, the general before the specific, and the simple before the complex (National Foreign Language Center, 1993). Many native English speakers who have been raised in the United States have relatively little background in linguistic terminology; it is important to make use of the learners' knowledge of their native language, but teachers should be clear in their use of terms and show where the target language is similar to the base language and where it differs. Coherent presentation of the language is more effective for the learners.

The FACT class provides a good opportunity to display and discuss artifacts of the target culture as they relate to the accompanying performances. FACT classes and ACT classes are substantially different in terms of content and teacher/learner interaction, but they complement each other and are intended to provide the learners with a solid foundation for developing self-managed learning skills and culturally sensitive interactions.

EVALUATING DAILY PERFORMANCE

Establishing a method to hold learners accountable for their in-class actions, which in turn holds them accountable for how they prepare for class, facilitates effective performance in the classroom. Evaluation and feedback become the impetus for careful, solid preparation and more serious performance. We have found that evaluating learners on their daily performance—whether it be speaking, responding to speech, reading, or writing—provides this necessary encouragement to prepare and perform with consistency. It also instills in them the importance of these daily performances. Again, learning a language is learning a skill, not just acquiring a body of facts, such as words and grammar patterns. What a student can do on a few examinations during a course is not the best measure of what that student has really learned, internalized, and can actually do in a given situation. Though quizzes and exams are part of the academic setting, they ultimately should constitute a relatively small portion of a student's overall grade (perhaps 20%). What makes the difference in language learning is consistent effort over time. Daily evaluation of performance reflects this fact and both rewards and encourages the learners in their preparation. The vast majority of a student's grade should be based on the bulk of the effort, which is preparation and performance. This is reflected in the average of daily performances during the course. Because there are so many individual scores given throughout an academic term, no one score will significantly affect the overall average. The daily evaluation program encourages and rewards consistency. Neither occasional bursts of brilliance nor the inevitable stumbling on a given day will unduly influence the measure of the ability of the learner (the overall performance average). This system gives the teacher a better idea of what a learner can really do with the language and also provides important feedback that can be used to adjust teaching and learning experiences throughout the course. Most important, it can provide the learner with frequent, current feedback about how performance and preparation compare with the desired goal.

We have found that using a four-point grading scale is an effective way to evaluate daily performance. The emphasis of the performance scale is on cultural coherence; that is, the learners should be taught and encouraged to perform in such a way that native speakers who are not necessarily accustomed to communicating with foreigners would not have to adapt their behavior, linguistic or otherwise, to negotiate intentions and meanings. In the performed culture approach, it is not just the linguistic code that is evaluated, but also the associated behavior necessary for appropriate cultural communication. The outline that follows describes the preparation and performance ability for each level, with 4 representing nativelike communication within the domain and range of the learners' experience, and 1 indicating no real ability to communicate. It should be noted that achieving a score of 4 is wholly possible for the true novice learner who may know only one brief greeting consisting of two words, so long as that greeting is performed in such a way that no discomfort or misunderstanding arises in the target native interlocutor.

In-class performance standard

4.0   Solid preparation is evident and performance is fully culturally coherent, that is, speaking, writing, and responding to speech in ways in which natives of the target culture expect people to speak, write, and respond. It would present no difficulty, discomfort, or misunderstanding for a native. Repair (restating) is self-managed.

3.5   Good preparation with solid performance, such that there would be little to create difficulties, discomfort, or misunderstanding in interaction with a native. However, a few noticeable errors could hinder smooth interaction. Most repairs are self-managed.

3.0   Good preparation with good performance. Some aspects of the performance would create difficulties, discomfort, or misunderstanding in communication with a native. Evident weakness or patterned error requires occasional repair/correction from another (teacher, classmate).

2.5   Some preparation is evident and performance enables communication, but also presents several clear sources of difficulty, discomfort, or misunderstanding in communicating with a native. Repair is largely a matter of correcting problems, and comes mostly from others.

2.0   Weak preparation and performance create definite obstacles to communication that would result in more than simple discomfort. Utterances would cause puzzlement that the native is at a loss to resolve (what is this person trying to say?). Repair requires guidance from another (mostly the teacher), usually with multiple, often repeated, corrections.

1.5   Barely any preparation, with performance that would create considerable difficulties, discomfort, and/or misunderstanding in communicating with a native. Communication is achieved only with repeated correction and guidance from the teacher. Clearly not in control of the assigned material.

1.0   Attended class, but did not participate or failed to perform with any viable degree of competence.

0   Absent

Learners need to receive frequent feedback in order to benefit from the evaluations. Teachers have the responsibility to explain at the beginning of the course what will be evaluated, when and how it will be evaluated, and why. Of course, learners should not feel that they are always under the microscope. The feedback should be constructive. Everyone makes mistakes in learning a language, and everyone misspeaks, even in one's native language. A mistake does not necessarily result in a lower score. Note that the goal is to facilitate the development of self-managed learning skills. What we look for is the ability to recognize that a mistake or a slip was made and then self-correct.

Regardless of the skill being practiced, a performed culture approach can be successful. With regard to reading, we must get beyond the intense focus on the text and the linguistic parts that make up the whole, and learn the importance and value of top-down learning strategies. When reading a text, we need to consider the social implications. In other words, when we read something, what do we do with that knowledge? Do we discuss it with others, share it, or ask questions about it? In a performed culture–based class, we may discuss the mechanics in a FACT session, then talk about the text and apply it to everyday living in the target language in ACT sessions. We discuss the issue of reading and writing in more depth in Chapter Four.

CLASSROOM MANAGEMENT:
THE ROLE OF THE TEACHER AND THE STUDENT

In a performance-based classroom, the roles of teacher and student differ from those in a traditional classroom. The teaching and learning process can be viewed as a theatrical performance; the classroom is the stage, the teacher plays the role of the director, and the students are the actors. Before the actual performance, there is a period of rehearsals during which the director coaches the actors in their various roles and performances. As with an actual theatrical performance, the director is usually off stage, the actors on stage. Likewise, the teacher in a performance-based classroom plays a peripheral role on the sidelines, coaching, correcting, and even modeling the performance. But it is the actors (the learners) who are on stage performing. The performed culture classroom is a learner-oriented setting where learners do the bulk of the speaking (or performing). One of the roles of the teacher is to provide opportunities for learners to use the language they have been introduced to in the instructional materials. In other words, the teacher is responsible for creating the contexts where learners can perform in a variety of communicative situations. The teacher then also plays the role of stage manager. The teacher is a manager of the time learners are in the classroom. ACT class time is not wasted on reading through vocabulary lists or dialogues, lengthy grammar explanations, dictation exercises, and so on. Learners are expected to prepare outside of class by memorizing dialogues, learning vocabulary, studying grammar patterns, reading assigned texts, considering the five elements of performance for the given scenarios, and so on. They should come to class prepared to *apply* this information in authentic and useful situations. Language performance should be contextualized; in other words, the teacher provides a context for each performance (i.e., sets the stage). Learners in these kinds of classes understand that performing is an integral part of the learning process and that a great deal of responsibility for learning lies with them.

CONCLUSION

Learning to speak a foreign language involves a variety of skills and behaviors. To communicate with native speakers in the target environment requires that learners know not only what to say, but also how to behave. This linguistic and cultural knowledge includes knowing what kind of language to use in a variety of circumstances (genres) and with a variety of people (styles). It also entails knowing what to do with oneself in a communicative situation. All four skills (listening, speaking, reading, and writing) are an inextricable part of the language maze. Furthermore, the cultural code is evident in every aspect of the linguistic code. With culture and performance as part of a framework for teaching East Asian languages, learning becomes more than memorizing vocabulary and grammar patterns, reciting dialogues, and reading aloud passages in the target orthography; it becomes an exercise in learning how to behave as a native of the target culture. It not only involves self-expression and interpretation of native intentions, but also includes the social function and reaction to language artifacts that require one to act upon that information as a native would. Our learners cannot become natives. However, it is possible and desirable for them to interact with target natives according to the conventions of the target culture in a way that will not cause any discomfort or embarrassment.

In the subsequent chapters, we discuss each of the four skills as well as the importance of context, grammar, and discourse strategies, and the role materials play in the learning process. We link all that we describe in these chapters to the performed culture framework we have established here and in Chapter One. It is our hope that the reader will come away with a more holistic view of the language-learning process and how to better teach these important principles in the classroom.

Chapter Three

SPEAKING AND LISTENING IN CULTURE

In this chapter, we discuss ideas for presenting speaking and listening activities to help learners perform in culture. We also outline aspects of the spoken language that need particular attention in beginning language courses. These are important in fostering the development of speaking and listening skills in order to promote natural conversational ability in culturally appropriate performances in East Asian languages. They also give a foundation on which to build reading and writing skills, which are discussed in the next chapter.

DISCOURSE-BASED ACTIVITIES

A primary goal of the performed culture approach is to help learners interact naturally in the target culture in ways that help native speakers of the target culture to feel comfortable. The basic unit for activities to develop speaking and listening skills is the dialogue. Social interaction consists of more than simple strings of sentences; utterances are combined in coherent ways and include discourse markers and other signals for turn taking. Also, with dialogues, learners have the opportunity to practice natural intonation patterns, which are determined by the dialogue as a whole, not merely individual sentences. Through dialogues, learners can use language naturally right from the beginning within the domain and range of the topics, structures, and situations that have been introduced.

As we have stressed, the dialogues should be authentic and useful. When learners practice such dialogues, they are able to develop repertoires that they know are authentic and accurate and they are able to develop automaticity with various scripts and situations.

Setting the Context

The key component in the presentation of the dialogues is contextualization. The first step is to consider what outcomes are desired in the learners as a result of the performances. What linguistic and cultural behavior should the learners experience and internalize as a result of the day's activities? Once this is determined, the teacher then considers contexts that will enable performances leading to those outcomes. It is essential that the learners understand the five elements of performance that are involved in each activity. Setting the context is the foundation for all activities. As learners understand the context, they can answer the following questions:

What is the occasion for this exchange?
Where is the exchange taking place?
What is the relationship between the people involved?
What is the purpose of the exchange?
Who else may be listening to the exchange?

In other words, *why* am I saying this and doing it in this way? The process of establishing context will change as the learners gain proficiency. Remember that in ACT classes, all interaction takes place in the target language. In the early stages of learning, therefore, the context will be set using visual aids, including perhaps simple signs written in the base language. For example, the teacher may display a sign or write on the board to communicate the aspects of performance; it may indicate the location ("at the office") or the occasion ("morning," "3:00 pm," "greeting your boss," etc.). Nametags are a useful way to indicate roles ("boss," "employee," "teacher," "student," "friend," etc.).

As the learners gain more proficiency, the contextualization can be done verbally; the teacher can outline the elements of performance by simply saying (in the target language) something like "Now we are at the office preparing for a meeting with overseas clients. You are discussing with a colleague the language abilities of the staff." It is important to remember that if the context is not clear to the learners, their use of the language becomes mechanical. They may say the appropriate dialogue but may not understand *why* they are saying what they are saying. The context is crucial in helping the learners to see the cultural appropriateness of the language they are using.

Role of Memorization

We recommend that learners come to ACT class having memorized the assigned dialogue. Currently, most text series include multimedia materials. Such materials provide visual and audio input that allows learners to hear native models and see the interactions take place in the culture. The multimedia materials provide the basis for memorizing dialogues. More advanced materials enable learners to record themselves as a participant in the dialogue, and they can then compare their utterances to the native model. The memorized dialogue becomes the basis for the day's activities, but it is the means to an end, not the goal in and of itself. The dialogue can be performed as it has been memorized, and then the learners can expand on what they have memorized and apply what they have prepared in new situations so that it becomes a part of them.

Most learners expect that language learning will require a great deal of memorization, although many seem to consider it only in terms of vocabulary and perhaps grammar structures. However, when it comes to learning dialogues, some students are apprehensive; they have difficulty understanding the purpose. It is important at the beginning of the course and perhaps periodically afterward to talk about why learners are asked to memorize.

Many will say something like "I am a visual learner and I can't memorize." This is understandable, and is probably true of most of us. Those who have participated in the U.S. educational system have generally had little opportunity to memorize. However, this does not mean that learners do not have or cannot develop the ability to learn aurally. Learners may not think they are good at memorization. However, most, if not all of them, have in fact memorized a large number of poems in the form of song lyrics, even though they may have never intentionally done so. They have memorized these lyrics, not as the result of an overt effort, but by repeated, contextualized exposure. The context includes music, which is a powerful context for memorizing, as well as learners' associations between the songs and experiences they have when listening to them. This example helps learners see that they can memorize under the right conditions, and it reminds teachers of the importance of contextualized repetition in fostering memorization. The context of the visual images in the multimedia materials can be very effective as the learners memorize in preparation for class. Providing useful contexts in class activities helps learners to further solidify associations between their experiences and what they have memorized. Even those who consider themselves visual learners and who have had little experience in memorizing text can be successful through repetition in appropriate contexts. When learners memorize segments of discourse based on aural models from multimedia materials, they gain a repertoire that can be relied on as both linguistically accurate and culturally authentic and that fosters automaticity. An important benefit of memorization is that learners practice producing correct intonation patterns for units of discourse beyond isolated vocabulary words. We discuss this later in the chapter. When dealing with TFLs such as East Asian languages, to simply to practice speaking without regard for cultural appropriateness will lead to a performance that is unlikely to put native speakers at ease and may well result in giving offense. Memorization helps learners know *what* to apply in new situations because they have a repertoire of discourse units that they know are authentic. As we have already noted, the memorized dialogue is not the goal, but rather the starting point for applied activities. The memorized discourse units are *applied* in contextualized activities to help learners see the social and cultural functions of the given performance.

Recognizing that there are variations in learning styles and that teachers need to be sensitive to those differences in course planning, it is also important to remember that the mind can adapt to new ways of learning. We are not restricted to only one learning style, even if we are more comfortable with one style than with another. Part of our responsibility as language teachers is to help learners learn how to learn and become self-managed learners so that they can continue to progress in interactions outside of class and after leaving our programs. We need to help them learn effective and efficient ways to learn, even if this requires some stretching on their part.

Building on the Context—Expansion and Variation

Following the context set up in ACT class, the teacher can take one role in the dialogue and select a student to take the other, or a student could be selected for each role. The context should provide the motivation for the exchange so that the dialogue will flow naturally. To help the learners to gain a more complete view of how the language is used to accomplish culturally appropriate interaction, it is helpful to expand the memorized dialogue to include utterances that naturally precede and/or follow the given dialogue; these can be as simple as a greeting leading into the dialogue or an expression of thanks after making a request or an acknowledgment that the request has been received. Expanding the dialogue helps the learners to fit the performance into a more comprehensive framework.

Following the first performance, the teacher can select two other students to perform. After a couple of performances, variation can be introduced. At first, one of the five elements of performance can be changed, which will result in a change in language use. For example, the location might change from the office to an encounter on the street; the occasion might change from a greeting to a parting, or the roles might change from work colleagues to friends. Where there may not have been anyone else overhearing the exchange in the first context, in a variation, a boss, teacher, or parent may be present. Similarly, the script might change so that a customer needs to buy four large notebooks rather than two small ones.

Different pairs of students can be asked to perform each time. These kinds of variations demonstrate how changes in certain aspects of performance affect language use and allow the learners to apply in new ways the material they have prepared. Note that when we talk about asking learners to memorize dialogues, the purpose is not for them to merely parrot back memorized sequences of sounds. The first pair or two who perform the dialogue as it was memorized do so in a clear context, and then later pairs apply the basic dialogue in the variations the teacher introduces. The learners need to think about the variations in order to make the necessary changes in performance. The memorized dialogue is the foundation for the activities, but the situations in class require the learners to demonstrate an understanding of what they have memorized. Memorization for its own sake is not the goal and, in fact, is discouraging to the learners and not very helpful in the learning process. Memorization for application in performance, on the other hand, is very valuable in providing the learners with a repertoire that they can use productively.

After applying the memorized dialogue through expansion and variation, the context can be changed further to allow learners to apply what they have learned in a more open-ended way. The teacher can establish settings that allow the learners to draw on what they have prepared and practiced in new performances. Through all of these activities, the teacher acts as the coach or director for the learners as they perform.

Normally, there will be a number of related activities during a given ACT class. Ideally, the various activities flow seamlessly and naturally from one to the next. This makes the day's activities more effective in helping the learners to establish memories of their performances that will benefit them in the future.

Of course, the building blocks for the dialogues are grammar structures, vocabulary items, and pronunciation and intonation patterns. It is helpful to have rehearsals for performances that focus on individual building blocks as need be. Much of this may be done out of class using software or other resources. The teacher may have some activities prepared as part of the flow of linked performances for the class, or some may be introduced when the teacher sees a need for further rehearsal with specific elements of a performance. Additionally, we recommend build-up exercises in learning dialogues wherein learners can participate in step-by-step progressions of phrases that they repeat after listening to a recording of a native model. Build-up exercises are discussed further in Chapter Six.

In summary, the process of establishing the context and then providing opportunities to perform in context is essential in helping learners to see the connection between language and culture and to develop self-managed learning skills, including identifying the elements of performance and the relationship between societal factors and culturally appropriate interaction. In the following sections, we discuss some aspects of East Asian languages that may require particular attention in order to help learners speak as naturally as possible, focusing on pronunciation and vocabulary issues. Grammar is treated more extensively in Chapter Five.

PHONETICS AND PHONOLOGY—BUILDING BLOCKS
OF THE SPOKEN LANGUAGE

Learning to perform in a new language and culture (especially truly foreign languages) requires far more than knowing lexical items and grammar structures in the target language. Learners must also train the vocal tract to articulate new sounds, the body must develop new habits related to nonverbal communication, and learners must learn new ways of viewing interpersonal interaction.

In considering the phonology of English in comparison with that of Chinese, Japanese, or Korean, there are several areas that require special attention in learning pronunciation and intonation. East Asian languages contain sounds and sound combinations that don't occur naturally in English. For native English speakers learning these languages, instruction is important for overcoming the challenges that these differences pose. Learners benefit from specific help in understanding how to produce and recognize the sounds of the new language.

The underlying motivation for attention to pronunciation and intonation is the recognition that the medium is the message. Communication is more than "getting one's message across" by merely "saying what one wants to say." *How* something is said is as much a part of what is communicated as *what* is said. Interaction is a performance, and all elements of the utterance are part of that performance. The way the message is phrased, grammatically, phonologically, and otherwise, constitutes the performance and plays a role in interpersonal interaction. Learners of East Asian languages should understand that what they are communicating goes beyond the propositional content of the message (the *who, what, where,* and so on); pronunciation and intonation are important as well in establishing and maintaining personal relationships. Language is the means for building and maintaining relationships, and if native speakers of the target culture are not comfortable with the language learner, or if they feel that interaction requires too much work because they cannot understand the learner's pronunciation, the learner's ability to achieve intentions in the target culture will be compromised. We have the responsibility to help learners understand the significance of each element of their performance and help them develop skills that are as nativelike as possible.

When dealing with East Asian languages, learners are required not only to produce new sounds, but also to learn "new types of sounds that utilize completely unfamiliar articulatory gestures" (Jorden and Walton 1987, 115). Jorden and Walton point out that the techniques commonly used to teach the phonological systems of Indo-European languages, such as comparison with English sounds, repetition, and extensive listening, are generally inadequate when dealing with East Asian languages. Most often, the descriptions found in textbooks are either inadequate or are highly technical and make sense only to those trained in linguistics. However, Jorden and Walton suggest that to best help the learners, teachers should be trained in articulatory phonetics, which includes a thorough introduction to mouth geography—that is, an understanding of the functions and placements of the various articulatory organs (lips, teeth, tongue, throat, and so on). Teachers untrained in phonetics typically rely on repetition and then wonder why their learners have a hard time mastering pronunciation, including tones in Chinese. Jorden and Walton also suggest that pronunciation practice should rely on self-generation rather than mere mimicking. Learners need to understand not just how a syllable should sound, but also how to actually produce that sound. Teachers lacking in this kind of knowledge will not be able to train their students effectively. Not all learners will need intensive training in this regard, but many will benefit from such instruction.

There are several differences between the phonological features of English and those of Chinese, Japanese, or Korean, many of which may require special attention. We next consider some of these features in the three languages.

Chinese Sound System
The two most troublesome sounds for learners of Chinese are the palatal and retroflex initial sounds; these are Romanized as *ji, qi, xi* and *zhi, chi, shi, ri,* respectively. Because these sounds are not normally produced in the English language, learners will often substitute what they perceive as similar sounds from English. Native English speakers tend to substitute the English initial sounds *j, ch,* and *sh,* as in the words "job," "chip," and "ship" (Chin 1972), resulting in little or no distinction between retroflex and palatal initial sounds. For example, the words *shou* and *xiu* or *zhang* and

jiang end up sounding the same. When learners understand where the tongue is supposed to be and how the sound is formed, they will generally have greater success in producing the Chinese sounds appropriately. For example, the retroflex initial sound *zhi*, as in the word *zhīdao*, ("to know"), is made in the back part of the mouth, with the tongue pulled back and curved lengthwise. This type of verbal explanation can be supplemented with a diagram of the relevant elements of the vocal tract. A palatal sound, such as *jī* ("chicken"), is produced at the front part of the mouth with the tip of the tongue placed on the gums below the lower front teeth. It is also useful for learners to know that one must nearly smile when producing palatal sounds. These types of explanations can be very useful in helping learners generate accurate, nativelike sounds in Chinese.

Japanese Sound System
English has several vowels, including diphthongs (single vowel sounds that start in one vowel position and end in another, such as in "crowd" or "joy"), and these can be tense or lax ("beat" as opposed to "bit"). Japanese, however, has only five vowel sounds, all of which are tense, and there are no diphthongs. Learners of Japanese as a foreign language (JFL) often tend to use English vowel sounds between certain consonants when pronouncing Japanese words. Japanese also has consonants not found in English (e.g., bilabial and palatal fricatives /hu/ and /hi/, alveolar affricates /tu/ and /du/, the uvular stop /n/, palatalized consonants, and geminates). Likewise, English has consonant sounds not native to Japanese (e.g., labiodental and interdental fricatives *f, v,* and *th*; the alveolar liquid [l]). In addition, some consonants that are found in each language are pronounced differently. For example, the stops [p], [t], and [k] are not aspirated in Japanese as they are in English. Also, the alveolar stops [t] and [d] are articulated with the blade of the tongue rather than with the tip. The alveo-palatal fricative /sh/ is not formed with rounded lips in Japanese as it is in English. Another significant difference is related to the liquid /r/ sound. In Japanese, this consonant is pronounced as a flap, quite unlike the English /r/. The labio-velar approximant /w/ is formed with less lip movement than in English. These differences often lead to difficulties in pronunciation for JFL learners.

Korean Sound System

Korean phonology also is substantially different from English (see Choo and O'Grady 2003 for discussion). In Korean, there are eight basic vowel sounds, some of which are similar to English and others that are quite different. Diphthongs are also prevalent. Korean differentiates between tense and lax vowels, and vowel length is also important in distinguishing words. In terms of consonants, aspiration and voicing are areas that require special attention. Other aspects of phonology that can pose challenges for learners are consonant relinking, where a consonant can shift to the next syllable, even across word boundaries, diphthong reduction, neutralization, assimilation, and contractions.

For some of these sounds and concepts from Chinese, Japanese, or Korean that do not appear in English, learners may benefit from specific instruction and guidance in articulation. In the early stages, there is a role for focusing on certain sounds to develop an awareness of appropriate pronunciation, both in perception and in production. However, after initial attention on the sound itself, we recommend contextualized practice, at least in the form of actual words, rather than strictly as isolated sounds. This can be done even in the early stages before the learners have been exposed to a variety of structures. For this kind of practice, learners do not need to know the meaning of the words used to practice the given sounds. This type of practice should always involve an authentic aural model rather than relying solely on visual input; visual input alone cannot provide the proper model for pronunciation.

Learners often seem to think that as long as the words and the structures they use are correct, they are communicating successfully. However, they need to understand that pronunciation and intonation are also part of the message, as is body language. Pronunciation and intonation patterns are part of the message that is sent and are therefore important for establishing and maintaining relationships. To achieve their intentions in the target culture, they must be aware of the importance of natural intonation and the ramifications of errors.

Sound Systems and Vocabulary

Japanese borrows liberally from other languages, and ironically, one of the most difficult areas in teaching Japanese pronunciation relates to words borrowed from English (*gairaigo*): Many learners begin to pronounce a borrowed word according to the Japanese pronunciation but then often revert to the English pronunciation of the corresponding word. Another common problem is the use of English vowel sounds in attempting to pronounce the borrowed word; the result is that the pronunciation falls somewhere between the two languages, not quite Japanese, yet not English. This is partly a lexical issue; learners must understand that once a word is borrowed, it becomes the "property" of the borrowing culture, which will often alter the pronunciation as well as the use of the word. This is a common occurrence in Japanese, including borrowings from both China and the West. Chinese, particularly Cantonese, also borrows words from English, which can be troublesome for learners.

English has also borrowed from other languages, as is seen commonly in names. Examples include *Montana* and *Los Angeles* from Spanish, and *Notre Dame* from French. Borrowing often accompanies increased contact with the other culture, including familiarity with foods (e.g., *chow mein, sushi, sashimi, sukiyaki, kimchi*), clothing (e.g., *kimono*), or other things (e.g., *tai chi, gung ho, futon, karaoke, tsunami, kamikaze, harakiri, pokemon, t'aekwondo*). As happens when foreign words are borrowed into Japanese, the pronunciation of these terms in English has been altered from the original to match the phonological system of English. Most native Japanese speakers would not recognize the English pronunciation of *karaoke* and *harakiri* as referring to the same things they know by these terms. The meaning or use may change also, as seen in the use by some Americans of the word *karate* as a generic term for martial arts. Changes in pronunciation and use come naturally with borrowing. When learners understand this fact, it becomes easier to pay attention to the borrowed form as an element of the target language rather than relying solely on knowledge of the original form and its use in the base language.

Borrowed words can be given new meanings or undergo a shift in usage, and the borrowing culture may even create new expressions using the borrowed words. For example, words borrowed from English might undergo the kinds of changes shown in the following table using Japanese examples (Shibatani 1990; Tsujimura 1996).

Semantic Shifts	English	Japanese	Japanese Use
Narrowing	stove	*sutoobu*	used for heaters only, not cooking stoves
Extension	handle	*handoru*	also used to refer to a steering wheel
Transfer	mansion	*manshon*	condominium
Pejoration	boss	*bosu*	used to refer to a crime boss
Japanese Creations			
		buronzu gurasu	from "bronze glass"; used to refer to tinted windows
		puraisu daun	from "price down"; used to refer to reduced prices
Simplification			
	puncture	*panku*	(as in English)
	supermarket	*suupaa*	(as in English)

Part of teaching pronunciation in Japanese is teaching the importance of using the Japanese pronunciation of borrowed words and the phonological rules involved in borrowings (see Quackenbush 1977).

√ Chinese, on the other hand, generally coins new words to represent the concepts being borrowed, and as a result, there are fewer foreign words appearing in Mandarin Chinese. For example, the word for "computer" in Mandarin Chinese is *diànnǎo* (literally, "electric-brain"), and the word for "cell phone" is *shǒujī* (literally, "hand-device"). Some dialects of Chinese, Cantonese in particular, have a tendency to use transliterations of foreign words. For example, the Cantonese term for "bus" is *bāsì*, and "taxi" is *dīsì*; the Mandarin terms for these words are *gōngòng qìchē* ("public car") and *chūzūqìchē* ("private car"), respectively. In recent years, however, the younger generation of Mandarin speakers has begun to use transliterations as well as newly created words. These examples show the new Chinese creations and the corresponding transliterations.

English	New Chinese Word	LiteralMeaning	Transliteration
e-mail	*diànyóu*	electric-mail	*yī mèi ér*
Internet	*wǎngluò*	net-net	*yīn tèwǎng*

The transliteration for "Internet" is interesting in that it combines a transliterated portion *yīn tè* as well as *wǎng*, the Chinese word for "net." The younger generation is more likely to use the transliterated terms rather than the newly created terms.

Korean, as with Japanese, has borrowed a significant number of words from China (see Lee and Ramsay 2000 for discussion). Many Japanese words have been adopted as well, although currently, most loanwords tend to come from English. In general, Korean speakers attempt to approximate the pronunciation of loanwords in the original language, but sounds are modified to fit Korean phonology, and some borrowings end up sounding quite different from the original.

In summary, East Asian languages have aspects of pronunciation and vocabulary borrowings that require special attention because of differences between these languages and English. We point out some of these differences as a reminder that developing pronunciation and vocabulary use that are as natural as possible will be a great asset as learners interact with natives of the target culture.

ACCENT

An important area related to intonation is accent. Accent is realized in a language in one of three ways: stress, tones, or pitch (Tsujimura 1996). English is a stress accent language, Chinese is tonal, and both Japanese and Korean are pitch-accent languages. In English, words have primary stress and often secondary stress to indicate accent. In some cases, accent distinguishes words, such as the noun *produce* and the verb *produce*, or the noun *subject* and the verb *subject*.

Chinese Tones

In Chinese, accent is realized through a system of four primary tones. This system is perhaps the most challenging part of Chinese phonology for the second language learner to master. The challenge is compounded by the interaction (and interference) of the English intonation system. The first tone in Chinese is considered a high tone, the second is a rising tone, the third falls and then rises, and the fourth is a falling tone. Among the few empirical studies that have been done on the acquisition of Chinese tones by learners, there is little agreement on which tones are the most difficult to acquire. Shen (1989) reports that tone four is the most difficult for learners to produce, followed by tone one. She explains that the most common errors are pitch or register errors, which she attributes to the small natural pitch range of the English language. These errors are due to the lowering of the pitch range when speaking Chinese to fit the pitch range of the English language. On the other hand, Miracle (1989) reports in his study of learners of Mandarin Chinese that there is an equal distribution of contour (the shape of the tone) errors and register (the pitch of the tone) errors, and that the rising tone (tone two) is the most problematic for learners. McGinnis (1997a) supports Miracle's claims, reporting that the majority of errors found in his study are with tones two and four, the rising and falling tones. Our experience reflects McGinnis's findings: rising and falling tones seem to be the most problematic for learners.

All three studies agree that learners generally have difficulty learning Chinese tones well. In Miracle's (1989) study of elementary-level learners of Chinese (the equivalent of one year of study), there was a 42.9% error rate. In other words, nearly half the time, learners made tonal errors in speech. The other two studies reveal similar rates, indicating that there is much room for improvement in teaching tones.

There are a number of possible reasons for the high error rate that has been observed. One explanation is that the English intonation system interferes with the production of Chinese tones; this possibility has been raised and discussed persuasively by White (1981). She argues, as does Shen, that the pitch range of Mandarin

Chinese is much wider than that of English. Second, she reports that "stress in English is associated with pitch height; because of this, the English speaker will hear the Mandarin high tones as stress. Emphatic stress is expressed with a high falling contour in English" (1981, 52). She further explains that when English intonation patterns are superimposed onto an utterance in Chinese, the tones are affected and are no longer accurate in Chinese. She provides a simple example of this, which we have seen frequently in the classroom: English speakers often have a desire to emphasize or stress the word "very" as in "very good." This results in a stress on *hěn* so that *hěn hǎo*, which should have a second-third tone sequence, becomes a fourth-third tone sequence. Many other errors of this nature also occur, such as when learners use rising intonation in posing questions in Chinese, and in other situations where emotion is articulated through intonation in English. This does not mean that we teach that the Chinese do not express emotion when they speak. On the contrary, learners need to understand that the Chinese express emotion in other ways, such as through the use of modal auxiliaries and sentence-final particles. Of course, Chinese also has intonation patterns that are an integral part of the language. Though there are studies that have been published on Chinese intonation patterns, none have attempted to address the pedagogical issues involved. A detailed discussion of intonation analysis in Chinese is probably best left to intermediate to advanced learners.

Another important question is how to teach tones most effectively. Numerous proposals have been suggested, ranging from the carefully considered approach of tonal spelling (DeFrancis 1986; Johnson 1985), in which tones are integrated into the Romanized spelling of the word, to less scholarly proposals, such as a musical approach (Woo 1976), in which learners are encouraged to sing their lessons. Another approach uses creative diacritic marks that employ musical note notation and other grammatical markings, such as a question mark to indicate the second tone and an exclamation mark to indicate the fourth tone (Bar-Lev 1991).

One of the common ways in which we introduce tones is with the Y. R. Chao five-point notation scale, where 5 represents the highest pitch and 1 the lowest pitch. In this notation system, the four tones of Mandarin Chinese are represented as follows:

Tone 1: 55
Tone 2: 35
Tone 3: 214
Tone 4: 51

This method is convenient in that it accurately represents the contrasting pitch levels as well as the contour of each tone. Shen (1989, 39) challenges this approach, however, arguing that "actual production of tones in the speech stream does not correspond in a one-to-one manner to the phonological prediction." She goes on to say that a third tone does not have an absolute 214 contour; rather, in speech it sometimes may be pronounced as 213, 313, or 314 depending on the individual. Shen argues that each individual will have a unique pitch range that must be figured out. She proposes a register approach, in which learners are taught that there are three general tone registers: high, low, and mid tone, and that they should pay attention to the starting, ending, and turning points of the four tones. She explains, "Tone 1 starts with a high key and remains in this high key; Tone 2 starts with a mid key then moves up to a high key" (1989, 40), and so on. Based on his findings, Miracle (1989) suggests that we not abandon Chao's five-point scale, but rather supplement it with Shen's register approach. We have found that both approaches can be useful when teaching tones to beginning learners. Chao's scale illustrates effectively the general pitch and contour variations among the four tones, and Shen's register approach can be used to help learners understand their own individual pitch range.

Some students will naturally pick up on tones without a great deal of explanation, whereas others seem to need significant instruction and individual practice with a teacher. Regardless, important aspects at the beginning level of instruction include the following:

1. A systematic and thorough approach to the phonological system of the language
2. Early emphasis on accurate pronunciation (providing feedback by grading pronunciation accuracy helps learners focus)

) 3.   Providing additional help outside of class to work on tones as needed

Speech recognition software can be a valuable tool for showing learners the actual contours and pitch levels of the tones they produce compared to those of a native speaker. Learners can also benefit from comparing a voice recording of their performance with that of a native model. Learners often have difficulty distinguishing between good and poor pronunciation in their own speech. Hearing their own voice on tape and comparing it with an accurate model will foster the development of self-monitoring skills, which are essential in becoming a lifelong language learner.

Japanese Pitch
In the case of Japanese, accent is realized through changes in pitch, rather than by tones, as in Chinese, or stress, as in English. As already noted in relation to Chinese, JFL learners also seem to commonly use English intonation patterns when speaking Japanese. For example, when beginning JFL speakers express questions, they often use rising intonation, as in English, even in cases where Japanese does not use rising intonation (such as in questions with the *ka* marker). In standard Japanese (Tokyo dialect), there are three rules governing pitch-accent. First, there is always a difference in pitch between the first and second *morae* (sound units in Japanese, roughly analogous to syllables). If the first *mora* is lower in pitch, the second will have high pitch, and if the first *mora* is high, the second will have low pitch. Second, once the pitch contour drops in a given word, it will stay low for the remainder of that word. Third, some words do not drop in pitch. That is, some have an initial low pitch, the second *mora* is high, and the remainder of the word remains at a higher pitch. Again, a common error for JFL learners is the tendency to use English intonation patterns, including stress-accent, rather than the pitch-accent contours of Japanese. When learners understand that accent in Japanese is fundamentally different from accent in English, it will help them recognize appropriate patterns in their own speech and as they listen to native models.

One factor in evaluating materials is the way learners are given assistance in recognizing and producing appropriate accent patterns. This is something that cannot be learned adequately simply from visual input of written forms. It is helpful, however, to have some kind of written representation of accent patterns in beginning-level texts as a reminder of proper accent, but it is critical to have abundant audio/video materials to enable learners to *hear* those patterns. Learners benefit from modeling and feedback. Certainly, this can be part of class time, but the more exposure learners have, the better. Materials that provide this exposure will help learners improve more rapidly in areas of pronunciation and intonation. One of the most important aspects of the development of self-managed learning skills is the ability to monitor one's pronunciation and intonation based on a target-language native model.

As noted here, one reason for having dialogues as the basic unit of instruction is that learners are able to hear and practice intonation contours as they occur naturally. Inaccurate pronunciation or intonation can affect how natives of the target culture feel about interacting with the learner. Natural-sounding pronunciation and intonation are an important part of performance. Mistakes can lead to misinterpretations.

Korean Pitch
Korean is also considered a pitch-accent language (see Lee and Ramsay 2000 and Choo and O'Grady 2003 for discussion). In earlier times, tones were part of the language, and some dialects still use tones today (Lee and Ramsay 2000). In Korean, the initial syllable of a word carries higher pitch. Once the pitch falls within a phrase, it remains low. The final syllable of a phrase is generally longer. Length can indicate emphasis or emotional involvement on the part of the speaker. Higher pitch also expresses focus. A syllable with a low pitch can be followed by a particle spoken at a higher pitch, and a syllable with a high pitch can be followed by the same particle spoken at a lower pitch.

Pitch Summary
Given the significant difference between accent in English and accent in East Asian languages, learners of these languages face challenges in developing nativelike intonation. When learners are

aware of the fundamental differences between the base and the target language in the way accent is realized, it becomes much easier to understand and monitor appropriate accent without relying on habits from the base language.

As noted, a misconception among many teachers, particularly native speakers of East Asian languages, is that the written language should be the focus of instruction and that oral and aural skills will come naturally or automatically alongside literacy skills (see the discussion of native paradigms in Chapter Six). As we discussed in Chapter Two, we recommend that introducing the writing system be delayed until learners develop an understanding of the phonological system, with special emphasis on tones in Chinese and pitch differences and intonation patterns in Japanese and Korean.

In the case of Chinese, we recommend initial exercises providing learners with practice in hearing and identifying tones. Before learners can be expected to produce tones accurately, it is important for them to practice listening and distinguishing between the different tones. For example, learners can listen to individual syllables; these syllables may be written in *pinyin* but without the diacritic marks. Learners can practice placing the correct tone mark over each syllable as it is read by the teacher or heard from a recording. These types of exercises can build up to the point that learners listen to syllables and write out the *pinyin* together with the correct tone mark. As already noted, we do not advocate spending a great deal of time working with syllables in isolation. Most learners seem to be able to identify and produce correct tones at the syllable level, but the real issue, which is more difficult, is the correct identification and production of multiple syllables linked together in sentences or longer lengths of discourse, such as dialogues. For this reason, it is important to practice pronunciation and listening skills in meaningful discourse units.

We do not advocate spending a great deal of time exclusively on phonology in general. The importance of context in meaningful learning applies to the learning of phonological features of the language as well grammar and vocabulary. Excessive focus on isolated, noncontextualized language units becomes boring and provides little benefit. In short, learners will not remember meaningful language when learned in a hit-and-miss manner. Correct pronunciation can be emphasized and practiced as learners perform dialogues and participate in contextualized exercises.

Pedagogical Application for Pronunciation and Intonation

As we have explained, to help learners develop pronunciation and intonation that are as nativelike as possible, it is important to provide opportunities to practice with discourse units such as dialogues, rather than isolated characters, words, or sentences. Part of learning intonation patterns, including tones and tone sandhi rules (tone change rules) in Chinese, is learning how such patterns are realized through discourse, not merely at the sentence level. It is one thing to adequately mimic the pronunciation of a single syllable in isolation, but maintaining the proper intonation contour over an extended sequence is more challenging. Another important reason for always having students practice with structurally accurate and socially appropriate discourse, and at normal speed, is the development of appropriate intonation skills.

To foster a sense of proper intonation, corrective feedback on intonation errors is very valuable and aids in the development of self-managed learning skills. It is helpful to explain to learners initially the importance of pronunciation and intonation in the target culture, and that the learners can expect to be given feedback on their intonation during the course. Without an understanding of why we correct intonation and pronunciation, learners may wonder why they are receiving corrective feedback when their use of vocabulary and structure is accurate. We strongly recommend that learners always repeat the correct utterance following the feedback. Learners often simply nod to acknowledge the feedback; however, because developing intonation skills includes training the muscles involved in articulation, it is important that learners repeat the utterance following the feedback in order to train the body to do what the mind understands. Passive assent acknowledging a cognitive understanding of the feedback serves only half the purpose.

ACCURACY AND FLUENCY

The distinction is often made between *accuracy* and *fluency* when discussing the development of speaking skills. *Accuracy* refers to correct use of language structures, and *fluency* refers to smoothness in speaking at a natural pace. Different methodologies over time have usually focused on one or the other. Traditionally, the focus in much of foreign language education seemed to be on accuracy, as seen in the so-called grammar-translation method. An emphasis on fluency seemed to grow out of a response to this structural approach that was common a few decades ago. With the grammar-translation method, learners' attention was focused on syntactic patterns with little regard for situated use; students were able to recite dialogues but were not as successful in applying what they had learned to other situations. The pendulum has swung the other way, and some now suggest that "communication" is all that matters—that learners should focus on the development of fluency through abundant and free use of the language. Currently, some materials and approaches seem to favor accuracy and others fluency. However, language learning is no more "communicating" than it is memorizing grammar "rules" (see Hammerly 1985). Attention to accuracy need not impede fluency, and a focus on fluency need not negatively affect accuracy. It is desirable and possible to achieve both.

The approach to cultural performance we are outlining reflects the awareness that in order for target natives with whom learners speak to feel comfortable, fluent, structurally accurate, and socially appropriate speech is essential. Before we discuss questions related to accuracy and fluency, it is helpful to first consider the idea of "communication." An approach that maximizes speaking opportunities certainly reflects an understanding of the importance of practice in the development of performative skills. However, when a learner is merely saying what he or she wants to say, the resulting "communication" may be completely inappropriate in the target culture. Communication must necessarily take into account all parties in a conversation. Even though the learner may feel successful in saying what he or she wants to say, the listener may have misunderstood the speaker's message or intent. Communication is a negotiated process. For target natives to feel comfortable, which is an important step in developing long-term relationships and achieving one's intentions within the target culture, *how* something is communicated can be just as important as *what* is communicated. This is particularly true when seeking to participate in a truly foreign culture, where behaviors one has grown up with may not have significance in the target culture or may even be interpreted negatively in that culture. Stewart and Bennett (1991, 2–3) express this idea as follows:

> For most people, including Americans, the distinguishing mark of cross-cultural interaction is the disappearance of the familiar guideposts that allow them to act without thinking in their own culture. Routine matters become problems that require planning or conscious decisions. They may not know when to shake hands, nod their heads, ask a question, express an opinion, or maintain silence. ...Faced with these cross-cultural uncertainties, people tend to impose their own perspectives in an effort to dispel the ambiguity created by the unusual behavior of host country nationals. They are unlikely to suspend judgment about differences in behavior because they assume unconsciously that their own ways are normal, natural, and right.

Even from the early stages, learners of East Asian languages need to develop a sense that merely expressing their thoughts using the target language will not ensure understanding on the part of the target native listener, nor will it ensure acceptance of the message on a sociocultural level. The received message may be much different from what the speaker intends. Certainly misunderstandings can occur even between two native speakers of a language. However, when dealing with TFLs, much frustration and discouragement can be avoided when attention is paid to cultural accuracy as well as fluency.

It is important to emphasize accurate, precise pronunciation from the very beginning so learners will know that this is an essential part of successful communication. As learners participate in performances in the classroom, phonological features of the language will be contextualized and made an integral part of the overall communication process.

One's feelings about accuracy and fluency determine the extent to which learner errors are corrected. If one believes that "communication" (saying what you want to say) is the ultimate goal, then there may be a tendency to place less emphasis on accuracy, and therefore less emphasis on error correction. It is important to help learners speak as much as possible, but we believe that accurate pronunciation is an important element of fluency. We must remember that one of the primary reasons we learn a foreign language is to enable us to develop relationships with members of the target culture. If we are able to "communicate," but our speech is full of mistakes and poor pronunciation, it is less likely that native speakers will be eager to spend time with us. Conversely, when we speak and act as much as possible like the natives of the target culture, they will be more at ease and more likely to want to develop and continue the relationship.

Some teachers may even be less inclined to correct pronunciation errors at the intermediate and advanced levels, perhaps assuming that pronunciation should be taught only at the beginning level, or that if learners did not develop good pronunciation skills at that stage, there is no hope of improvement later. Not only do we need to place great emphasis on pronunciation early in the learning process, but we must also continue to emphasize accurate pronunciation throughout the learners' career. Improvement can be made at the intermediate and advanced levels, and it is the responsibility of teachers to guide and coach learner performances in all areas—correct grammar, accurate pronunciation, appropriate cultural behavior, appropriate vocabulary usage, and so on. Only when this is done will learners truly be able to progress in their understanding and ability to communicate in the language so as to make others comfortable.

Most teachers of Japanese have probably had a student approach them and say *arigatoo* ("thank you") or *ohayoo* ("good morning"). In terms of propositional content, the meaning is easily understood. The student is likely very sincere in expressing thanks, for example; however, the form of the message is socially inappropriate in Japanese culture for a student when addressing a teacher. Knowing the Japanese form for "thank you" and simply practicing saying what one wants to say will not adequately prepare learners for the proper cultural performance in such a setting. In the cases noted here, learners should address teachers with the more respectful *arigatoo gozaimasu* or *ohayoo gozaimasu*. Although teachers certainly understand the speakers' intent and the nature of the errors, native Japanese colleagues report that just such errors can be offensive because socially and culturally, the expected expressions are deeply ingrained in members of the target culture. At an emotional level, the initial response is one of discomfort, even among those who understand the kinds of mistakes that are part of the language-learning process.

This particular type of error may seem relatively insignificant. However, other far more serious problems can occur at the interpersonal level, as reflected in the following example. Watabe (1997) reports a situation where a consul general from Japan visited a university and gave a speech in Japanese. Afterward, a student who had learned Japanese primarily through exposure and practice, with little formal training (therefore, with little training in issues of accuracy), approached the speaker and said, "*anata no hanasi, totemo yokatta yo.*" The propositional content, which the student intended as a compliment, was essentially, "Your speech was great!" Watabe reports the perplexed look on the face of the consul general: He did not know exactly how to respond, and was obviously uncomfortable. Presumably, he understood the student's intended compliment; however, given the socially inappropriate way in which it was delivered, it seemed to cause some consternation and was embarrassing to more experienced Japanese speakers nearby.

We wish to stress that cultural and linguistic accuracy are equally important, and are as important as fluency. The message that is communicated involves more than words and structures; pronunciation and intonation are also part of the message, as are sociocultural appropriateness and body language. Everyone can think of cases in one's own language where body language or intonation can suggest sarcasm, the opposite meaning of the words and structures as customarily used. Even when a sentence is structurally correct, the choice of words or even the choice of sentence structure may render the utterance socioculturally inappropriate. When dealing with truly foreign languages, such as Chinese, Japanese, and Korean, the question for learners is not simply "How do you say X in Chinese (or Japanese or Korean)?" but rather, "What do the Chinese (or Japanese or Koreans) say in this situation?" Structure, lexical use, pronunciation and intonation, social appropriateness, and body language are all part of the message that is communicated. When learners have the idea that they are "communicating" as long as they are saying what they want to say, they miss the role of the target culture in the exchange as well as the role of the listener.

Jorden (1986, 146) speaks of "abominable fluency"—the ability to speak fluently, but with structurally inaccurate and/or culturally inappropriate speech. When the speaker is "fluent," he or she feels comfortable. The "abominable" description applies because the target native interlocutors are not comfortable, and perhaps are even offended. Hammerly (1985) points out that practice "doesn't necessarily make perfect, but it makes permanent" (120), noting that practice speaking beyond one's level of competence results in permanent imperfections. More will be said about this later in the chapter.

Virtually every theory or teaching methodology has some merit, which is why almost any theory generates interest and gains followers. To gain legitimacy, a theory should be grounded in sound principles. We must be careful to avoid taking an extreme position, which then might result in overlooking or even disavowing important principles on which competing theories may be based. In determining what approach to use in language teaching, the methods advocated for implementing the given approach must be examined as well. Usually there are beneficial elements that can be drawn from a variety of approaches. Good ideas and good methods can be found in both the so-called structuralist approach and the communicative approach.

The effort to foster structural accuracy must not overshadow the importance of the application of language in situated use. Likewise, the effort to foster fluency must not diminish the importance of accuracy, either structurally or culturally.

Discussion of the relative merits of the two areas of focus usually includes the issue of error correction. There is an extensive literature about error correction, with strong feelings on both sides of the issue (Brown 1994a; Omaggio Hadley 2001; Lee and Van Patten 1995). Some feel that error correction detracts from "communication," and others feel that mistakes are part of what is being communicated and that learners should *strive* for accuracy. Error correction gets at the heart of one's ideas about language. In Chapter Two, we referred to the question "What is language?" We spoke of the differences between the spoken language and the written language. In fact, everything teachers do in the classroom reveals their view of what language is and how it is learned. If a teacher does not consciously examine his or her views of language, methodological decisions will happen by default, not as a result of thoughtful reflection.

√ (One of the advantages of the communicative approach is the attention given to fluency.) This approach seeks to maximize learner speech in an effort to develop the ability to speak smoothly, without one's train of thought being interrupted by correction. One potential problem in the communicative approach, however, is precisely this focus on saying what you want to say. When learners from the United States are simply encouraged to speak for the sake of speaking practice, the only recourse they have is to base their comments on what they know from the base culture. Their experience in U.S. culture, however, may not help them to know what is appropriate in the target culture and may even give them wrong ideas about what is appropriate. If such speaking practice does not take into account the aspects of communication mentioned here, the potential exists for serious miscommunication. The learner may be sending unintended messages. Jorden and Walton (1987) discuss how learners "filter" the target language through their native mind-set. Just as we seek to reduce the affective filter in language learning, we advocate seeking to reduce the base culture filter as well, in order to optimize appropriate target culture performance.

JFL learners with experience in Japan have noted situations where associates with less experience in the language and culture have not been successful in making themselves understood by native speakers, even when using accurate structures. The reported problem in such cases was that the speaker used Japanese words and structures to say things in a way that would be appropriate in English, and the native Japanese listener, while obviously knowing the words, could not quite understand what point was being made. The more experienced JFL learner essentially must "translate" the Japanese spoken by the associate into more natural Japanese. The native speaker then was bemused that the foreigner had to translate the Japanese for the native Japanese speaker. The first speaker was saying "what he wanted to say," but it was not understandable. The more experienced associate was able to retranslate because he understood both the cultural perspective underlying the message and the cultural perspective of the native Japanese. He was able to bridge the gap between the two.

LEARNER FEEDBACK

When the focus is on accuracy, a certain amount of error correction is required in order to help learners understand errors in structure, lexical use, pronunciation and intonation, social appropriateness, or body language. However, some express concern that such correction may inhibit learners and therefore impede fluency. In considering error correction, it is important to distinguish what we will call "mistakes" from "errors." Everyone makes mistakes. Even native speakers of a language make mistakes, as seen in false starts, repairs, repetition, and so on. Mistakes are certainly an expected part of the language learning process and are part of normal language use. Learners need to understand that and know that teachers realize it as well. A mistake is a failure to perform appropriately, whereas an error is a failure to realize what is appropriate in the given context (structurally, lexically, socially, and so forth). Mistakes are occasional and suggest that natural use of the element in question (e.g., pronunciation of a particular sound, a lexical item, a grammar structure, a gesture) is not yet automatic or may merely suggest a slip of the tongue. Errors are systematic and suggest that the element in question has not yet been learned. Feedback should take this difference into account.

Language learners develop a set of internal hypotheses that are refined through testing. For that refinement to occur, feedback is important. It is commonly known that those from East Asian cultures generally will not give feedback to learners concerning language use. Brown (1994a) notes the "overpoliteness" of native speakers in generally avoiding giving feedback. This seems to be true particularly in East Asia. If a learner commits errors, Japanese will usually try to understand what was intended, without suggesting that anything was wrong (again, an important cultural trait!). It is important, therefore, that learners have the opportunity to test and refine hypotheses through receiving feedback in the classroom.

There are different types of feedback and differences in the manner of giving feedback. Feedback can be formal or informal, delayed or immediate, overt or implicit. The way the feedback is given can contribute to learner inhibition or reduce concerns about being corrected. Regardless of the type, manner, or degree of feedback, learners will benefit most and be more at ease if they understand why, when, and how they can expect such feedback. It is helpful to explain to learners why and how they will receive feedback, and the areas in which they will receive it. Teachers should help learners know what to expect and why. With this understanding, those serious about their learning will welcome feedback rather than dread it.

Formal feedback can be given regularly, orally or in writing, to help learners understand generally positive aspects of their performance and specific suggestions concerning ways to improve. Some kinds of feedback should be immediate, in order to help learners understand something that may not be remembered or be clear after time passes. Feedback can be a direct statement, or it can simply be a look, gesture, or question to help the learner realize there was a problem (see Omaggio Hadley 2001 and Brown 1994a for discussion). When possible, it is desirable to encourage and elicit self-correction; this helps in the development of self-managed learning skills. After providing corrective feedback, it is important to have the learner repeat the correct utterance, as previously noted. Language use is far more than a cognitive understanding of what is appropriate; it also is important that learners have the experience in training the tongue and physical gestures through actual production as they develop the ability to perform in the target culture. Feedback need not be intimidating. When the teacher is viewed as one who is there to coach better performance rather than as someone hunting for errors, learners are more accepting of correction.

Accuracy and fluency need not be considered as mutually exclusive. One should not be sacrificed for the sake of the other. In the performed culture approach, our goal is to develop learners who are both accurate and fluent. Appropriate feedback, while giving the learners opportunity to use language in culturally appropriate contexts, can help them to develop both fluency and accuracy.

As one teacher of Japanese has said, the goal is not for our learners to be comfortable in speaking Japanese, but rather for the Japanese to feel comfortable when those learners are speaking with them in Japanese. The former usually occurs before the latter. It may be said that fluency relates to the learner's comfort, and accuracy to the listener's comfort. Both will occur when we approach pedagogy with the idea in mind that accuracy and fluency are both possible and desirable.

In the case of China, Japan, and Korea, generally speaking, the more fluent the learner is, the higher the expectations of target natives that the speech be accurate as well. An exchange student related an experience when studying in Kyoto. The student noticed that the teacher corrected his (mis)use of honorifics far more than that of any of the other students. The teacher explained that this student was more advanced than some of the others, and that given his level of fluency, native speakers expected a greater degree of accuracy. She said that if he continued to make errors (in honorifics, in this case), the native speakers would assume that he was intentionally violating societal norms and therefore intending to be rude. Her correction reflected her concern that his ability to build and maintain relationships not be compromised because of inaccurate speech.

SPEAKING SKILLS

In all language-learning activities, it is important that learners understand the aspects of the context and the various elements of performance, which were discussed in Chapter One. In providing speaking activities, teachers should explain or otherwise contextualize the situation sufficiently so that the learners understand the social factors influencing the discourse. Inasmuch as language use and style vary based on genre, learners should have the opportunity to participate in a variety of generic situations, always with a clear understanding of the genre and its role in the L2 culture.

Different types of activities can play an important role in the development of speaking skills. Activities can range from *mechanical*, which provide form practice through focusing on expected responses and have the goal of developing automaticity, to *meaningful*, which focus more on meaning than on form, and to *communicative*, which allow for open-ended responses. In any case, even with the more mechanical activities, interaction should be prompted in context, which may be as simple as showing a picture that illustrates what is expressed by the language used in the mechanical exchange. The mechanical kinds of activities are considered "scaffolding" or skill-getting activities, which build toward skill-using activities. Just as scaffolding is important in the construction of a building and taken away once the building is complete, scaffolding activities can help in skill development and are not needed after a skill is acquired.

Speaking activities should also provide practice in a variety of styles and genres that are important for the learners to know. These might include making purchases at a store, telephoning a friend, telephoning a business to obtain information, visiting the home of an acquaintance, giving directions to a taxi driver, making reservations for an airline ticket, greeting a superior, and making an apology.

LISTENING SKILLS

The preceding sections have covered some issues that are important in the development of speaking skills. These same issues are important in the development of listening skills. The principles discussed are just as relevant for listening. There can be no (conversational) listening without speaking. As we discuss the role of dialogues in speaking, remember that dialogues are also important in listening in that they provide context and allow learners to hear the use of grammar structures, vocabulary, pronunciation, and intonation in natural settings. It is important to remember, however, that listening is a different skill, and even though many activities foster both speaking and listening skills, some activities should focus on listening itself. The following section discusses some ideas for activities that will foster listening comprehension.

Listening Comprehension

As with speaking, listening involves far more than understanding pronunciation, vocabulary, and sentence structures. An awareness of each of the aspects of the performance, including the social relationship between the speaker and the audience, and awareness of rhetorical devices within a specified genre are important components of listening comprehension. The significance of changes in intonation, knowledge of how irony and sarcasm are expressed, and so on, are also important elements of listening. As already noted, oral communication necessarily involves the hearer. Just as in speaking activities, learners need to have speech contextualized in their listening activities in order to understand the kinds of moves being made by the speaker and how these constitute, maintain, or alter social relationships.

The teacher, then, must take care to contextualize listening activities. As with speaking, these may range from more mechanical to more communicative types of activities, yet each must be performed in an identifiable, understood context. As noted, the dialogue is considered the basic unit of instruction. When learners participate in dialogues, they have both speaking and listening opportunities. We have discussed the role of expansion, variation, and application in performance activities. Another valuable activity relates to comprehension. That is, following a performance activity, questions can be asked about what has taken place as a way to gauge learner comprehension. These questions are in the target language and are most helpful if they take place within the context of the performance, rather than being a teacher–student type of exchange. For example, the setting might be one where a company official is sending a subordinate to purchase some supplies for an upcoming meeting; the primary performance relates to making purchases. When the employee "returns" from making the purchases, the one filling the role of the supervisor might ask a variety of questions relating to what took place at the store.

In thinking about listening activities for learners, it is useful to consider three modes of communication: *interpersonal, interpretive,* and *presentative* (Kubler et al. 1997). The interpersonal mode involves direct interaction between two people; dialogues are a common example. The interpretive mode does not involve interpersonal interaction, but appropriate cultural interpretation is still essential. Examples of this type of communication include watching movies, listening to the radio, and listening to formal speeches. The presentative mode includes making noninteractive presentations, such as speeches. The classroom performance activities we have talked about are primarily interpersonal in nature. The interpretive mode also is important in the development of listening skills. Many of these activities can be done outside of class. For example, learners can watch films or listen to radio broadcasts (including over the Internet). These opportunities are most productive when there are prelistening activities as well as follow-up questions, discussions, or other activities. We discuss some of these here.

Interpersonal – dialogues (interaction btn ≥ ppl)

interpretive – appropriate cultural interpretation (movies, radio)

presentative – speeches

A distinction is made between *input* and *intake* in listening activities (Brown 1994b): *Input* refers to what is heard, and *intake* refers to what the learner actually processes mentally. Input is important, but intake is what really makes a difference in skill development. Listening activities should focus on intake to help learners listen interactively. When a person encountering a new language has little background in vocabulary or structure, it is extremely difficult to make anything out. The utterance usually is heard as just a long string of sounds. Activities that focus on intake, that is, language that is meaningful to the listener, can be helpful at all stages of learning.

The variety of listening activities also includes intensive and extensive listening, or local and global listening. In intensive listening, learners participate in activities that help them develop skills in listening for, identifying, and understanding discrete, isolated elements of language. These may cover the range of language levels. Extensive listening activities are more general and involve listening for meaning at a higher level. These involve top-down processing and foster comprehensive listening skills.

Listening activities at the beginning stages where learners are encountering the sound system might include listening to identify a certain sound or pronunciation, a certain tone, or a certain relationship in pitch. Learners might be presented with minimal pairs, differing slightly in pronunciation or accent (tone or pitch) and be asked to distinguish between the two. They can be given tasks to focus their listening for a certain vocabulary item, sentence structure, or discourse marker. The text for the listening activities might be something the teacher says, a conversation between other classmates, a movie or television program, a radio broadcast, or a recording of a public announcement.

In considering performed culture, the primary purpose of all of these activities is to help learners understand the language as it is used in its cultural and social context. The elements of performance are important in listening activities also. Exercises might require learners to identify some aspect of the performance based on what is heard, for example, listening for a certain speech style that reflects a particular relationship between speaker and listener.

As with performances for speaking, reading, and writing, the curriculum should cover a variety of genres in listening tasks.

Dialogues are a major component of performances. During the normal course of a curriculum, these generally will include a range of social relationships, situations, and functions. Movies, television programs, and radio have been mentioned. These also include a range of genres: listeners might be exposed to news programs, dramas, talk shows, comedies, variety shows, travel shows, documentaries, advertisements, weather reports, music, interviews, and so on.

As already noted, these activities are most productive in the development of cultural sensitivity and linguistic skill when pre- and postlistening activities are included. (Prelistening activities can incorporate discussions about the topics involved, from both a linguistic and a cultural standpoint) Discussions can prepare the learners to focus their listening by helping them to think about the content and context of what they will hear. (Postlistening activities can include discussions or other activities where the learners must act on what they have heard) Their performance will reflect the extent of their linguistic and cultural comprehension.

Listening activities can cover the range from isolated sounds to extended text, such as a movie or speech. They can focus on individual linguistic or cultural items or require a holistic response. Pre- and postlistening activities help the learners maximize the effectiveness of the listening. The underlying motivation for the development of listening skills is to further increase the learners' sensitivity to culturally appropriate performances.

CONCLUSION

Speaking and listening are distinct skills. Developing each skill requires contextualized practice in performing, based on identified, specific cultural parameters. These should be varied in order to help learners develop a sense for rhetorical devices across different genres. Learners should always be able to identify relevant aspects of the setting, including the relationship between the participants. As learners become sensitive to variations based on role and setting, they will be more adept at developing self-managed skills.

Chapter Four

READING AND WRITING

In Chapter Two, we discussed differences between the spoken language and the written language. In this chapter, we treat issues related to reading and writing and how they are related to the idea of performed culture. Our discussion addresses the social nature of reading and writing, the importance of social appropriateness in reading and writing tasks, and the importance of avoiding premature reading and writing activities.

READING: ACTIVE OR PASSIVE?

Of the four language skills, speaking and writing were traditionally referred to as active skills, and reading and listening considered passive skills. From the perspective of the language learner, this division seems natural, because with speaking and writing, language is being produced and with listening and reading, language is being interpreted. As noted in Chapter Three, however, listening is much more than a passive activity. The interpretation involved in listening requires mental activity on the part of the listener in bringing to bear knowledge of pronunciation, intonation, morphology, lexicon, syntax, style, genres, cultural context, and background in order to interpret what is heard. Similarly, reading comprehension requires active mental processing that involves knowledge of orthography, morphology, lexicon, syntax, style, genres, world knowledge, culture, and so on. In recognition of the mental activity required, listening and reading have come to be treated as active skills (Omaggio Hadley 2001; Brown 1994b; Carrell, Devine, and Eskey 1988; Iser 1978; Eco 1979). Listening and reading activities are more effective and efficient when learners understand the active role they play in the listening or reading process.

As discussed previously, in a language curriculum, integrating all four skills—listening, speaking, reading, and writing—is certainly important, but the issue involves finding the appropriate balance between these skills at each level. All are essential, but it does not follow that each should receive equal coverage at each stage in the curriculum. The ratio of course activities among the four should vary based on the level of instruction, as noted in the foregoing discussion about Learning Model Instruction and Acquisition Model Instruction. In this chapter, we further explore the relative roles of reading and writing in comparison with speaking and listening.

BUILDING ON THE FOUNDATION OF THE SPOKEN LANGUAGE

Given the primacy of speech in development and interaction, it is helpful to have speaking and listening activities precede reading and writing. The greater importance placed on speaking and listening in the earliest stages of language learning (particularly in the case of these TFLs, which use different writing systems) does not mean that reading and writing need to be postponed inordinately. It merely suggests that reading and writing activities should have as a foundation language that the learners have already practiced in speaking and listening activities. Reading and writing activities should be based on the domain and range of the learners' understanding of the target language system. Some activities that focus on skill and strategy development, such as hypothesis formation, may involve unknown lexical or other elements. In such cases, however, the content should be carefully controlled at the earlier stages of reading development, in order to meet the objectives of the activity in question.

Using the native script as the means of presenting information in the early development of conversational skills saddles learners with an unnecessary burden that can complicate and slow the learning process. When reading and writing activities are introduced immediately in the beginning course, learners are required to deal simultaneously with both spoken and written conventions, the orthography itself (which is a significant issue in the case of East Asian languages), vocabulary, grammar, sociocultural appropriateness, and pronunciation and intonation issues.

Learners can learn both the spoken language and the written language more effectively and efficiently if they are not forced to deal with the entire range of issues simultaneously. Without knowledge of the issues related to the writing system and written conventions, learners have no recourse but to resort to decoding rather than actual *reading*. Having the writing system constitute the only gateway to the language can be a problem for learners. An existing foundation in the spoken language is a great help in developing functional reading and writing skills later on. The development of skills in speaking and listening should not be dependent on knowledge of the writing system.

ORTHOGRAPHY

Knowledge of the orthography is certainly an essential component of reading and writing. However, simply knowing characters, being able to identify the reading (pronunciation) and meaning of characters, does not guarantee skill or fluency in reading or writing. Fluency in these skills also requires knowledge of the language as a system for making meaning, independent of the writing system, as well as discourse conventions. In addition to processing a different orthography, learners must also develop different physiological reading patterns in encountering texts written vertically, from right to left, and with no spaces delimiting words.

As we have pointed out, there are important reasons for delaying the introduction of script until learners have a solid foundation in the sound system of the language, and also for basing use of the writing system on what the learners already understand about how the language is organized as a system of making meaning. Walker (1991) identifies three reasons for delaying the introduction of characters. First, such a delay follows the order of natural language acquisition; in all cultures, oral and aural skills are learned before literacy skills. Second, it allows learners to focus on the orthography without having to worry about grammar and vocabulary, which they would have already learned; this is related to the skill mix already discussed. Third, it provides a review of previously learned material. For example, in the approach we are recommending, if learners are introduced to characters during the fourth week of class, they would be learning the characters associated with the vocabulary from a previous lesson, which means they would already be familiar with the phonology and with grammar and vocabulary items learned in that lesson. Rather than having to learn the shape, sound, and meaning of a character all at once, they are simply adding the shape of the written representation to what they already know (its sound and meaning).

A notable study that examines the effect of a delay in introducing characters was conducted over one academic year and evaluated two sections of a first-year Chinese course (Packard 1990). Learners were tested in all four skills at the end of each of two semesters. The no-lag group was introduced to Chinese characters simultaneously with the other skills beginning in the first week of the semester, and the lag group was introduced to characters three weeks after the course began. By the end of the second semester, the lag group had studied the same number of characters as the no-lag group. Consequently, they ultimately had less time to learn the characters than the no-lag group.

At the end of the first semester, there were no significant differences between the two groups in listening comprehension or in knowledge of grammar and *pīnyīn*. In the area of phonetic discrimination, the lag group scored significantly better than the no-lag group. At the end of the second semester, again, there was no significant difference in the listening comprehension and grammar and *pīnyīn* categories, nor was there a significant difference in character reading or character writing. Even though the lag group had less time to learn the characters, they scored just as well as the no-lag group in reading and writing skills. Of even more importance is the finding that the lag group scored significantly better in the phonetic discrimination category. This means that they were better at transcribing syllables and were more fluent in spoken Mandarin. According to this study, there were no benefits associated with the immediate introduction of characters in a course, but there were significant benefits resulting from a delay in the introduction of Chinese characters. This study suggests that delaying character introduction in the initial few weeks allows learners to become more familiar with the sound system of the language, which results in better oral skills, without any detriment to their learning or retaining characters, either in recognition or production.

There are several aspects of reading and writing that can be taught before characters are introduced that can be of significant benefit (Mickel 1980). For example, learners can profit from an introduction to the basic historical development of the writing system, a familiarity with the radical-phonetic composition, which is common to a majority of Chinese characters, and an introduction to common radicals, general stroke order patterns, and proper counting of strokes. All of these kinds of exercises can be taught and practiced during the lag portion at the beginning of the course. When learners are later introduced to specific characters in a lesson, they will better understand the writing system in general and be more confident in recognizing and producing characters.

Delaying the introduction of characters presumes the use of some other representation of the language. In the case of Chinese, one option, discussed in Chapter Two, is *zhùyīn fúhào*, a phonological representation of the language, and in Japanese, individual words can be represented in *kana*. In the case of Japanese, certainly most would argue for the introduction of *kana* before *kanji*. The question then becomes whether to begin with *hiragana* or *katakana*.

These two *kana* systems have different functions. *Hiragana*, which seems to be the starting point for most Japanese materials, is used primarily to represent conjugated forms and function words. (Content words are usually represented in *kanji*.) Presumably many materials begin with this system because it can be used to represent entire sentences, although generally, only texts for children actually appear entirely in *hiragana*. *Katakana* is used primarily to represent words borrowed from languages other than Chinese (Tsujimura 1996; Shibatani 1990). Despite the popularity of starting with *hiragana*, an important advantage to starting with *katakana* in the curriculum is that it can immediately be used naturally to represent language units familiar to the learners, including their own names and borrowed words (e.g., "bus," "taxi," "ice cream," "computer"). However, as already noted, even *katakana* should not be introduced until the learners are familiar with the sound system of the language. *Hiragana* can be introduced later and still be used naturally. For example, words written naturally in *hiragana* can be combined with words written naturally in *katakana* into meaningful units that use the natural script in natural ways (e.g., ワープロがありますか。 *Waapuro ga arimasu ka*).

An important aspect of the idea of performed culture is that language use is situated in authentic contexts. Reading and writing texts and tasks also should be based on natural situations. It follows that use of the writing system itself should be as authentic as possible. Therefore, *katakana* seems to be a better choice because it can be used for its usual purposes from the beginning. Starting with *hiragana* usually means that the script is used in inauthentic ways. In summary, in the case of Japanese, we advocate introducing *katakana* first, followed by *hiragana* and then *kanji*. With each script, its introduction should follow the development of conversational abilities in the language units being represented with the respective scripts.

Although both *zhùyīn fúhào* and *kana* can be learned sufficiently to be put to use more quickly than the Chinese characters used in either language, the fact remains that these are new orthographies for learners, and the same arguments can be made that premature use results in decoding rather than reading. In any event, it is impossible for learners to develop actual reading skills using these scripts because neither one is used exclusively in the native texts the learners will eventually read. With these scripts, learners do not have the natural segmenting into language units that they would see in natural texts.

As noted earlier, learners need aural input for developing speaking and listening skills; they cannot develop communicative conversational skills in a second language merely from visual input of the language forms. Even with ample aural input, however, there is a role for a visual representation as a notation or reminder of that aural input. This is helpful in text materials in explaining the use or function of a given pattern, for example. Textbooks need to represent the forms of language visually *as a reminder* of the sound shapes of the forms involved. When this visual representation is in the native script, in the case of Chinese and Japanese, development of conversational ability can be impeded if there are any difficulties in reading the native script. Even though *kana* is introduced before *kanji* in a Japanese course, it is important to remember that *kana* should not be used to teach pronunciation, only as a reminder of pronunciation (just as with Romanization). If *kana* is introduced before learners have a concept of the nature of the language, the processing of *kana* is nothing more than a character-by-character decoding. Learners cannot process the native script in meaningful units until they understand what the meaningful units are and how they function together in the language. We recommend that the primary input, especially in the beginning levels, be aural input from audiotapes, CDs, or video media, rather than relying on visual processing of script. Given the role of visual input as a study aide and the inappropriateness of starting beginning courses with either Chinese characters or other representations (e.g., *kana* or *zhùyīn fúhào*), as noted in Chapter Two, we recommend using *pīnyīn* as a pedagogical script for Chinese and Romanization for Japanese as the visual *reminder* of what is *heard* from other audiovisual media. The role of the pedagogical script is to support the audio media—*not* the other way around. Any script can only approximate pronunciation. The relationship between the sounds of a language and their written representation is ultimately arbitrary. We stress again that a pedagogical script is intended only as a *reminder* of pronunciation and that it is inappropriate for *teaching* pronunciation and intonation. Communicative conversational skills are not developed through visual input of a pedagogical script any more than they can be through a native script.

Reading involves a sense of language as a system. It is more than simply knowing the symbols of the orthography: It also involves top-down skills and familiarity with textual conventions. Research has shown that even native readers can have difficulty processing native script when such strings do not follow the phonological rules of the language (Watabe 1996). Immediate introduction of the script for its own sake will not necessarily further reading and writing skills. The teaching of the writing system is an essential element of reading. We are arguing against premature "reading" that leads only to decoding, and for an approach to reading that pays attention to generic conventions, social conventions, and cultural contexts.

TEACHING CHARACTERS

In this section, we discuss issues related to teaching characters themselves and then return to issues related more generally to reading and writing skills.

Knowing individual characters is an essential part of reading and writing. However, as already noted, mere knowledge of characters does *not* constitute the ability to read or to write, just as being a good speller in English does not equate necessarily with effective or efficient skills in reading or writing. Reading and writing require more than just knowing the shape, sound, and meaning of individual words.

Chinese characters are composed of three elements: a graphemic component (shape), a phonemic component (sound), and a semantic component (meaning) (Ke 1996). Often the graphemic component receives the most attention in teaching the writing system. However, research has shown that native Japanese and Chinese readers seem to rely more on the phonemic component of a character than on the graphemic or semantic (Matsunaga 1994, 1995; Horodeck 1987; Ke 1996). This suggests the importance of a prior foundation in the spoken language before reading and writing.

Radicals, stroke order, and stroke count are important elements in teaching the writing system. Given the burden of learning these elements, and the evidence suggesting the relative importance of the phonemic aspect of characters, it seems desirable to teach the written representation of a word *after* the learners are familiar with the pronunciation and the meaning of the word in question. Adding the graphic component to an existing foundation that includes the phonological and semantic components is desirable. This eases the memory load and also serves as a review for previously learned vocabulary through exposure at different times and in different contexts (recycling).

In the case of Chinese, another important issue is whether to teach simplified or traditional characters, or if both are to be taught, which to start with and when to incorporate the other. To become fully proficient in dealing with Chinese texts, familiarity with both simplified and traditional Chinese characters is required (Kubler et al. 1997, 104):

A knowledge of both types of characters is important not only to be able to read writings from *both* mainland China and Taiwan—because the mainland uses primarily simplified and Taiwan uses primarily traditional—but also to be able to read a *full range* of writings from *either area,* because both systems are used to some extent in each area.

We suggest that traditional characters be learned first because it is easier to learn simplified characters after the traditional forms have been learned. In most cases, simplified characters have been derived from traditional characters, thus making the transition less challenging for learners than learning the simplified forms first. Learners can effectively make the transition to simplified characters during the intermediate level of instruction. We do not recommend learning the two kinds of characters simultaneously because trying to remember two different graphs for each character places a difficult burden on the learners. Recently, it has become popular for text developers to provide the text or dialogues of lessons in both simplified and traditional characters; this makes the text appealing for those learning either system. However, this apparent strength may also be a weakness: When learners have their choice between the two systems, they naturally will rely on the one they are most comfortable with, regardless of the intentions of the teacher to emphasize one system over the other. In short, having the systems side-by-side creates a crutch and can actually prolong the learning of the system being taught.

In the process of learning characters, we recommend having the learners do as much as possible outside of class in the repetitive activities they can do on their own, so that class time can focus on applied, practical use of the vocabulary items involved. Of course, this suggests that learners are given some guidance about what characters are, how they are composed, their role in the language, the role of the radical, and the three components of a character (sound, shape, and meaning). With a foundation in the basic elements of characters, learners can study the various aspects of individual characters on their own, including stroke order. It is also important to teach accuracy in stroke count, stroke order, and stroke direction to help ensure better handwriting. Knowledge of these elements is helpful when reading handwritten texts, especially those written in a cursive style: if learners do not know the appropriate stroke order, reading cursive handwriting can be very challenging.

It is important to remember that good penmanship, calligraphy, and general writing skills are not the same things; each has a role, but they should not be confused. *Calligraphy* is an art and is best left to specialized classes. *Penmanship* refers to the ability to accurately form reasonably legible characters. *Writing skills* refer to the ability to compose coherent and culturally appropriate texts, not the ability to form characters accurately.

We highly recommend that as characters are taught, learners be exposed to a variety of known vocabulary items using that character. Knowledge of characters for their own sake is not particularly helpful; the purpose for knowing characters is to read and write texts, not single characters. Learning the writing system is most effective when characters are contextualized. The importance of knowing characters cannot be overstated; however, keep in mind that reading and writing involve far more than knowing the orthography. The learning of characters is not a one-shot experience (Schank 1976, 1982); retaining the knowledge of characters requires a great deal of repetition and reinforcement. We recommend consistent recycling of previously learned characters, including in new vocabulary contexts as new words are learned.

Because most learners have more opportunities to read than to write, it is expected that the set of characters they can recognize will usually be greater than the one they can produce. It is helpful to point out to learners that this is generally true of native speakers as well. Repeated exposure to characters in a variety of contexts is essential. Many learners also benefit from mnemonic devices as aids in remembering the shape, sound, or the meaning of a character or word. Flash cards can also be an effective study tool, and useful as quick review aids. On flash cards, it is important to include examples of the given character in context—that is, in a variety of vocabulary, rather than relying on isolated characters out of context.

Learners will find that regardless of their level of experience, they will eventually encounter unfamiliar characters or combinations of characters. As we teach learners *how* to learn characters and also *how* to use their knowledge of characters to form hypotheses concerning unknown words, we will better prepare them for future learning and help them to become better self-managed learners.

BUILDING AUTOMATICITY IN LOWER-LEVEL SKILLS

An important element in fostering reading skills is the development of automaticity in lower-level skills. These include the skills involved in dealing with the orthography and the actual text. Automaticity is certainly fostered when knowledge of characters, vocabulary, and linguistic structures is maximized. This involves the ability to recognize and interpret meaningful segments of language as units, rather than as isolated characters or words. Automaticity is also developed as learners are able to recognize textual structure and orthographic conventions—the use of punctuation in the target language, which may include symbols or uses not found in the base language, the use of *katakana* in Japanese for emphasis, similar to the function of italics in English, and so forth. Research suggests that even intermediate-to-advanced learners of Japanese have problems processing lexical items expressed in *katakana*, including words borrowed from English, even though they may tend to think that such words are easier to understand (Warnick 1996, 1999).

Developing automaticity in dealing with these elements of a text requires exposure and practice. Through scanning or other directed intensive reading activities, learners can foster lower-level processing skills. Such activities also are useful in developing strategies for dealing with unknown elements in a text. The greater the automaticity in processing meaningful units of a text, the more attention can be given to higher-level cognitive processing, which is also important in reading.

A variety of activities and games can be introduced to help build automaticity in recognizing shapes, pronunciations, or meanings associated with a given character. Many learners benefit from activities and materials that reinforce recognition of similarities in radicals or other components of the character, similarities in meaning, or similarities in the phonological component.

AUTHENTICITY IN READING AND WRITING

Cultural authenticity is as important in reading and writing activities as it is in contextualizing conversational activities. It has been suggested that before we discuss the "what" of reading, we need to address the more fundamental question of *why* people read in the first place (Eskey 1986). Eskey claims that for any approach to the teaching of reading to succeed, we must consider the motivation for reading. In most studies of reading a foreign language, there is little, if any, discussion of how the text itself (including its genre) and how motivation to read affect the reading process. Many studies discuss the implications of their results as though reading can be characterized as a single kind of act, constant across genres and independent of motivation, interest, or purpose.

For any approach to reading to succeed, we also should account for social and cultural factors. We should consider how a society deals with the given text, and why and how members of the culture read that text. We read the way we have been taught to read (Scholes 1982), hence the crucial nature of authentic tasks in the L2 curriculum. The L2 reader may come from a culture that has a very different view of reading, how it should be done, and what the purposes of reading are (Eskey 1986), so teachers have a responsibility to help L2 readers bridge any such gaps.

Ochs (1990, 308) states that "language socialization entails both socialization *through* language and socialization to *use* language." In a similar manner, the socialization associated with (L1) reading and writing can be thought of as entailing socialization through these activities and socialization to read and write. L2 learners also need to become socialized to reading and writing in the context of the target culture.

We suggest that reading and writing can be considered as social activities, even though most reading and writing is done alone. Reading and writing can be considered social activities for several reasons. First, language itself is social: Words mean what they mean because of how they are used in society. Uses and meanings change based on social contexts. Second, writers write and readers read in a social context. Writers make assumptions about the audience; they write based, in part, on what they expect the readers to know and the experiences they expect the readers will have had. Third, social conventions influence reading and writing behavior in terms of where and why and when certain texts are generally read or written. Fourth, we are socialized to read and write. In normal conditions, children grow up experiencing how texts are used in society. They develop an awareness of the relationship between reading and writing and participation in societal events and experiences. Fifth, reading can be considered a social activity because we react to what we read. Ideas, attitudes and opinions are often influenced by what is read, which in turn affects future social interactions. Reading can spur conversations or lead to writing activities, such as recording thoughts in a letter to a friend or writing a letter to the editor of a newspaper. Reading and writing can be social in that book clubs or poetry circles are often organized as social means for discussing texts.

When considering a performative approach to reading and writing in order to help learners develop a culturally appropriate sense for the role of the given text in the target society, authenticity is important in three ways: in the use of orthography, in the texts themselves, and in the tasks based on those texts. It is important to remember that the written language is not merely a representation of the spoken language. Each has its own styles and features, and these vary based on the genre. In developing reading and writing skills, learners need to understand the conventions and stylistic differences among genres.

In terms of the orthography, authenticity relates to the manner in which the writing system is used. As previously noted, using Romanization for reading and writing activities is an inappropriate use of that script. Also, using *hiragana* (or *katakana*) to represent entire texts is inappropriate for adults. The use of *wakachigaki* style, which includes spaces between words, or extensive use of *furigana* to indicate the reading or pronunciation of the given word may have a pedagogical use in helping to develop lower-level skills, but are not authentic.

Learners need to be prepared to access the kinds of texts they will encounter in the target culture and interact with them in ways natives do. The kinds of texts learners see and the tasks based on those texts will vary depending on the relative ratio of LMI and AMI.

Using realia is an excellent way to expose learners to natural texts. Tasks can be based on the kinds of interactions native readers have with these texts. For example, as learners develop competency in giving directions or handling shopping scenarios in the beginning stages of language learning, they can use actual department store information guides that show where in the store certain departments or merchandise are located. In the case of Japanese, many of these items are written in *katakana*. Even without having been exposed to *kanji*, learners can use authentic "texts" in authentic ways in asking and giving directions. Also, brochures for ski resorts in Japan, many of which include information written in *katakana*, may list the level of difficulty of the various runs; such brochures can be used in tasks focusing on making comparisons. We strongly recommend that such kinds of realia be introduced into the curriculum as the basis for tasks involving reading (and writing). They provide an excellent basis on which to promote communicative oral activities and enable the early, frequent, and effective use of texts in the development of both spoken and written skills. Train or bus schedules, signs, menus, and advertisements, to name a few, can be introduced in a principled, authentic manner, based on the linguistic level of the learners. Even relatively early, learners can be exposed to authentic texts without requiring immediate introduction of the writing system in a beginning course.

Texts and tasks should always be geared to the level of the learners' development. However, this does not mean that they necessarily need to comprehend the entire text. Learners definitely should have a foundation in the elements of the text that are the focus of the task (such as the orthography, lexical items, and structures), but the task can be tailored to match their level. The same text can be used at different points in the curriculum with an expanding scope, based on increased knowledge of the writing system and the language features involved. To repeat, tasks can be geared to the learners' level and can be adjusted for working on certain skills as the focus changes, without necessarily requiring complete understanding of all elements of the text.

Selecting Texts
As explained in Chapter Two, Noda (1994) discusses the relevance of pedagogically created materials to the notion of authenticity. Such materials can be used in authentic tasks as well, and are particularly appropriate for beginning learners in LMI instruction. In addition, realia can be used effectively in a variety of ways. Issues involved in text selection include the degree of fit with the learners' experience with the orthography, lexical items, sentence structures, organization, style, content, and exposure to the genre. There are many authentic artifacts that can be used effectively; some examples include signs, labels, maps, ads, handbills, memos, faxes, invitations, want ads,

announcements, comics, graphs, charts, lists, train schedules, and letters. These can be obtained from a number of sources, such as the Internet, newspapers, magazines, reference works, literature, academic writing, and phone books.

The purpose of the task is the fundamental consideration in text selection. What are the objectives for the reading activity? What skills are the learners to focus on? Are the text and the task appropriate for their level? It is helpful to expose learners to a cross-section of text types so that they develop an understanding of textual conventions for a variety of genres in the target culture.

It is essential that learners gain a sense for the text in its cultural setting; different genres have different social conventions. They also need to see that different texts can be read in different ways. For example, we do not read newspaper articles and advertisements the same way, nor do we read college textbooks the way we read novels for enjoyment or shopping lists the same as the phone book. However, when reading Chinese or Japanese, we find that without guidance, learners tend to approach all types of texts the same way, often character by character, usually stopping at each unfamiliar character or word to consult a dictionary.

APPROACHES TO READING

Over the past few decades, researchers have suggested different models of reading. It is difficult to thoroughly characterize the reading process because reading can be observed only indirectly or incompletely. Research has sought to understand both the product (comprehension) and the process of reading.

Reading models are generally classified into one of three types: bottom-up, top-down, and interactive (Warnick 1996). Stanovich (1980), Kamil (1986), Samuels and Kamil (1984, 1988), Eskey (1986), Rayner and Pollatsek (1989), and Ruddell, Ruddell, and Singer (1994) provide discussion of models, differences between the types, and the more influential models within each.

The first type of model to appear is known as a bottom-up model (Gough 1972). In this type of model, it is hypothesized that the sequence of processes involved in reading proceeds from the perceptual processing of print to the higher-level cognitive operations.) Reading is said to originate in the lower-level skills of combining smaller units (beginning with the letter) into larger and larger units as the eye processes the print on the page. Processing is considered to be unidirectional, and the bottom-up model traditionally has not accounted for the role of background knowledge or contextual information.

The failure of this type of model to account for some empirical observations (such as readers' use of world knowledge in reading) prompted a rethinking of this view of reading. A top-down model was then proposed, which hypothesized that rather than proceeding serially from lower- to higher-level processes, reading consists of higher-level processes that direct the flow of information through lower-level processes. It was suggested that readers approach a text with certain hypotheses in mind, and then sample only enough of the text as necessary to confirm their hypotheses (Goodman 1970; Smith 1971).

Further research addressed deficiencies in top-down and bottom-up models by proposing interactive models of reading. Such models incorporate the best features of both bottom-up and top-down models. Interactive models assume that readers utilize both kinds of processes in order to achieve comprehension (Rumelhart 1977; McClelland 1986; Just and Carpenter 1980). Discussion of the interactive nature of reading has expanded beyond the interaction of bottom-up and top-down processes to include the interaction between reader and text, the interactive nature of the text itself (i.e., what makes the text a text and not just a collection of sentences) (Grabe 1988), and also the relationship of the text with other texts (intertextuality).

These reading models have been developed primarily with L1 reading in mind; L2 reading research has traditionally been based on the framework provided by L1 reading research. Coady (1979) and Bernhardt (1986) propose models specifically related to second language reading.

READING SKILLS AND ACTIVITIES
As a variety of reading tasks are incorporated into the curriculum, learners can be exposed to a range of activities that will help them develop an assortment of important reading skills. Reading activities are often divided into local and global reading, or intensive and

extensive reading. (Local, or intensive, reading focuses on specific information or specific kinds of information, which may include grammar patterns or vocabulary items that learners have encountered. Global, or extensive, reading encompasses the text as a whole and examines it in its entirety.)

Scanning exercises are an example of intensive reading. In these activities, readers look for specific information instead of reading the text in its entirety. For example, readers scan an advertisement to look for a phone number, price, or location. Skimming is an example of extensive reading. In this kind of exercise, readers quickly read the text as a whole and make generalizations about it. The purpose is to get the gist of the text.

In the effort to help learners develop self-managed learning skills, it is important to provide opportunities for them to learn to use contextual cues to resolve ambiguities or hypothesize concerning unknown elements of the text. Activities might require learners to identify discourse markers or utilize knowledge of conjunctions. Teachers could also create tasks that focus on the use of the orthography, the lexical items or linguistic structures in the text, the rhetorical devices, and the style, organization, or content. We recommend that the activities always be contextualized in a manner appropriate to the target culture. Most learners approach reading with the goal of understanding the propositional content of the text. This is certainly essential, and reading activities can help them develop their ability to do so. It is important to keep in mind, however, that understanding the content of the text is not the ultimate goal: The next level is to help learners understand what to do with the text *after* the content is understood (Walker 1984). Texts are produced to fill a particular role in society(To become participating members of the target culture, learners need to understand the social role of the given text. They need to understand why natives of that culture read the text and what they do as a result. Reading activities in the foreign language curriculum, therefore, should be sociolinguistically appropriate and should focus on the social nature of the text.)

Reading activities have three elements or aspects—the prereading phase, reading the text, and the postreading phase. In the prereading phase, teachers "prime the pump" so learners will start thinking about language, social, or cultural issues that will prepare them to better understand what they will read. Teachers can help the learners understand the genre, its role in the society, why natives read this kind of text, what the conventions are for the genre, what lexical items and structures might be expected, and how the content might relate to experiences they have had.

The actual reading phase, particularly with extensive reading activities, is generally best completed outside of class. Learners can do the actual reading of the text on their own. Class time is most effective when used to prepare the learners for their interaction with the text and to provide opportunities to promote social involvement following the reading of the text.

The postreading phase is probably the most overlooked, yet it is the most important of the three stages. When postreading is discussed in the literature, the focus is generally on exercises that help gauge comprehension. However, as we have noted, it is important to help learners gain a sense of *why* natives read this text and how it affects them (see Walker 1984). If the focus is simply on extracting the propositional content of the text, learners will likely not see the social application of reading.

To summarize, we recommend that class time devoted to reading activities be focused on the pre- and postreading phases, which necessarily involve more social interaction. Whether the reading phase itself takes place in or out of class will depend on the purpose of the task, the nature of the text, the level of the learners, and the type of activity (local vs. global, and so forth).

In our experience in observing a variety of courses, we have found that learners are often asked to read aloud and then discuss the content of what was read, often in English. This method seems to be used in an effort to help the teacher see the extent to which the learners understand what they read in the text. Certainly there is a role for reading aloud. However, oral reading is processed in the mind differently than silent reading. It is commonly seen after having a learner read aloud that when a question is put to the reader about what was just read, he or she often needs to look at the text again silently before answering. Oral reading provides a check on the understanding of the pronunciation of characters; however, teachers need to understand the different roles of both silent and oral reading. Reading aloud and then translating into English is not a culturally authentic process, nor is that process very beneficial for long-term skill development.

Sample Activities

This section reviews ideas for activities at different levels.

For beginners, menus, particularly those with several items written in *katakana*, provide various possibilities. As a prereading activity, learners might discuss the kinds of foods they like or experiences they have had with the cuisine of the target culture. The learners might ask others about the types of restaurants they like or ask for recommendations concerning specific dishes. Discussion might include the different types of restaurants there are in the target culture and what kinds of behaviors are appropriate. For example, in Japan, many restaurants are very small, often seating a dozen or fewer customers. Some restaurants have a vending machine where the customer inserts the money, selects a menu item, and then takes the ticket from the machine to the counter to place the order with the attendant. In Japanese restaurants, customers are often given a hot, damp cloth to wash one's hands prior to eating. It is also acceptable to pick up one's bowl and to slurp noodles. In discussing types of restaurants where there is a server, topics might include sample exchanges that take place between servers and customers in the target culture. These kinds of issues could be discussed as a precursor to reading a menu. The reading phase would be looking over the menu itself. A postreading activity might involve placing an order, or asking the server questions about different dishes, giving the learners opportunities to practice the kinds of exchanges that were discussed in the prereading phase.

Another beginning-level activity would be to provide learners with a train schedule that shows locations, departure and arrival times, and departure and arrival gates or platforms. The context could be set by telling learners that they are expecting a friend from a specified location, and then they could report when and at what gate the friend will arrive. A prereading activity might ask students to describe what they could expect to see on a train schedule or to discuss the role of train transportation in the target culture.

Reading different genres at different levels will have a variety of purposes, but a primary goal in reading activities generally is to help learners see how the texts are used in the target culture. There may not always be a significant difference between cultures in they way that they respond to a given text. For example, the way customers deal with a menu in Korea and in the United States may, in fact, be similar in many respects. In those kinds of cases, cultural similarities should be pointed out as well. Another primary goal is to help learners develop a repertoire of experiences that will help them to have natural social interactions as a result of their reading and writing experiences. Social exchanges as part of reading and writing activities help learners see how texts are used in a culture.

At the intermediate level, short essays can be used effectively. As a prereading activity, for example, the learners might discuss the issues addressed in the essay and talk about their own feelings regarding those issues, or they might discuss the author's background and the circumstances in which the essay was written. Learners also might discuss aspects of the culture that make the issues relevant. One important aspect to cover in the case of Japanese relates to ellipsis: Much is usually left unsaid in Japanese writing because of the expected shared experience of the readers. In this case, prereading discussions might explore challenges presented to readers who don't share that same experience and review the kinds of information that might be omitted.

Postreading activities that accompany short essays might compare the author's and the learners' views or address why the author might feel that way. Learners also might compare their reactions to the author's opinions with those of native readers. A follow-up writing activity could have the learners write a letter to the editor in response to the essay, with discussions about how cultural viewpoints affect the content and style of the letter.

Advanced learners might read newspaper or journal articles or short stories. Prereading activities could include a discussion about the author or the genre or how the author is viewed by readers or by his or her peers. Postreading activities might include giving opinions about the text in oral reports or debates, or writing a synopsis in a letter to a friend.

In developing reading and writing activities, we recommend that texts and tasks help learners understand how a given text is used in society and how reading that text affects social interactions. For example, when planning a newspaper-reading activity, teachers can help the learners understand the roles of a newspaper, and the type of article selected, in the target culture. If it is an editorial, do natives of the culture read and then discuss the views presented? Do they write their own letters to the newspapers to express their views about the original article? The role of a given text in the target culture may be similar to that of the base culture; if so, this should be pointed out to the learners. To the extent that the text may have a different role, activities should provide experiences that help learners see the difference.

READING STRATEGIES

Research has shown that readers use a variety of strategies (Davis and Bistodeau 1993; Mori 1995; Warnick 1996, 1999; Everson and Kuriya 1998). Instruction can help learners become aware of what strategies are effective and efficient and increase their repertoire of reading strategies, which will contribute to the development of self-managed learning skills. Language learning is a lifelong task. Particularly in the case of Chinese and Japanese, it is not possible in four years of the university curriculum to adequately provide exposure to every genre or text that will be useful to the learners as they continue to interact with Japanese or Chinese society. As a result, it is imperative that we help them develop the skills and strategies to continue to learn effectively after leaving our programs, inasmuch as reading is "absolutely crucial to the life-long maintenance of language skills and the increase of knowledge" (Walker, 1984, 68).

Several strategies or behaviors have been identified at various levels of reading: bottom-up, top-down, metacognitive, and socio-affective. Bottom-up strategies relate to a focus on orthography, resolving word or phrase meaning, paying attention to grammar structures, paraphrasing, and translating. Top-down strategies include prediction, inference, and association with prior knowledge. Metacognitive strategies relate to an awareness of the reading process itself, including reference to one's own use of strategies, commenting on the reading task, and monitoring one's comprehension. Sociocultural strategies relate to the social aspect of reading as well as the affective state of the reader, including expressing his or her level of interest in the text, making associations with prior personal experience, reactions to the text, and references to interactions with others based on the text.

As we have mentioned throughout this book, sensitivity to context and the ability to look beyond the linguistic code are essential for effective retention. Reading exercises should be more than just a focus on grammar and vocabulary. As learners develop automaticity in recognizing vocabulary and grammar and pay more attention to the content of the text, they are able to better comprehend discourse strategies and the social role of reading in the target culture. For example, instead of assigning a long list of vocabulary that students must learn in association with a reading passage, a more effective task would be to identify important points that were brought up in the passage. The discussion about those points will require use of the important vocabulary, but the focus shifts to a more practical application of the material. Learners begin to focus on why the content is significant, what it means to them, and how they can put the information to use in interactions with natives of the target culture. Vocabulary and grammar naturally become contextualized because learners are not just memorizing words from a list, but are trying to understand those words in the larger context of the passage. The focus shifts from the linguistic code to meaning. Learners are not necessarily expected to give the English equivalents for a list of target language words, or vice versa, but rather are expected to do something with the information in the passage by using the appropriate vocabulary and grammar items. They may be required to summarize the passage orally. They might respond to questions based on the content of the passage. Questions can be posed in English or the target language depending of the level of instruction and the purpose of the exercise. As previously noted, it is beneficial to have students read the passage outside class so that the bulk of class time can be used for pre- and postreading exercises that provide for interaction. Because we read silently in our native language most of the time, it makes sense for language learners to do the same. However, there is a benefit in occasionally having learners read out loud so the teacher can monitor pronunciation and character recognition.

WRITING

Writing is a learned skill. Knowing how to produce a given character or set of characters does not equate with "writing." Writing includes knowledge of sentence structure, style, genre, rhetorical conventions, and organization. It is also important to differentiate between the ability to produce a character (with the correct strokes in the correct order) and penmanship. Although a focus on calligraphic skills has its place, it is not the focus of language instruction, nor is it necessarily helpful in developing facility with the writing system of a language.

Because writing is perhaps the least used of the four skills, and the one most dependent on foundation skills in the others, it is natural that writing receives somewhat less attention in the average language curriculum. Writing activities can focus on the process or the product of writing. Both are important. The writing process involves prewriting, drafting, and revising. Intermediate feedback is important at each of these stages in order to develop natural writing skills. Not all areas need to be stressed with each task, however. Feedback can be formal or informal, and may be provided by the teacher or by peers.

As we have stressed with every skill, authenticity is important. Writing something using the words and sentence patterns of the target language in the native script is of little benefit if the result does not match the cultural conventions for the given genre. To achieve their intentions in the target culture, learners need to understand the role of the given genre, its conventions, and how natives view that kind of text. Simply using target language elements in an American style of writing will not prepare learners for interaction within the target culture.

As with reading, it is important to avoid premature texts or tasks. For example, if learners have never seen a Japanese diary or journal, and if they do not know the functions Japanese diaries serve, asking them to keep a journal in Japanese has little performative value. Exposure, generally with explicit discussion, at least in the earlier levels of language study, should precede asking the learners to write. Given the differences in rhetorical organization between the base language and the target language (see Hinds 1983), learners benefit from instruction in how to organize their writing at the discourse level, instead of merely focusing on grammaticality at the sentence level.

The distinction between *literacy* and *reading* (Walker 1984) when applied to writing would suggest that in LMI mode, learning to represent in writing what one is able to say is a useful writing exercise. Learners must understand, however, that this task is based on oral conventions and is different from AMI writing that conforms to genre-based conventions for different text types. LMI writing tasks serve as a bridge to literary language.

CONCLUSION

In this chapter, we have discussed issues related to reading and writing activities. We have stressed the need for contextualized activities and culturally appropriate tasks. We also have stressed that reading, as well as writing, is a social activity. It has been said that even thinking itself can be considered a social activity (Shore 1996)! This all may seem counterintuitive because most reading by adults takes place silently. However, what we read and the way we read are influenced to a large extent by societal factors. Decisions about what we read, where we read, when we read, and how we read are influenced by religious, political, or social conventions (Bennett 1995). Part of learning to read is learning what society does with different kinds of texts. We learn how society considers different kinds of texts. We learn the various purposes for reading different kinds of texts and what readers do as a result of their reading. We learn conventional responses to different texts. We learn the cultural norms and expectations associated with different genres. The way we read is influenced to a large degree by how we were taught to read, and the reasons we were taught that reading is valuable or important. The different facets of the social nature of reading vary across and within cultures. Greater distance between the culture of the reader and the culture that produced the text requires more attention to the social nature of the text within its own culture.

A pedagogical approach based on performed culture applies also to reading and writing. We consider performance as "a situated behavior" (Bauman 1977, 27) and "an approach to experience" (Schechner 1987, i). Reading and writing are behaviors that are situated in context, and therefore the act of reading itself and the act of writing itself, are types of performance. The five elements of performance addressed are applicable to acts of reading and writing. Just as a dance has no meaning except as it is performed by a dancer (see Fish 1980), and a drama isn't complete until it is performed (Turner 1987), for a text, the meaning develops as a process through the interpretive act as the reader interacts with that text, and it is this interaction that itself constitutes a performance. As a result, there are different kinds of performances, based on variations in readers, texts, and contexts. When reading is seen this way, we can account for differences in reading behavior based on context and content as well as for the relevant social and cultural issues. Reading and writing are cognitive, social, linguistic, cultural, and perceptual endeavors. Each of these areas should be given attention in the quest to help learners become more efficient and more effective in reading and writing.

Chapter Five

A PERFORMATIVE APPROACH TO GRAMMAR, VOCABULARY, AND DISCOURSE

The teaching of grammar is often a dominant focus in foreign language classrooms. Learning a foreign language in American high schools has often focused on the rote memorization of abstract structural patterns and vocabulary. Traditional attitudes toward grammar instruction can be summed up in a statement made by American clergyman Jason Chamberlain in an inaugural address at the University of Vermont in 1811: "Morals and manners will rise or decline with our attention to grammar" (Knowles 1999, 200). There has been a great preoccupation with proper grammar not only with the learning and teaching of English in the United States but also with the learning and teaching of foreign languages at both the secondary and the college levels of instruction, which has resulted in a great deal of emphasis on the structures and patterns of a language and less emphasis on actual language use. This was obviously evident in the grammar-translation method, which viewed the study of language as an intellectual exercise and a passport to great literature. In the latter half of the twentieth century, methodologies that developed in reaction to grammar-translation, such as the direct method, audiolingualism, and the communicative approach, focused instead on language use with little or no regard to the overt learning of grammar. The audiolingual method was centered on an audio-oral component, but many see it as being very pattern based, even if not overtly so. (For detailed descriptions of these approaches, see Omaggio Hadley 2001 or Richards and Rogers 1993.)

We begin this chapter with a brief discussion of the differences between prescriptive and descriptive grammars. This is followed by a discussion of two general ways of teaching grammar, inductively and deductively. These sections allow us to understand the basic principles behind grammar instruction in the foreign language classroom. The next section of this chapter addresses the issue of context, with regard to grammar and vocabulary instruction. We then review some of the research that has been conducted in the field of second language grammar acquisition, relating to Chinese, Japanese, and Korean. The implications of this research provide the basis for our approach to teaching grammar from a performed culture perspective, which puts the focus on discourse. This is the topic of the last section of the chapter.

PRESCRIPTIVE AND DESCRIPTIVE GRAMMARS

Grammar has traditionally focused on "parts of speech, the article, the noun, the adjective, the pronoun, the verb, the participle, the adverb, the preposition, the conjunction and the interjection" (Johnson and Johnson 1998, 146). This emphasis is on the parts of speech as they are used to form sentences; it is characteristic of a prescriptive grammar and entails what Chomsky regarded as *competence*, or the innate ability for a native speaker of a language to know implicitly the proper and correct patterns and structures of speech (Omaggio Hadley 2001, 3). Most grammar books (of any language) deal with this idealized sentence and word class–based notion of grammar. A typical example of a prescriptive grammar in Chinese is Li and Thompson's (1981) important work, *A Functional Grammar of Mandarin Chinese* (though they do deal with some discourse-related issues as well); Samuel E. Martin's (1975) *A Reference Grammar of Japanese* is an example from Japanese. Prescriptive grammars describe how the language is supposed to be, the proper, formal, and prescribed way of forming sentences. The advantage of a prescriptive grammar is that it is uniform and standard, though it usually does not consider dialectal variation or other nonstandard usage of a language. From a learner's perspective, prescriptive grammars provide a standard, though generic, look at the grammar structures of the target language. They provide the building blocks on which the learner may rely when performing (whether orally or in writing) in the target language. There is usually little fear of not being understood linguistically when basing one's performance on a prescribed grammar of the language, even though the performance, at times, may not be exactly as a native would communicate.

The drawback of a prescriptive grammar is that it most often deals specifically with sentence-based structures, providing little help to learners when it comes to producing discourse beyond the sentence level. Nativelike discourse strategies are not usually considered, thus leaving learners on their own to link well-formed sentences into cohesive and coherent segments of realistic discourse.

A descriptive grammar is one in which the language is described and analyzed as it is actually used by native speakers of that language. This correlates with Chomsky's notion of *performance*, that is, language in action (Omaggio Hadley 2001, 3). This kind of language is replete with false starts, self-correction, hedging, and what some may regard as ungrammatical speech. Grammar of this nature exists on street corners, in school cafeterias, and among friends; it is full of slang and other nonstandard usages of the language. Furthermore, this kind of language is typically looked down upon by traditional grammarians. Regardless of the many attitudes toward performative language, this is the language that is living and in actual everyday use by natives. People all over the world and from every walk of life seldom speak in complete sentences. In fact, most people are usually surprised when they see a written transcript of their informal, spontaneous speech. The advantage of paying attention to descriptive grammars is that we get a more accurate view of how the language is being used by native speakers. However, descriptive grammar explanations can be challenging for the beginning learner of the target language because they may vary from standard grammar rules the learner has been taught.

Both types of grammar have their strengths (and their weaknesses). Some believe that it is not in the learners' best interest to expose them to descriptive grammar explanations at the elementary level of instruction. However, some involved in foreign language education feel that grammar should be prescriptive in nature at all levels of instruction. A review of materials that are available in Chinese, Japanese, and Korean, reveals that the vast majority deal with grammar at the sentence level. There is also a belief among some teachers that learners will "pick up" the discourse strategies associated with descriptive grammars on their own, particularly if they spend time in the target country. They think that these kinds of grammar strategies are too hard to teach in the classroom and simply must be learned through experience. Here we present research arguing that learners may not, in fact, pick up such skills through informal exposure alone.

We believe that both prescriptive and descriptive grammars are important at different learning levels. There is an appropriate time and place to introduce both to learners.

INDUCTIVE AND DEDUCTIVE APPROACHES TO TEACHING GRAMMAR

There are two general approaches or methods for teaching grammar: a deductive approach and an inductive approach. Proponents of a *deductive* approach maintain that learners should develop an explicit knowledge of the grammar of the language being studied and have a firm grasp of the various grammar "rules." With this kind of approach, considerable class time is spent talking about the language, or what we call a FACT-oriented approach to the language. Grammar principles are explained, drilled, and reproduced on quizzes and exams. An extreme example of a methodology that maintains a deductive approach to grammar is the appropriately named grammar-translation method. With this methodology, most of the class time is spent explaining and discussing grammar and translating passages from the target language to the native language. Much contrastive analysis is used with his methodology.

A purely *inductive* approach to grammar also maintains that "rules" are important, but the process of learning them is different from a deductive approach. In this approach, learners are expected to induce the rules as they are exposed to carefully organized and introduced language input. In other words, learners are exposed to the language and are expected to figure out the grammar rules by repeated exposure and reproduction. Proponents of this approach point out that native speakers of a language learn without any explicit instruction in grammar; thus, learners of a second language should be able to do the same (Johnson and Johnson 1998). This approach is most closely associated with what we call a purely ACT-based approach to language teaching with little or no explicit explanation or discussion on grammar; that is, with few FACT sessions.

Both of these approaches, in their purest forms, fall short of utilizing an efficient and learner-friendly method (for adult learners) for learning a foreign language. A purely deductive approach to grammar utilizes so much time in the classroom talking *about* the language that learners have little time to actually apply the rules to practical, communicative situations they will likely encounter in China, Japan, or Korea. A completely inductive approach can be frustrating to learners as they are left on their own to figure out the many grammar rules. Some learners may be able to understand the grammar in the end, but a great deal of time could be saved if grammar structures are explained to them sometime during the learning process, preferably before they will be expected to creatively use the pattern or rule in question.

The obvious solution lies somewhere between the two extremes. Explanations of grammar can be very useful, and at the same time, ample opportunity for learners to practice using the grammar in realistic communicative applications is essential. As we explain in Chapter Two, our solution to this dilemma lies in the ACT/FACT approach. Approximately one day per week (for a ratio of one FACT session to four or five ACT sessions) is spent discussing grammar, vocabulary, and the social and cultural implications of the language introduced in the lesson that is being covered. Students have the opportunity in FACT sessions to ask questions (in their native language) and participate in discussions about the language and the culture. This helps learners to better understand the language they are expected to use in the classroom during the rest of the week or instructional cycle. In fact, most adult learners prefer some kind of grammar explanation and benefit from such discussions. Another advantage of the FACT session is that it does not distract from or disrupt the target-language speaking environment of an ACT class where learners are expected to perform entirely in the target language. Discussing grammar and other structural issues (in the learners' native language) in an ACT class tends to break the flow or momentum created by speaking entirely in the target language. An ACT session is far more efficient when learners are allowed to speak only the target language.

This balance of grammar instruction allows learners not only to discuss grammar and vocabulary but also to spend the majority of the time practicing it in meaningful performances. In that the performed culture approach places emphasis on performance, the instructional cycle usually begins with an ACT class, or a performance (as shown in Chapter Two). Learners perform a dialogue or other communicative exercise, which allows them to understand the communicative situation they are participating in (the five elements of a performance). This session is followed by a FACT session that reinforces and supports the performance. It also reinforces the idea that grammar and vocabulary must be learned in context, not learned first then placed in a context later.

TEACHING GRAMMAR AND VOCABULARY IN CONTEXT

In a FACT-based teaching approach, such as the grammar-translation approach, grammar and vocabulary are the focus of instruction. The linguistic code becomes the emphasis of not only instruction but also assessment. Grammar and vocabulary treated separately from the appropriate contexts in which they occur have the potential to create misunderstanding and result in a lack of skill using them in real-life communicative situations. Knowing about the grammar and knowing the meanings of words (declarative knowledge) do not always equate with knowing how to use that knowledge (procedural), that is, knowing when and with whom it is appropriate to use certain vocabulary items and structures. Presenting new vocabulary and grammar patterns in appropriate social and cultural contexts helps learners understand *how* to use this information as native speakers of the language would. Next we discuss how grammar and vocabulary can be treated to ensure that performance remains the focus of language learning.

Grammar and Context

In grammar classes, grammar explanations at the sentence level must often be clarified by stating that the specific meaning depends on the *context* in which the structure or grammar item occurs. This can be very confusing for students and argues for not only discussing the prescriptive characteristics of a grammar item, but also comparing it with various descriptive characteristics. There are many grammar patterns in Chinese, Japanese, and Korean whose meaning depends on the context in which they occur. Following is an example of how context ultimately dictates the function of a structural pattern.

The statement *tā lái le* in Chinese can have at least five meanings depending on the context of the utterance. Without the social and cultural context, one can only guess at the function of the particle *le* at the end of this utterance. Here are five possible interpretations from Chan (1980, 58), all depending on the context in which the statement is uttered.

> 他来了。*tā lái le.*
> a. She comes (now). (She didn't used to). Inchoative aspect—new habitual situation.
> b. She's coming. (About to come). Inchoative aspect—imminent action.
> c. She's coming (now). (On her way). Inchoative aspect—action underway.
> d. She came. Perfective aspect—clear termination point.
> e. She has come (has arrived). Perfective & inchoative aspect—result phase of the action.

When using only a prescriptive, sentence-based grammar, learners may not understand all the various meanings implied by context. By supplementing a prescriptive grammar with a descriptive component, learners can get a better feel for how a grammar feature functions. In the case of *le* in Chinese, there is little consensus on the function of this aspect marker in all its various contexts. By relying wholly on prescriptive grammar explanations of this feature, one lacks access to other important functions that this marker can express. For example, some have even argued that the perfective aspect is a discourse marker in that it functions as a means of guiding the reader or listener through the text. It is the perfective aspect that gives a narrative a sequential ordering (Hopper 1979). Foregrounded clauses utilize the perfective aspect *le* by narrating the actual events in a story, and backgrounded clauses utilize the imperfective aspect and provide supportive or supplemental information about the story but do not carry on the story line. These uses of aspect marking in Chinese can vary considerably among prescriptive descriptions. Furthermore, learners can gain a better understanding of a grammar feature by examining it, not only in prescriptive manifestations, but also as it occurs naturally in discourse.

Korean, like Chinese, is a very context-rich language. This is evident by examining the use of anaphoric reference—specifically pronoun deletion, topic chaining, and ellipsis. Japanese is similar in this regard. Sentence-linking strategies in Japanese also are highly context dependent.

In Japanese, the meanings of verbal gerund *–te* + *imasu* will vary depending on the context of the communicative situation.

Script	Interpretation
Tabete imasu.	I'm eating. OR I've eaten.
Matte imasu.	I'm waiting. OR I will be waiting.

In these examples, the correct interpretation depends on the context.

There are numerous other features of prescriptive Chinese, Japanese, and Korean grammar that exhibit different characteristics when encountered in discourse contexts. It is for this reason that using descriptive explanations and discussions along with exercises is beneficial to learners.

Vocabulary and Context

Just as it is difficult to ascertain the true meaning or function of a grammar feature without the context in which it appears, it is likewise difficult to determine the true meaning of a word or phrase without its accompanying context. We are very accustomed to vocabulary lists in the target language with the native language equivalents conveniently printed alongside; seldom is more than a one-word gloss provided to explain the vocabulary item. This strategy reinforces the dangerous idea that there are ready-made English equivalents to all the vocabulary items that we introduce in East Asian language textbooks. This practice also contributes to the erroneous attitude that learning a foreign language is merely learning how to say *X* in language *Y*. This produces learners who are very adept at speaking Chinese (or Japanese or Korean) in English; that is, they may be using Chinese, Japanese, or Korean words but they are communicating in a way that Americans communicate, not like natives of the target culture. When learners are left to their own creativity in the language too early, or without sufficient guidance and supervision, they often create dialogues or monologues in the target language, but they say things that a native would never say, or at least they would not say it in that manner. Spending several years learning Chinese or Japanese devoid of contextual and cultural implications will create learners who irritate and anger natives with whom they come in contact.

In her important works *Understanding Cultures Through Their Key Words* (1997) and *Semantics, Culture, and Cognition* (1992), Wierzbicka argues that every language and culture has key words that reveal much about the culture's core values. She shows that cultures can be understood by studying certain words in those cultures. There are many words in languages that simply cannot be translated with a one-word English equivalent; sometimes a paragraph or more is necessary to convey the true meaning and implications of a single word in the target language. Wierzbicka uses the following Japanese words as examples: *on, giri, amae,* and *wa*. Can these words, with all that they mean and convey, be simply interpreted in English with words such as *gratitude, justice, honor, dependence,* and *harmony*? Do these concepts in English give a clear idea about what these Japanese terms refer to, or do they merely confuse the matter (1997, 235)? She goes on to show that the Japanese word *amae* simply cannot be explained easily and that its meaning and essence are so deeply rooted in the Japanese mind-set and culture that whole books have been written on the subject.

Even if a word can be interpreted with a single-word equivalent, its cultural connotations are oftentimes very different. Wierzbicka uses the example of *hierarchy*: Although this word may have negative connotations in American society, there is no such meaning in Japanese society. She goes on to say, "If one does not move from these approximations and vague analogies to something more precise one remains locked in one's own cultural perspective" (1997, 236). Jorden and Walton (1987) have used the analogy of a filter when referring to the cultural baggage that we all carry with us: We perceive the Japanese, Chinese, or Korean language and culture through our own American cultural filter. It is unconsciously and automatically in place. The role of the foreign language teacher thus is to train learners to be able to see more clearly through that filter and to guide their thinking and perceptions to reflect native paradigms, perceptions, and intentions.

Walker and Noda (2000, 190) provide a useful examination of the Japanese expression *sumimasen* that illustrates how the same term can have a wide range of meanings depending on the context in which it is uttered. They provide four distinct functions of the word depending on variant contexts.

1. Context: Teacher asks for student homework at the beginning of class

Script	Interpretation
Hai, shukudai o teeshutsu-shite kudasai.	OK, turn in your homework assignments.
Sumimasen.	I apologize for not turning in my assignment.

2. Context: Customers in a restaurant trying to get the attention of the waiter/waitress

Script	Interpretation
Sumimasen.	I want attention (service).
Hai, omatase itashimashita.	Yes, sorry to have kept you waiting.

3. Context: A group of passengers just boarding a train

Script	Interpretation
(standing) **Sumimasen.**	I want you to move over to make a space for me.
(sitting) *Doozo.*	Please (go ahead).

4. Context: Secretary gives office worker a typed document

Script	Interpretation
Hai.	Here you are.
Sumimasen.	Thank you.

These examples clearly show that a one-word gloss of *sumimasen* does not account for the various interpretations given. The English term generally used to gloss this Japanese word is *sorry*. However, if learners are left with this vague gloss, they will be in for many surprises when they step off the plane in Japan.

A Chinese word that has a variety of meanings is *guānxi*. This word is usually glossed as *relationship* or *connections*, which in some contexts is correct, but it also carries a number of meanings depending on the context of the communicative situation. Consider the following.

1. Context: A teenager talking to her close friend about her mother.

Script	Interpretation
Wǒmén hěn shú, ***guānxi*** *hěn hǎo.*	We're very close. We have a good relationship.

2. Context: A person bumps into another, knocking something out of the person's hand.

Script	Interpretation
Zhēn duìbuqi ya.	I'm really sorry.
Méi ***guānxi***.	Don't worry about (it's no problem).

3. Context: One person seeks the advice of another on how to get something done through another person.

Script	Interpretation
Nǐ yīnggāi gēn tā lā yíxià ***guānxi***.	You should build your connections with him.
Wǎ gāi zuò shénme?	What should I do?
Qǐng tā chī fàn ba.	Why don't you take him out to eat?

In each of these examples, a one-word gloss of *guānxi* does not suffice because the meaning changes depending on how the word is used.

A related vocabulary phenomenon occurs when a learner assumes that an English term will readily translate into an equivalent in the target language, when in fact many English words and phrases simply do not translate clearly into East Asian languages. For example, apologizing in Chinese is not as simple as translating *I'm sorry* into a Chinese expression and using it whenever you would apologize to someone in American culture. In Chinese, there are at least four "translations" of *I'm sorry*: *Duìbuqi, bàoqiàn, bùhǎo yìsi,* and no response at all. These terms all can be used to apologize depending on the situation in which they occur; the appropriate one to use depends on the context of the communicative situation. Each of these terms is appropriate in different situations, and likewise one term will not be sufficient in all situations. Usage depends on the five elements of a performance discussed in Chapter One: the time and place of the occurrence, the roles of the interlocutors, the script, and the audience. Consider the following examples.

1. Context: You step on someone's foot in a busy market.

Appropriate term: *Duìbuqi.*

2. Context: You have to call and cancel a meeting with a client (in a business setting).

Appropriate term: *Bàoqiàn.*

3. Context: You call a close friend to cancel a dinner appointment.

Appropriate term: *Bù hǎo yìsi.*

4. Context: A teacher arrives ten minutes late for class. Students have been waiting patiently.

Appropriate term: *no response*

Likewise, there are times in a Chinese cultural context where one would not even use the same expression that would be used in American society. For example, it may be appropriate in American society for a store clerk to apologize to a customer if the store did not have what the customer was looking for; in China, however, this simply would not be an appropriate time or place to make such an apology. Americans also are notorious for their frequent use of the term *thank you*. In American society, it is quite common to thank a store clerk for helping you, but in China, this is not an expression that is used so casually.) Greetings in Chinese are another area where Americans often misuse language. Learners sometimes use *nǐ hǎo* in Chinese whenever they would use the expression *hello* or *hi* in English; but by so doing, they overuse this greeting, saying it in contexts where native speakers would not.

De Mente (1996) has chronicled what various words in Chinese really mean, that is, the alternate meanings that they carry in different contexts. Though his work is titled a dictionary, it is really more of an encyclopedic reference of what he calls *China's Cultural Code Words*. He does much more than define the word; he tells about its origins and, more important, how the word is used in modern society. For example, under the entry for the expression *kǎolǜ, kǎolǜ*, this term has the heading "we're looking into it." He goes on to describe government bureaucracy in China, rules and regulations, and how decisions are made. What is not implicit in the definition, he explains, is that there is no clear time frame implied in the expression: It may mean a week, a month, or never. In other words, learners should know that if they receive this response to an inquiry, proposal, or other information-seeking act, it may mean "no," "maybe," or that the other person may not want to deal with the situation right now. When learners are armed only with the strict definition of a word, they are bound to meet with frustration, and perhaps even anger. Another example De Mente provides is the Chinese word we equate with *freedom*: He captures this word, *zìyóu*, with the phrase "license to be bad." De Mente explains that the term *zìyóu* has negative connotations in both traditional Confucian-based Chinese thought and in communist Chinese thought. This is far from the connotations that *freedom* implies in the West.

As we teach learners of Chinese, Japanese, and Korean, it is essential that they understand not just an English approximation of a word or phrase, but also how, when, and with whom it is appropriate to use it. One textbook that explains vocabulary according to the elements of a performance is the five-volume *Spoken Cantonese*

(Jian and Christensen 1995; Christensen and Fung 1995, 1996) series. Next we cite three examples of vocabulary items introduced in Cantonese with the accompanying explanations. The words all appear in a dialogue for student performance.

pok　　　　　Originally this word was a noun meaning *gall bladder.* In traditional Chinese thought, the gall bladder was considered to be the source of courage and bravery. The phrase *gau pok* in the dialogue means *having guts*; literally it means *have enough courage.* This expression is typically used among lower classes of people, such as among vendors in a market. It is also used occasionally in a joking manner among close friends.

hohk yahn　　A common phrase in Cantonese. Literally it means *study-person,* but it has the meaning of following someone's behavior or actions even though you may not be qualified to do so. In this phrase, then, the customer is saying that even though Daaih Giu has this medical condition, she still thinks she can do business as usual.

wo　　　　　This sentence final particle indicates surprise on the speaker's part and also adds a teasing or sarcastic tone to the utterance.

Christensen and Jian (1995, 15)

∨ (As we have shown, even the function and meaning of grammar patterns are determined by social and cultural context. It is important always to present the language in authentic cultural and social contexts.) At the elementary and intermediate levels, this can be done effectively in realistic dialogues. Dialogues that are realistic and authentic enable the presentation of patterns and vocabulary) items in a controlled, appropriate cultural context. After learners are familiar with the material provided in the dialogues, they can be guided in the use of those patterns and vocabulary in other contexts. Eventually learners should be able to create their own contexts in which to use the material, and they will have an understanding of the appropriate elements of the context. At the advanced levels, incorporating authentic discourse data—natural recorded conversations, television and radio, newspapers, literature, essays, and so forth—automatically provides an authentic context. With this type of material, it is important that we train learners to interpret the message according to the context in which it is presented, both socially and culturally. In other words, learners must understand how native Chinese or Japanese or Koreans would likely interpret it, and what they would do with the information gained. Learners must understand the appropriate social implications of the information presented.

RESEARCH IN THE ACQUISITION OF L2 GRAMMAR

The proper use of grammar is dependent on the communicative situation at hand. The type of grammar structure one decides to use will depend to some degree on the performance and the five elements that create the social and cultural context of that performance. Grammar, like vocabulary, is meaningless without a cultural context to provide meaning. Learning to use grammar correctly requires opportunities to use it in meaningful contexts. There has not been a great deal of research in the acquisition of grammar features in Chinese, Japanese, and Korean as foreign languages, despite the need for solid research in this area. However, more and more studies are addressing these issues. In this section, we describe a few studies that examine the acquisition of discourse grammar features. *Discourse grammar* refers to grammar structures and strategies that go beyond the sentence level and are relevant in larger segments of language. Without skill in the use of grammar at the discourse level, learners will not progress to advanced levels of proficiency.

With sentence-based grammar features, learners can usually become fairly adept at using grammar in the target-language environment. However, it is the discourse grammar features that are particularly troublesome for learners of East Asian languages. These features include the marking of temporal reference (most specifically the aspect system), anaphoric reference (pronoun deletion and topic chaining), sentence-final particles, the use of sentence-linking strategies, narrative strategies (the order of presenting material, as well as narrative voice), the use of discourse particles (*wa* and *ga* in Japanese; subject and object markers, emphasis, contrast, conjunction markers, and sentence markers in Korean), the *n desu* construction in Japanese, and ellipsis.

It is commonly assumed that some of these features are too difficult to teach in the classroom and must simply be "picked up" by learners when they are in the target-speaking community. This assumption may seem reasonable because there is very little published information about these types of discourse grammar features, thus making them more difficult to explain and practice in the classroom. Several recent studies (noted here) have found that even with considerable experience living in the target-speaking cultures, learners in fact do not pick up these features on their own.

Bourgerie (1996) conducted a study on the acquisition of modal particles to determine if these discourse features were indeed being "picked up" by learners. He analyzed the acquisition of four sentence-final particles: *a/ya*, *me*, *ba*, and *ne*. His subjects consisted of sixty-five students studying at the upper intermediate level (second year, second semester at the college level). Most had spent an average of twenty-two months abroad living as missionaries in a Mandarin-speaking community (Taiwan). The average time spent in formal study of Chinese was sixteen months. These subjects completed a cloze test where they were to add the correct modal particle in a series of sentences and longer passages. According to Bourgerie's statistical tests, "the data show that there is not a significant difference to conclude that students perform differently based on their years in a Mandarin environment or years of formal study" (116). His findings clearly show that not only are learners not acquiring these discourse markers in the classroom, they are likewise not learning them on their own through exposure and regular contact with native speakers. Bourgerie concludes by saying, "If our intent is to have students learn Fps [final particles] when they are in the Chinese environment, then deferring the acquisition of Fps seems an unsuccessful strategy" (119).

Christensen conducted two studies concerning the acquisition of other discourse marking to determine if time spent in the target community or in the formal classroom would influence acquisition. The first study (1997) focused on the acquisition of temporal reference marking, particularly that of perfective aspect marking. In this study, Christensen analyzed oral narratives produced by native Chinese speakers as well as intermediate and advanced learners of Mandarin Chinese. Twenty-seven narratives produced by learners were compared with native speaker narratives. Three factors were analyzed to determine how they affect acquisition of perfective aspect marking: the amount of formal (classroom) Chinese study, whether there is improvement over time, and whether experience abroad makes a difference. The learners were divided into three groups: advanced learners, intermediate learners with experience in a Mandarin-speaking environment, and intermediate learners without experience abroad. The advanced learners were all Chinese majors, had an average of four years of formal study, and averaged 23.6 months in the target environment (Taiwan). The intermediate group with experience abroad had an average of 1.7 years of formal study and an average of 19.6 months in a Mandarin-speaking environment. The intermediate group with no experience abroad had an average of 1.65 years of formal training. The results of statistical analyses make three issues clear:

> One, learners of Mandarin Chinese in this study are not learning to use temporal reference marking as natives use them. Two, time spent in a Mandarin speaking environment does not significantly affect the acquisition of these markers, and three, the amount of time learning Chinese does not significantly affect the learner acquisition of these markers (12).

The second study (1998) used the same subjects and database to determine the acquisition of anaphoric reference marking. The results were similar in that there was a statistically significant difference between the learner groups and the native group with regard to anaphoric reference marking. The primary problem learners had was with topic deletion: they simply used the pronoun in excess compared to the native narratives. Likewise, there was no significant difference in the performance of the three learner groups: neither experience in a Mandarin-speaking environment nor amount of formal study improved the acquisition of these discourse devices. These findings reinforce Bourgerie's findings about what our students are not learning in the classroom or in the field on their own.

These findings also reinforce those of an earlier study by Xie (1992), which reported that "English speakers learning Chinese repeatedly and excessively use pronouns in Chinese discourses in the same way they do when they produce narratives in English" (25). For example, personal pronouns appear three times in the English sentence "*I* gave *my* book to *my* brother"; the corresponding Chinese sentence would have no pronouns. When pronouns are used in Chinese wherever they naturally occur in English, the resulting sentence sounds awkward. What is normal for English sounds excessive in Chinese. Both Xie and Chu (1990) indicate that native Chinese children also use pronouns excessively. Xie further speculates that if it is true that this discourse strategy (pronoun deletion in Chinese) is acquired later, then English speakers who are at more advanced stages of their Chinese education should perform better than those at lower levels (29); this reasoning corresponds to the general belief that learners will pick up these kinds of discourse strategies on their own through increased contact with native speakers of the language. This reasoning seems sound, but Bourgerie's and Christensen's results refute this idea. Though learners at the advanced level did perform slightly better than intermediate learners, the results were not statistically significant.

This research sends a clear message that we as language teachers are not doing a sufficient job in the classroom teaching discourse strategies. We believe that our students are not learning these discourse strategies for a variety of reasons. First, we are still fixated on sentence-based grammars. We are dependent on these grammars because they are more plentiful and because sentence grammars are easier to teach and grade. Second, there is a significant amount of research on discrete points of grammar, such as the *bǎ* and *bèi* constructions, modification, and aspect marking. Third, because there is such a lack of research and materials on discourse grammar, we as teachers do not seem to understand it nearly as well as sentence-based grammar features. Nevertheless, grammar features at the discourse level are an extremely important part of advanced-level cultural performances in the target language. Sometimes the acquisition of modal particles, sentence-linking strategies, pronoun deletion, and so on, makes the difference between a mediocre learner of the language and the kind of learner who truly puts the native speaker at ease, who opens doors, and who builds lasting relationships.

Two other studies have shown that narrative style may be rooted in the cultural context of the speaker or writer. Narrative style may also influence the syntactic marking that speakers (or writers) choose to use. Erbaugh (1990) conducted a study using the well-known "pear" film as the basis for narrative production. She discovered that when Chinese natives produce narratives in their native language, the narratives are more story oriented, that is, they sound more like a story. But when native English speakers created narratives, they were more memory oriented, that is, the English speakers were more concerned with reporting the events that transpired in the film than with telling a cohesive story. Because of this orientation, the Chinese narratives followed a more sequential ordering of events. Whitlock (1993) also conducted a study comparing narrative production of native Chinese and native English speakers; she recorded native Chinese narratives, native Chinese English narratives, native English narratives, and native English Chinese narratives. She found that native Chinese narratives were more theme oriented, that is, they were more likely to have a prevalent theme, which makes for a more storylike narrative. She also reported that the native English narratives focused more on describing events and event-oriented conclusions. These results ~Chinese complement Erbaugh's observations concerning story-orientation and memory-orientation. Christensen's research with narrative production also found that native Chinese narratives stick to a more sequential ordering of events structured with the perfective aspect marking. Native Chinese speakers seem to view the events in a film as completed states and narrate them in a real-world sequence. On the other hand, native English speakers tended to view the events in the film as a series of ongoing processes or events, which was reflected in their Chinese narratives by an unnaturally high number of imperfective aspect devices and a correspondingly lower use of perfective aspect marking than the comparable native Chinese narratives. This is significant in that it tells us that grammatical marking is tied to cultural perspective as well.

American [handwritten annotation next to "complement"]

INTRODUCING SENTENCE GRAMMARS
AND DISCOURSE GRAMMARS

It is evident from our discussion that learners need better instruction in the classroom to learn discourse-based grammar and narrative features. Following is a list of some of the discourse items that may be particularly useful for learners to understand and be able to use.

Chinese
- anaphoric reference (pronoun deletion, topic chaining)
- sentence-linking strategies (forward, backward, and other means)
- modal particles (sentence-final particles, modal auxiliaries)
- aspect marking (especially perfective marking)
- stress and intonation patterns

Japanese
- particles (*wa* and *ga*)
- anaphoric reference, use of ellipsis
- sentence-linking strategies
- aspect marking
- *no da* pattern

Korean
- particles (subject and object markers, emphasis, contrast, conjunction and sentence markers)
- grammatical relations expressed with case particles
- anaphoric reference (pronoun deletion, topic chaining, ellipsis)

Walker (1989) has suggested that at the initial stages of instruction, grammar should be introduced at the sentence level. Few would argue with this suggestion. At the lower levels of instruction, a Learning Model Instruction (LMI) approach should be employed. LMI deals with an item-based learning approach, that is, fundamental vocabulary, structures, and pronunciation are encountered and learned in order to form a base or foundation on which to build. LMI calls for using pedagogically created materials for elementary-level instruction with a gradual exposure to cultural artifacts (recorded materials that were not intended for pedagogical purposes). With regards to grammar, an LMI approach calls for introducing grammatical items at the sentence level because it is important for learners to develop a foundation of fundamental knowledge in the target language. As learners are gradually introduced to cultural artifacts, they are likewise exposed to grammar features that may vary from the prescriptive norms. Acquisition Model Instruction (AMI), or strategy-based instruction, deals with this type of material, with the goal of teaching learners to be able to deal with cultural artifacts (i.e., recorded material for natives) of Chinese, Japanese, or Korean. Instead of focusing on specific items, learners are trained to develop sound strategies to successfully interpret these kinds of materials. At the upper levels of instruction, an AMI approach is dominant, and thus descriptive grammar explanations are more applicable. We wish to emphasize that authenticity and authentic materials (artifacts) are not the sole domain of upper-level instruction. Noda (1994, 170) has noted that "the authenticity of materials is an important part of making activities authentic, but the authenticity can be created with scripted materials." She argues for authenticity of activities, or the type of classroom activities that lead to participation in authentic situations. These are the types of activities that should be planned at all levels of instruction. With LMI instruction, the activities may be scripted, as in dialogue performances, but those scripts should reflect authentic situations that will likely be encountered in the target language environment. In AMI instruction, learners are exposed to artifacts and trained in how to interpret them and incorporate them into authentic cultural behavior.

The figure that follows (Walker 1989, 49) shows that the more time is spent learning, the more exposure there is to artifacts, with longer stretches of discourse and the accompanying descriptive grammatical features. The issue of how to introduce discourse-based grammatical features is explained next.

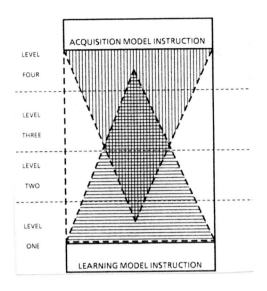

Introducing Grammar at the Sentence Level

At the elementary and intermediate levels of instruction, a three-step progression from highly controlled exercises to open-ended, creative use of the language has proven successful in many classrooms. Here are the three types of activities:

1. Dialogues (highly controlled)
2. Role Plays (semicontrolled)
3. Improvisational tasks (open-ended)

In the first step, learners are exposed to the grammar and vocabulary items as they learn to perform realistic dialogues. Dialogues work well because they provide the appropriate social and cultural context needed to understand the function and meaning of the patterns and vocabulary items (as discussed in Chapter Three). As learners memorize the dialogues, they learn these items in a controlled context that they can fall back on in the future. Walker and Noda (2000, 190–191) refer to this as compiling a memory of culture.

After learners are familiar with the material in a controlled context, they are then exposed to other contexts where the grammar patterns and vocabulary items are also appropriate. This second step can be done through role plays where learners are assigned a specific role and specific communicative tasks to complete. In other words, learners receive detailed instructions to compete the task. They have the opportunity to practice in this kind of controlled environment until they are comfortable producing appropriate language with the correct grammar patterns and vocabulary items.

The third step is to allow learners to create their own contexts while using the patterns and vocabulary from the specified lesson. This can be done in at least two ways. For example, teachers can provide open-ended situations where learners must improvise their responses on the spot in order to complete the task. These exercises are broader than the preceding type; they allow learners more freedom to respond and to use the language creatively to express their own ideas, opinions, and feelings. A second exercise of this nature asks learners to create their own dialogues based on the dialogue, topics, patterns, and vocabulary items presented in the lesson. This type of exercise is the culmination of all that they have learned in a particular lesson and provides a good format to show that they understand and have internalized the information that has been presented and practiced. The most important thing to remember with this kind of activity is that learners need to present the language in culturally and socially authentic contexts. If this is not emphasized, learners can very easily get into the habit of speaking English in Chinese (or Japanese or Korean). That is, they will simply translate into the target language what they would say in a Western cultural context, which defeats the purpose of emphasizing the cultural factors that are so important in any communicative situation. Learners must be given sufficient time to learn and practice the material in controlled contexts before they are allowed to create contexts on their own. Next we provide a simple example of how each of these steps can be implemented in the classroom.

Chinese Example
Grammar pattern: verb + *le* (indicating completed action)

1. Dialogue (excerpt)
   A: *nǐ zhōumò zuò shénme?*   What did you do over the weekend?

   B: *wǒ **kàn le** sān běn shū.*   I read three books.

2. Role Play
   You run into a friend from school on a Monday morning. The person asks what you did over the weekend. Since you went to a film festival, tell him/her that you watched six movies.
   (*wǒ zhōumò **kàn le** liù bù diànyǐng.*)

3. Improvisational Task
   You run into a friend. Tell him/her about what you did over the weekend.
   (answer will vary by student)

Japanese Example
Grammar pattern: *~te iru* (indicating continuing action)

1. Dialogue (excerpt)
   A: Tanaka kun, nani site iru?   *What is Tanaka doing?*

   B: tosyokan de benkyoo site iru yo. *[He]'s studying in the library.*

2. Role Play
   You telephone a friend one Saturday afternoon. She asks what you are doing. Tell her that you are watching TV. Ask what she is doing.

3. Improvisational Task
   You run into a group of friends at the library. Discuss what everyone is studying.

Though these grammar patterns can be drilled mechanically, with scaffolding drills, activities should progress as quickly as possible to exercises that are contextualized culturally and socially.

Introducing Grammar at the Discourse Level

At a minimum, it is the responsibility of teachers to identify these kinds of discourse-level grammar features as they arise in the texts (oral or written) that are prepared and studied in class. A three-step process can be useful in bringing these strategies to light.

1. Identifying discourse devices
2. Exercises in identification and usage
3. Creating texts using discourse devices

The first step is for the teacher to identify when and where these discourse devices occur in a text. It is important for learners to get as much exposure as possible to these discourse features. However, exposure alone is not enough; a skilled teacher must identify these features so that learners recognize them and their significance. Once learners have seen numerous examples of the feature in context, they are ready to move to the next step.

The second step is to provide exercises to practice identifying and using the discourse device, such as a cloze test where learners must fill in the blanks with the appropriate features. For example, for students learning about topic chaining and pronoun deletion, teachers could provide a sample of discourse text with all the anaphoric reference markers replaced with blanks. Learners would be instructed to place a pronoun or noun phrase in the blank or to mark an X if nothing is required, to indicate the zero anaphora. The learners' results can then be compared with native performances. Stylistic issues can be discussed as well as variation according to discourse genre. The appendix of Bourgerie's (1996) study shows an example of this kind of exercise for modal particles.

In the third step, learners create their own texts incorporating the discourse strategies being studied. Using the example of anaphoric reference marking, learners can create narratives (either oral or written) based on an assigned topic that then can be transcribed, analyzed, and discussed. Examples of native speaker narratives can be used for comparison and further analysis. If students are in the practice of writing essays or journal entries as part of the curriculum, these can be used to teach and analyze discourse features. When using student writings, it is best to identify problems by circling or underlining, rather than correcting all the mistakes; this enables learners to analyze their writing and correct mistakes themselves. It can be highly beneficial for learners to turn in an initial draft for feedback before turning in a final draft; this more closely resembles the writing process in the native language, namely, planning, drafting, revising, and editing.

An example from Chinese illustrates how these three steps work. The text used here comes from a spontaneous oral narrative and shows how pronoun deletion and topic chaining work in Chinese. In the English translation, the pronouns in parentheses indicate those that do not occur in the Chinese text.

> *Yǒu yíwèi qí zìxíngchē de xiǎo nán hái*
> *mānman de guòlái, guòlái,*
> *kàndào zhāi lí de rén zài méiyou zhùyì tā*
> *tā jiù kuàisù de bǎ tā chēzi fàng xià*
> *ránhòu ne bǎ nà yí dà kuāng lí fàng dào zìji de chē shàng*
> *jiù zǒu le*
> *qí chē jiù zǒu le.*

There was a little boy riding a bicycle. (He) slowly came over, (he) came over. (He) saw that the guy picking pears was not paying attention to him. So he quickly put his bike down. Then (he) took that big basket of pears and put in onto his own bike. (He) then left, (he) rode his bike away.

The same text can also indicate the usage of pronouns and the zero anaphora. Here, the underlined portions signify either the initial noun phrase or the pronoun. Ø indicates the zero pronoun, or places where the speaker has deleted the pronoun.

1. Identifying discourse devices
Yǒu yíwèi qí zìxíngchē de xiǎo nán hái
Ø mānman de guòlái, Ø guòlái,
Ø kàndào zhāi lí de rén zài méiyou zhùyì tā
tā jiù kuàisù de bǎ tā chēzi fàng xià
Ø ránhòu ne Ø bǎ nà yí dà kuāng lí fàng dào zìji
de chē shàng
Ø jiù zǒu le
Ø qí chē jiù zǒu le.

By identifying these features, either orally in a class discussion or in writing (as the previous example shows), learners understand how and when pronouns are deleted in Chinese narrative discourse.

2. Exercises in identification and usage

The same or a similar passage can be used at this stage. Teachers can simply have the learners underline the pronoun repetition and show where the pronouns may have been deleted.

3. Creating texts using discourse devices

In this step, learners are given the task, either orally or in writing, to create a narrative; this can be done with prompts or cues such as pictures, or a topic can be given. Learners then create a narrative following the examples regarding pronoun deletion that have been examined in class. The teacher can indicate where overuse of the pronoun occurs, and so on.

This three-step process can easily be incorporated into a course. It provides the opportunity for learners to learn discourse structures that research has shown are often left untaught and unlearned.

If one has the luxury of being able to offer a course solely devoted to grammar, one can provide a good environment for learning these kinds of skills. A mix of sentence-based (prescriptive) and discourse-based (descriptive) grammars can be used in this kind of course, which is optimal at the upper intermediate to advanced level. A sentence-based traditional grammar can be used as the foundation, giving students an explicit review of many grammar principles that have been introduced in the language classroom. It is helpful for students to be able to discuss these grammar items, ask questions, see a multitude of examples, and have contextualized exercises to practice using them. Once they have this experience, it is helpful to expose them to discourse-based grammar items as well. Because there are few texts or materials that explain discourse grammar items, teachers must be creative in selecting materials for learners to analyze. They can provide each student with several pages of natural discourse data, such as recorded conversations between native speakers in either Mainland China or Taiwan, or from Japan or Korea, as the case may be. Movie scripts can also be used, but they may not be as ideal as spontaneous discourse. The exercise can emphasize spontaneous oral discourse or (less ideally) written discourse. This allows learners to compare grammar features between different genres of discourse, thus seeing a more complete picture of how these features function in a variety of contexts and genres. (A successful format is to first spend time reviewing the grammar feature from the sentence perspective using one of the available grammar texts in print.) Students can read the material, give oral reports, and/or participate in discussions of the feature. After they are comfortable with this level of grammar discussion, students can analyze the discourse data they have been given. For example, after analyzing the prescriptive grammar description of perfective aspect marking, particularly postverbal *le*, learners then note all occurrences of this marker in the discourse data. Productivity of the aspect marker as well as how it functions in each occurrence can be compared with the prescriptive grammar. Learners can be instructed to pay particular attention to usages that are not described in the prescriptive grammar. A classroom discussion can be dedicated to the variation of the grammar feature in question. As a class, the teacher and students can note patterns and come up with descriptions of how the marker functions in authentic discourse data. Finally, learners can read current articles that deal with variant or discourse functions of selected grammar features. These articles can be discussed in class and tied to the prescriptive grammar explanations as well as to the descriptive discussions from the previous class.

This type of approach provides learners with a more comprehensive analysis of grammatical marking in the target language. It is particularly useful in helping learners understand the social and cultural applications of discourse devices as they are used in context. Even if it is not possible to devote an entire course to grammar, this mix of prescriptive and descriptive grammar elements can be utilized in any language class.

Focus on the Task
The performed culture approach to language teaching that we advocate is similar to task-based instruction, particularly with regard to teaching grammar. The bulk of classroom time is used in the rehearsal of performing tasks, which range from pedagogical tasks to target or real-world tasks. As already mentioned, tasks should flow logically, that is, from highly controlled to open-ended. Put another way, reproductive tasks should precede creative tasks. Focusing on

the task rather than on the structural pattern can help learners remember how and when to use the structure in real communicative situations; this places the pattern in an authentic context. When context is built into the learning process, remembering later how to use it is more likely.

The four dimensions of a task—language, procedure, learner, and learning process—are related to the elements of a performance. In a performance, language and procedure are related to the script. The script provides not only the language but also the actions or procedure used in the communicative situation. The learner plays a specific role when communicating, and the role will determine or influence the other elements of the performance. The learning process is how the performance is structured in the classroom; it may involve the use of props and space and the sequencing of the activities (reproduction before creation).

We are not opposed to the use of drills. Mechanical drills can be viewed as scaffolding activities that provide important foundational skills and structure that aid in real-life communication. But drills are not an end. Ideally, learners have access to video and audio materials that allow them to do much of this scaffolding activity outside the classroom on their own. As we have said, the bulk of class time should be spent performing in the language, or in the rehearsal of performing tasks. As learners use appropriate vocabulary and structural patterns in realistic performances, learning and remembering will be enhanced. In the classroom, learners are in the process of creating memories of how to perform in given communicative situations. In so doing, the building blocks of the language (i.e., vocabulary and grammar) are systematically built into this memory.

CONCLUSION

We have demonstrated in this chapter the importance of both prescriptive and descriptive grammars and how to introduce them to learners. We have placed particular emphasis on descriptive and discourse-based grammar items because they are seldom taught or learned in the classroom, nor are they acquired by learners on their own, regardless of level of study or time spent abroad in target-language speaking environments. We have also raised the issue of context and why it is so important to present all language in appropriate and authentic social and cultural contexts. Training our learners to view grammar and vocabulary as part of a cultural performance places these sometimes abstract principles into a meaningful context that learners will be more likely to remember in the future.

Chapter Six

EVALUATING AND DEVELOPING MATERIALS FOR EAST ASIAN LANGUAGES

Materials, for better or worse, often shape not only what we introduce in the classroom, but also how we introduce it. Good materials make our job a pleasure, and bad materials can make it frustrating as we spend a great deal of time revising and supplementing inadequate lessons. The perfect textbook does not exist, nor is it likely to appear anytime soon. The reason for this is that teachers around the country come from different backgrounds, have differing levels of pedagogical training, and often have dramatically different teaching goals. As a result, it is inconceivable that a set of materials could be produced by any teacher that would satisfy all philosophical perspectives and methodological needs, or fit the circumstances of all learners. However, part of the problem is that many teachers simply do not know what to look for when selecting a text for a course. What constitutes good, pedagogically sound teaching materials is one of the questions we answer in this chapter.

The teaching of Chinese and Japanese in this country has a short history, at least compared to the more familiar Western European languages. Consequently, there are not as many materials available for teaching East Asian languages. Because the teaching of these languages is relatively new, the materials that have been produced often resemble ESL or European-language materials and do not deal with the issues that are characteristic of noncognate and culturally distant languages. Many educators assume that foreign language pedagogical theories apply to all languages and that there is no need to address language-specific issues. Some issues may apply generally to cognate languages sharing certain linguistic and cultural characteristics, but when dealing with cultures like those of China, Japan, and Korea, we run into considerable difficulties.

One of the most obvious problems we see is that materials developers introduce far too much new material in each lesson. Vocabulary lists commonly contain thirty, forty, or more new words, with a large number of new grammar items as well. This approach seems to have been borrowed from European language texts where this learning load may not be unreasonable (because there are a large number of cognates). It also naively follows the popular belief that it takes the same amount of time to learn Chinese as it does, say, French. Some believe that it is important to introduce a large number of vocabulary items from the start, but beginners are very limited in what they can do with those words without the support of grammar structures and an awareness of how the words are used. It is preferable to limit the amount of vocabulary initially and provide a solid framework of grammar patterns and discourse structures for using the vocabulary items before expecting learners to remember large lists of words.

Our discussion in Chapter One shows that truly foreign languages take a considerably longer time to reach a particular level of proficiency. We have argued that this fact alone calls for better methods for introducing and teaching these noncognate, culturally distant languages. In Chapter One, we described how we think languages such as Chinese, Japanese, and Korean should be taught. The materials we develop can reflect these attitudes and ideas, and existing materials can sometimes be adapted or supplemented to meet these needs.

Teachers often seem to be bound to the materials that are selected for a particular class. The less experience a teacher has, the more likely he or she will be to stick rigidly to the text whether or not it is a good text. Experienced teachers may also feel reluctant to diverge from what is "in the book." This rigid reliance on the text regardless of its intrinsic worth is also a characteristic of Asian language teaching and learning paradigms. (This point is discussed in more detail later). Because most currently available materials are less than ideal, it is imperative that we learn how to adapt these materials to suit the cultural and social needs of the target language and the specific goals of our courses and programs.

In this chapter, we first discuss the state of the materials available on the market today. We describe how most text materials are comprised and how they are intended to be used. This is followed by a discussion of native East Asian language paradigms; these are common assumptions that native developers of East Asian language materials have about their languages and about learning them. Next is a description of performance-based materials and how they can be utilized effectively. The role of video in the classroom also is addressed, with specific suggestions on how to best use authentic video for learning the language. We end this chapter with a discussion of how to evaluate existing materials.

When we use the term *text*, we are not limiting ourselves to traditional bound volumes of paper and cloth, but rather are referring to any materials that can be used in the classroom for pedagogical purposes—textbooks, audio programs, video programs and transcripts, computer programs, and so on.

THE STATE OF EAL MATERIALS

Most of the materials that have been produced in the past few decades depend on the theoretical frameworks and methodologies from teaching ESL and Western European languages. We see a great deal of grammar-translation methodology in current and past materials as well as the audiolingual approach and, more recently, the communicative approach.

Most textbooks follow a similar format: The main portion of any given lesson is often a dialogue or a similar written text. This is usually either preceded or followed immediately by a list of vocabulary words used in the dialogue. These lists typically present the target-language words and their English equivalents side by side. Grammar notes usually follow. These generally consist of a one- or two-sentence description of the grammar pattern with a few examples of the pattern used in other contexts. Some materials are more thorough, but most are terse and cryptic. Grammar notes are often followed with a series of drills and perhaps some exercises. Many textbooks do not go beyond drills, that is, using the vocabulary or sentence patterns in highly controlled, substitution-type drills. They usually require the learner to fill in the blank with a different noun, verb, or adjective. The following is a characteristic example for the pattern [*qù* + verb].

> *Tāmén zuótiān qù dǎ qiú.*
> They went and played ball yesterday.
> *Tāmén zuótiān qù* _____.
> *Tāmén zuótiān qù* _____
> *Tāmén zuótiān qù* _____.

Students place a verb in the open slot to indicate different [*qù* + verb] sentences. Sometimes the drills are very mechanical, with the substituted words provided, and some are more open-ended, where students can place any word that fits into the open slot.

Some materials also include exercises; these are the type of language activity that does not call for a predetermined or set answer, though context is always important. Exercises give learners more freedom to express themselves, which is important to their development.

If there are culture notes of any kind, they typically deal with aspects of achievement or informational culture such as the arts or history. Explanations of cultural behaviors that relate directly to language use are rare. If such notes are included, they are usually incomplete.

The kinds of materials just described focus almost exclusively on grammar and vocabulary and use a bottom-up approach. In other words, most of the materials available on the market today reflect the idea that learning the language is about learning grammar and vocabulary at the sentence level. We have provided arguments that this is far from an ideal way of learning how to communicate in another culture. In the vast majority of EAL texts, there is seldom an effort to place the language introduced into an appropriate social and cultural context. It is disappointing that some materials provide good dialogues with authentic language, only to omit other information about the dialogue, such as when, where, and with whom such an exchange might occur. These texts seldom provide additional material that offers variations to the dialogue to suit different genres with their accompanying roles, times, and places. Even texts that use a so-called communicative approach do not always provide a tie between the language and its social and cultural connotations. The best textbooks on the market likewise seem to heavily emphasize the linguistic code and neglect the cultural code. We addressed the issue of vocabulary in Chapter Five. To reiterate, it is simply not enough to provide a one-word English gloss for many Chinese, Japanese, or Korean words. Really understanding the meaning of many words, how and when they are used, and where to use them requires more explanation than a word or a short phrase.

Truly foreign languages such as Chinese, Japanese, and Korean are too culturally distant to be treated like any other foreign language. They require a cultural pedagogical foundation such as what we describe in Chapters One and Two.

In sum, the traditional approach that most texts follow starts with the parts (i.e., vocabulary and grammar), and gradually builds up to the whole via sentences. Vocabulary and grammar (i.e., the linguistic code) are emphasized first and sometimes exclusively, which leads to placing them into a dialogue or reading text.

NATIVE PARADIGMS

Noda (1994) has described native paradigms as assumptions that materials developers and teachers who are native speakers of East Asian languages tend to have about their native language and its study. These assumptions are readily seen in materials created by native speakers of East Asian languages. We do not mean that all materials developed by native speakers reflect these assumptions, merely that most have at least some of these characteristics.

Most native speakers with no training in teaching Chinese, Japanese, or Korean as a foreign language will naturally teach their native language in the way they learned as children. They can hardly be blamed for this because it is the only experience they have with learning the language. The problem with this approach is that first-language learners have no recollection of learning to speak; all that remains of language-learning memory is learning the written language. This then becomes the focus of teaching.

Furthermore, native East Asian attitudes toward education are vastly different from American attitudes. Traditional education in East Asia relies heavily on rote memorization with little emphasis on reasoning and analytical skills, especially the ability to ask questions, discuss varying viewpoints, and challenge the information presented in a textbook or lecture. Likewise, the traditional class in East Asia is conducted differently from the North American tradition. For example, the teacher in the traditional classroom is considered the "sage on the stage." In other words, it is the teacher's responsibility to convey knowledge. He or she is considered the authority on the subject matter and is not to be questioned. In a traditional classroom, students do not speak much unless the teacher specifically requests questions.

Students may find classes taught by inexperienced target native teachers to be especially challenging because these teachers often mimic the environment that they experienced as students. As a result, the classroom environment may seem harsh to Western learners because there is no tolerance for slouching, whispering to a classmate, reading the newspaper (even before class begins), and so on. Any behavior that detracts from complete attention to the teacher is unacceptable. Even asking questions may seem to annoy the teacher. In this kind of classroom, the learner may find conditions too stifling for active learning.

Hu and Grove (1991) provide a nice summary of Western and Chinese attitudes toward education and highlight the most drastic differences between them. Following is a modified version of that list (81–82). These differences help us understand not only East Asian teaching and learning styles, but also how many of these attitudes are reflected in the materials East Asians produce.

Asian Attitudes Toward Teaching and Learning

• The transmission of knowledge is oriented more toward theory than toward practice and application. The preferred mode of thinking is deductive, not inductive or operational as it is in the United States.

• Great emphasis is placed on details and facts, which are often committed to memory. Americans, conversely, worry little about remembering facts; instead, they focus on knowing where to find facts and how to use them creatively.

• A key learning objective is to know and be able to state facts and theories as givens, as wholes. Chinese students are rarely able to employ an analytical conceptual style, which Americans value.

• The content of learning is whatever is found in assigned texts or other readings; books are the sources of authority. Using books merely as sources of opinions or interpretations, as American teachers often wish to do, is not understood or appreciated by Chinese students.

• The teachers whose classroom style is most admired are those who give clearly structured, information-packed lectures with much information written on the blackboard (which students copy verbatim). Experiential learning, problem solving, case studies, and participatory teaching methods are distrusted and may be resisted by Chinese.

• Tests are extremely important because like the imperial examinations of old, they are viewed as the absolute determinants of a student's future. Chinese students do not understand that American teachers use tests primarily to gauge students' progress.

The native paradigms discussed next reflect many of these attitudes about education and the learning process.

Native EAL Teaching and Learning Paradigms

1.   *Writing represents the language.*
There is a common assumption among native speakers of Chinese and Japanese that the written language *is* the language. Textbooks include or begin with the written language as the default mode, and there is a heavy treatment of the written language. Romanization is not considered an acceptable presentation of the target language, and if it is used at all, it is limited to the first few lessons. Characters as well as written texts are simplified for beginning learners.

2.   *To study Chinese or Japanese is to go through literacy training. Speaking ability comes naturally; literacy does not.*
This also is a reflection of native speakers' experience learning their native language. There is the general belief that learning a dialogue requires reading it first, or at least a heavy reliance on the written form of the dialogue. Exercises likewise require answers written in the native orthography. New language should always present new information. In other words, it is believed that repetition practice is boring and not necessary. Finally, native speakers believe that university students should be engaged in sophisticated discussions rather than using the language to play games or do fun exercises that may not conform to the traditional, rigid classroom atmosphere.

3.   *A high level of foreign language proficiency is associated with reading and writing skills.*
This is a natural extension of the previous items. Consequently, writing compositions is considered important. In this paradigm, literary texts are incorporated into the curriculum as soon as possible. This is seen in many programs in which language learning is viewed as a means to access the great literature of a society.

4.   *Instruction is delivered through lectures.*
This is the "sage on the stage" syndrome, where the teacher is regarded as the unquestioned authority on the subject. Language materials such as textbooks should not provide too much explanation, otherwise this infringes on the responsibility of the teacher who should explain these things, especially topics such as grammar. Exercises often are written and can be done by students outside the classroom. Written exercises are the primary means of evaluating learners' performance. This is often seen in long, heavily weighted written midterm and final examinations.

5.   *Learning is accomplished through taking notes and reading books.*
Reading is the first thing learners should do with learning material. Textbooks are always the core of instructional materials, along with the teacher's word. Audio, video, and computer-based materials are supplementary to the textbook. Learning is always tested through written tests. An extreme example of this is a final exam for a

conversation class taught in the PRC where the entire exam was presented in Chinese characters with no speaking component at all. Although the language did represent spoken language, this exam became a reading comprehension and composition exam rather than the oral exam it purported to be.

6.   *The native behavior is the universal behavior.*

This statement corresponds to our discussion in Chapter One about ignored or covert culture. This is the idea that the way that natives speak or behave is the "normal" way to behave, which is challenged or questioned only when the native confronts someone from another culture who behaves differently. It also refers to natives' assumptions that the lexical and grammar changes required in polite speech are difficult but knowing when and how to use polite speech is not. Native speakers also tend to believe that translating the parts will produce the translation of the whole. This assumption favors a sentence-based approach to grammar: that understanding things at the sentence level will enable one to understand the language and grammar at the discourse level.

These assumptions are characteristic of the general attitudes of native speakers of East Asian languages. Examining materials published in East Asia immediately reveals many of these characteristics. Perhaps the most obvious is the use of the native orthography, even in beginning-level texts (see Chapter Four).

CULTURAL AND SOCIAL CONTEXTUALIZATION

Another deficiency we notice about many of the materials on the market is the lack of cultural and social contextualization of the language. The language is presented with little regard for who is speaking, where the communication takes place, the roles of the speakers, or the behavior that is associated with the communicative situation. If any cultural note is included, it usually consists of some note about the Great Wall or Chinese calligraphy, the Japanese tea ceremony, or the spiritual nature of Mt. Fuji. However, learners of East Asian languages need more information about behavioral culture. For example, most textbooks of Chinese have a lesson about drinking tea and include a dialogue with phrases such as *qǐng hē chá* (please have some tea). Though the language may be authentic, learners also need to know about how, when, and why tea is offered:

- Tea is automatically offered whenever one visits someone.
- The cup must be accepted with two hands.
- It is important to not refuse the hospitality of the host; even if the tea is not drunk, it is still important to accept it.
- Declining an offer for tea must be done politely, and a request is then made for an acceptable substitute, such as boiled water.
- Sometimes offering tea is more a social convention than offering the drink for refreshment.

These facts, along with other social behavior such as body language, are just as important as the words that are spoken.

In sum, most materials on the market, including the popular video guides, follow a structurally based, traditional approach. That is, the focus is on the forms of the language (the linguistic code), and instruction progresses from mechanical to more communicative. Learning begins with the intensive or internal elements and progresses to the extensive or external elements. The following chart summarizes this structurally based traditional approach.

Structurally Based Approaches

    1. Begin with structure
          • Learners memorize vocabulary and patterns
    2. Place the parts into the whole
          • Learners memorize or learn dialogues or study reading passages that use the vocabulary and patterns
    3. Communication: Focus on language use
          • Learners strive to use the language learned in meaningful communicative situations

Incidentally, there is often a huge gap between performing a memorized dialogue and being able to use that language in real communicative situations, (items #2 and #3), which is reflected in a major criticism of audiolingualism. Learning the structure devoid of the social and cultural context does not necessarily enable a person to know when, how, and with whom it is appropriate to use that language in the real world.

Materials that reflect an emphasis on performance focus on meaning and context from the beginning, with structures playing a supporting role rather than the main role. In other words, one begins with the external or extensive features and move to the internal or intensive features. This approach is summarized next.

Performance-Based Approach

> 1. Begin with the whole
>   - Learners familiarize themselves with the context and five elements of the performance that surrounds the situation
> 2. Performance of the whole
>   - Learners perform the dialogue, paying attention to how the vocabulary and patterns fit into the context of the communicative situation
> 3. Communicative practice
>   - Learners practice using the language in realistic and authentic communicative situations

This performance approach is more holistic in that learners are trained to see the big picture and not just the individual parts. This also is considered a top-down approach as opposed to a bottom-up approach.

In the next section, we discuss in detail this performance-based approach with regard to teaching materials.

CULTURE AND PERFORMANCE-BASED MATERIALS

Materials that reflect the performance and culturally based ideals described in Chapter One can be realized through four stages of development: presentation, performance, application, and review. These stages of development guide learners through steps that begin with a period of familiarization with the material, progress to performing and practice, and end with a review of the material.

173

Presentation

The purpose of this stage of learning is to familiarize learners with the communicative situation. For learning to be meaningful, learners need to know not only what they are saying, but also why. They must understand the social and cultural situation that dictates the language that is to be used. Because most learning materials teach the language through dialogues, it is important that learners understand the five elements of a performance—time, place, roles, script, and audience. In addition to the linguistic code, the cultural code, which includes the many nonlinguistic modes of communication such as gestures, body language, and proxemics, needs to be actively taught and stressed in the classroom. This familiarization during the presentation stage can be accomplished through classroom discussions, written descriptions, and video review. Video provides an ideal way to visually and aurally contextualize the language. The many modes of nonlinguistic communication can also be readily depicted in video: Learners can observe facial expressions and how people are dressed, how they walk, how they carry themselves, and how they bow. They also can observe streets and vehicles, buildings, furniture, and other items that may differ from Western society.

Performance

The performance stage is the most critical part of the instructional cycle. At the beginning and intermediate levels, it is appropriate to use the dialogue as the basis of the performance. After learners have been presented with the cultural and social background of the performance, including the roles, time, place, and so on, they are ready to begin performing in the target language. The dialogue is an ideal performance because it presents the vocabulary and grammar in a highly controlled and appropriate context. It is important that learners at this level have material that is controlled, such as the language found in a dialogue or monologue. If they are allowed to be too creative with the language too early, they will struggle in knowing how and when to use the language and appropriate cultural behavior. More important, they can easily lose sight of the cultural and social significance of a performance in the target language. In other words, they will rely too heavily on their own cultural perspectives and create target-language phrases that do not sound natural in a target-language communicative situation.

The performance stage can begin with a dialogue build-up type of exercise in which the dialogue is presented one phrase at a time, slowly building up to the whole exchange. So often materials on the market simply provide the complete dialogue on tape, which makes it difficult for learners to memorize the dialogue effectively and efficiently. If the material is presented in meaningful units, one short phrase at a time, learners can more readily internalize that material (through repetition) before going on to the next segment. A whole dialogue, or even one complete exchange in a dialogue, is often too long to repeat after the model on the tape. The old *Beginning Chinese* texts, by John DeFrancis, provide nice build-up exercises for the sentences introduced. The *Spoken Cantonese* series also utilizes these types of build-up exercises effectively.

Following is simple example of a typical build-up exercise. Such exercises can start with the end of the phrase and work backward. This kind of exercise is best done in the preparation phase (with audio- or videotapes), rather than during class.

> *kàn diànyǐng*
> *méiyou kàn diànyǐng*
> *zuótiān méiyou kàn diànyǐng*
> *Zhāang xiānshēng zuótiān méiyou kàn diànyǐng*

With longer dialogues at the higher levels, the phrases introduced can be longer because the learners are more able to memorize longer portions of discourse. Once learners have memorized the dialogue with the aid of the build-up exercises, they are ready to perform the dialogue in the classroom.

Learners inevitably are nervous to stand up in front of their peers and speak in a foreign language, which is why we believe it is important to get them performing in the classroom from the beginning of instruction. Teachers may want to remind students that when they get to China, Japan, or Korea, they will be performing in front of people from the time they step off the plane. They need to understand that at least in the classroom, they are in a comfortable and controlled environment, whereas in the target community, this may not be the case. It is also important to remind students that the more they perform in the language in the classroom, the more comfortable they will be when they perform in that communicative situation in the target culture. Teachers can do much to help learners relax and let go of some of the inhibitions that impede language performance by their manner of interacting with the learners and by how they prepare the learners for their language performances. Explaining clearly not only what students are expected to do but also why can help alleviate anxieties. Walker and Noda (2000, 209) refer to this as "remembering the future." Their premise is that the more you rehearse a predictable behavior, that is, some communicative situation that you will likely encounter in the target culture, the more you will be able to remember how to conduct yourself when you encounter that situation in the real world. In their words (190–191),

> Successful teachers of foreign languages create learning environments in which they present the particular things that are accepted in and typical of the target culture. Successful learners compile these presentations into memories that underlie acceptable behavior in cultures and languages that they have yet to experience outside their course or classrooms. *In short, they are trying to remember how to behave in a social environment that will occur in their futures.* [emphasis added]

Before students perform in the classroom, it is advisable that the teacher set the stage for the performance by providing appropriate visual aids and arranging the classroom to make the situation as realistic as possible. The teacher also should model the performance, or if the performance is available on videotape, show that portion of the tape as a quick review before the learners perform. The teacher should emphasize the importance of *performing* and not just reciting memorized lines. Dialogue performances should not be recitations. Too often, students memorize a dialogue and then stand in front of the class and recite the lines mechanically. Learners should strive to act. This is why visual aids are valuable and why the many nonlinguistic actions associated with the cultural code are important to learn when performing in the language. The more emotions and senses that are involved in a performance, the more likely it will be remembered in the future. How learners prepare outside the classroom will determine how they perform in the classroom. It is important to instruct learners in successful learner strategies and specifically how to prepare for in-class performances. The kind of feedback teachers give can also help in this regard. If learners know that just parroting the lines is insufficient, their preparation will go beyond that (assuming they care about what they are doing).

Dialogue performances can be followed by a brief session of correction. As a general rule, we do not advise correcting students in the middle of a dialogue performance. As students perform, teachers can note common errors and then address the class as a whole when making corrections; this strategy does not single out individual students. Besides, there often are troublesome parts of a dialogue where many students make errors. When individual correction is warranted, it can be done in a nonthreatening way after the dialogue is performed. A full exploration of error correction strategies is beyond the scope of this chapter. We advise readers to refer to Omaggio Hadley (2001) and Brown (1994a) for complete yet succinct discussions of error correction strategies for the classroom.

Application

In the application stage, learners apply the language they have learned to other contexts and situations not necessarily found in the classroom materials. It is important that learners know how to use the language in a variety of situations and contexts. For example, after students learn a dialogue that presents a basic greeting such as *konnichi wa*, it would be valuable to learn other types of greetings that are appropriate in other communicative situations. Likewise, when structural patterns are learned, it is important for learners to be able to use them in contexts outside the confines of the dialogue performed. This applies to vocabulary items as well. As mentioned in the previous chapter, it is helpful for many students to focus on the function of the pattern rather than on its structure.

At the beginning of the application stage, exercises should be tightly controlled. That is, teachers should have very structured exercises where learners do not have to create too much in the language before they are ready to do so. Important structural patterns and vocabulary that appeared in the dialogue can be practiced in controlled exercises where the learners will provide relatively predictable answers. Once they are comfortable performing using the vocabulary and patterns in a variety of contexts, they are ready to move on to more open-ended exercises such as role plays and improvisation exercises.

As discussed in Chapter Five, role plays provide learners with opportunities to perform roles that they will play in the target culture; in many cases, the roles will be student, traveler, or businessperson. Remember that these types of open-ended situations should not be practiced until learners have had the opportunity to perform within tightly controlled contexts so that they understand the cultural and linguistic parameters of the given situation.

An effective way to do role-play exercises is to first distribute cards on which the situation is described or give the instructions verbally, and then have students work in pairs to practice what they would say. The teacher should move about the classroom monitoring student performance, correcting, and coaching. After students have practiced the role plays, the teacher can select pairs to perform. The teacher can evaluate the performance, and the rest of the students have a chance to listen to and learn from others. In this way, the role play can also serve as a listening comprehension exercise. The teacher might even ask comprehension questions of the class when the role-play performances are complete; if the students know they will be expected to answer questions, they will pay closer attention to what their classmates are saying. As students are performing, the teacher can take notes to use when coaching the learners to a better performance and when evaluating their performance. At times, the teacher can participate in the role play and provide a model of authentic pronunciation, intonation, and body language.

Improvisation exercises can be defined in two ways. First, learners play a variety of roles that are not limited to the role they will play in real life. In an improvisation exercise, they may play the role of a student, department store clerk, or taxi driver. By playing the role of someone they are likely to encounter in the target community, they gain a better understanding of the communicative situation and the expectations and intentions of all roles involved. In terms of performance, learners need to understand the parameters well—because they may never be a taxi driver, they need to understand quite well the elements of the performance from a taxi driver's perspective in order to be culturally authentic.

A second way of looking at an improvisation exercise is to allow learners only a few minutes to prepare to respond to a given topic or situation. Learners must apply what they know about the situation to a different context, though it may be a related situation. These types of exercises can be conducted in the same way as role plays. They can also take the form of dialogues that learners create outside of class and perform in class. Students may be given a topic for their dialogues, usually the topic of the week's lesson, and they incorporate into them as many vocabulary items and patterns from the lesson as possible. We call these *improvisational dialogues* because learners are free to choose what to say and do, so long as they address the topic assigned. This allows learners to create their own contexts in the target language. As we have said, it is important that learners have the skills necessary to do this. When learners lack the necessary linguistic skills and, even more important, the cultural skills, they will end up performing an American skit while speaking the target language. These are invariably entertaining, but may not be culturally realistic.

Review and Evaluation
In this stage of instruction, it is important to regularly assess learners' understanding of the material that has been presented, performed, and practiced. Learners need regular feedback so they know how they are doing and how they can improve. Review of previously learned material is also very important. The process of learning East Asian languages can be very daunting, especially with the number of characters that must be committed to memory. It is important to build review sessions into the curriculum; this gives learners a chance to catch up on what they may not have internalized and better learn material they are familiar with. The goal in language performance is automaticity. Whereas the first time around, students may have learned the material well enough to perform it in class, during a review, they can focus more on natural performances and emphasize content in a greater way.

Evaluation can take many forms. As we advocated earlier, daily grading works effectively in determining students' overall abilities.

USING VIDEO IN THE CLASSROOM

There is not much debate these days about the benefits of video for teaching foreign languages. In recent years, we have seen a plethora of video materials geared toward foreign language learners. The use of video in the foreign language classroom has at least three distinct benefits. First, students are exposed to authentic language or artifacts—recordings of authentic language that are not created for pedagogical purposes. As discussed in Chapter Four, it is particularly important that intermediate and advanced learners be exposed to authentic language the way that it is used among natives in the target culture. Second, video presents language in its appropriate, natural social and cultural contexts. Learners are able to observe authentic contexts and perform based on those contexts. Third, cultural awareness is reinforced when learners observe native behavior in video; for example, kinesics (movement including gestures and body language) and proxemics (the use of space, for example, how close people stand to each other) are built in and readily observable. Tang (1996) presents a clear and convincing discussion of these factors with regard to video. Learners who view video materials are more able to make the connection between the linguistic code and the cultural code; that is, they learn not only what language to use, but also when and how to use it. As we have discussed, this is an essential part of an effective language-learning process.

Though there have been numerous pedagogically created materials based on Chinese language videos, the vast majority consist primarily of a movie script presented in Chinese characters, vocabulary lists with occasional grammar notes, and exercises, most often comprehension and/or discussion questions. These materials resemble traditionally oriented textbooks and do not take advantage of the video medium. A performance component is notably lacking. Video materials that are presented with a systematic, pedagogically sound approach, such as has been discussed here with reference to other materials, are sorely needed.

Video material should be introduced in manageable units. As with other materials, there should be presentation or familiarization activities, followed by a performance component where students are provided with the instruction and means to perform the language and cultural behaviors presented in the video segment. Finally, it is important to include a practice component where learners can personalize what they have learned.

Video and Performed Culture

Video can be used effectively with both extensive viewing activities and intensive viewing as the focus. Extensive viewing typically focuses on nonlinguistic factors such as viewing for specific information—identifying the speech act, body language, locations, or topics, as well as viewing to understand the gist of the language used. Intensive viewing deals with identifying the language code in the social and cultural context presented. Whereas extensive viewing typically deals with longer segments of video, intensive viewing focuses on shorter segments, some as short as thirty seconds to a minute.

Because of the ease of bringing video into the classroom, it is becoming increasingly common to use video in teaching. However, using video effectively is another matter. It is all too common for the teacher of Chinese, Japanese, or Korean to bring a movie into the class, put it into the VCR, and an hour later ask the class what they watched, what they got out of it, and so on. This results in a major overload of information that causes learners to become overwhelmed with the amount of new information they are bombarded with. Even a ten- or fifteen-minute video clip can be very intimidating. Remember that most feature films are not intended for learners of the language. Because authentic video material contains unedited language that is not geared to the learners' level, it can be intimidating and difficult to process.

For this reason, it is important to present video material gradually and in such a way that learners have the time and the skills to process it effectively. This is why it is important to introduce video with the same steps discussed in the preceding section: presentation, performance, application, and review.

Two mistakes commonly occur when using video in the foreign language classroom: introducing too much material, and showing video without a clear viewing purpose. Unless students are very advanced, it is simply not productive to show an entire movie or even a television episode and then ask questions about it. However, this activity may be beneficial if the purpose is to view for nonlinguistic culture behavior. When video material is presented without a clear viewing purpose, learners also tend to get lost trying to remember or process everything they see. Video material can be selected by segments that are culturally and linguistically rich and short enough that learners can process them without undue stress. We suggest no more than a few minutes per segment when the purpose is for learners to view intensively. When learners have a specific viewing purpose, they can focus on that task and tune out all the other information.

For example, the popular Chinese film *Strange Friends* can be used effectively for a variety of purposes, even at the beginning levels. After learners have learned place names, a short segment of the video that takes place in a train station can be shown. As the worker taking tickets at the platform gate calls out the various place names, learners can make a list of those places. When asking learners to view for a specific, focused purpose like this, it is important to emphasize that there will be much that they will not understand. Encourage them to ignore what they do not understand and focus on what they do, such as place names, numbers, and simple greetings.

As we have said, a problem with many video materials is that they consist of little more than the dialogue transcribed into characters, a vocabulary list, and occasionally some grammar notes and maybe some exercises. With materials like this, learners have little hope of really understanding the language used. They may be able to follow the story line, but there is little guidance in understanding the relationship between the language used and the social and cultural situations that are depicted. However, the potential of video in this aspect is nearly ideal: learners not only hear what is being said, they also can observe how people interact with each other, how close they stand to each other, how they carry themselves, the clothes they wear, and a myriad of other concepts and actions we may take for granted in our own culture.

EVALUATING AND ADAPTING EXISTING MATERIALS

Kubler et al. (1997, 123–129) provide a very thorough checklist for evaluating materials. Though this checklist was intended for Chinese, it applies equally well to any foreign language. It shows teachers what to consider and how to evaluate a text before adopting it for course instruction. In this section, we provide an abbreviated checklist of the most important elements to look for in a text. The list in Kubler et al. is arranged in categories: general considerations, cultural component, speaking, listening, reading, writing, and multimedia materials. Our checklist provides general considerations that are consistent with our discussion in this book. The detailed list in Kubler et al. is a useful reference for skill-specific considerations.

Though most text materials do not include much of a performance or cultural component, many do exhibit some of these characteristics. At the very least, one should be able to determine if a text can be readily adapted for these purposes. Our checklist will enable teachers to look critically at text materials to decide which will be the easiest to adapt and use in the classroom. This is the overriding principle in selecting a good text: Is this material adaptable to a performance-oriented approach?

- **Is the language introduced natural and authentic?**

This is the starting point. If the language in a text is contrived and unnatural, it will be very difficult for learners to do any realistic communication. We define authentic language as that which could be spoken by native speakers under common and normal circumstances. This may also include natural use by nonnatives—for example, "I'm an American," which a native would never say (Noda 1994). It is important that the language also emphasizes common usage over the rare examples of language use. If the language in a text is authentic and natural, it can generally be utilized in culturally accurate performances.

- **Is there a significant cultural component to the material?**

Is the language placed in a realistic social and cultural context? Most materials simply provide a dialogue with no supportive information, such as information about the roles of the speakers, when, where, and with whom such a dialogue would likely occur, and the specific behavior that would be a part of this kind of communicative situation. Some texts address some of these issues as notes that follow the dialogue. Look for materials that at least provide stimulating dialogues where the elements of a performance can be identified and reviewed. And if cultural issues are addressed in the text, are they accurate? Good materials will be contextualized both linguistically and culturally.

- ### Are the skills treated separately?

It is common for materials developers to freely mix the skills being learned. For example, learners may encounter listening and speaking exercises presented entirely in the native orthography. There is a time and a place for mixing the skills because they can reinforce each other, but care should be taken. If learners are doing a listening comprehension or speaking exercise, it may dilute the effectiveness of the activity if all the questions and materials are presented in characters. As a result, the listening or speaking exercise becomes a reading comprehension exercise—to understand the questions, learners must be able to read them first.

- ### Is new material introduced in digestible amounts?

Most materials available on the market today simply introduce too much in each lesson. Not only is it difficult to learn that much material in one lesson, it forces the teacher either to select certain parts of the lesson to be learned or to spend more time on each lesson than was originally intended. New material should be introduced in amounts that can be learned, and learned well, in a reasonable amount of time. Shorter lessons give learners a sense of accomplishment as they progress from lesson to lesson.

- ### Is the material interesting and practical?

Instructional materials should cover topics that are both interesting and practical. The content should be pedagogically sound. In addition, it is helpful and motivating to learners when the presentation and layout are visually appealing and easy to navigate; in well-designed materials, effective use of white space and font variety clarify and highlight the information presented. These may seem like small matters, but a good pedagogical design and layout can have a large impact on learner motivation and enhance the effectiveness of the materials.

- ### Are there a variety of communicative situations included?

So often materials provide examples of a single genre of discourse. To be comprehensive, materials should incorporate a variety of genres, from informal to formal, both written and spoken. For example, informal conversation with peers is important to learn, but it is also important to know how to conduct yourself at a banquet or when conversing with a professor. In writing, there should be both texts that represent the spoken language and more formal written genres. Learners must be exposed to and have guided practice in literary language as well, such as Chinese *shūmiànyǔ* (written language), and formal genres in Japanese.

- **Are vocabulary items presented in contexts that show proper usage?**

Vocabulary should be presented in appropriate cultural contexts, and explanations should be thorough enough to show how and when to use each word or phrase.

- **Are learners exposed to a variety of reading skills?**

To develop reading fluency in learners, it is important to expose them to discourse that is contextually supported. Individual sentences may be helpful at the beginning of instruction, but learners need to read a variety of materials that are presented in units beyond the sentence. Likewise, learners should be taught a variety of reading tasks, such as skimming to discern the general content of a passage (extensive or top-down reading) and scanning for specific information in a passage. This is in addition to reading for content and detail (intensive or bottom-up reading). These neglected skills are used every day and are an important part of general reading strategies in any language (see Chapter Four).

- **Are the video and audio materials presented naturally?**

Audio and video materials should be presented at natural native speed. It does learners no favor to slow the language down so they can more readily understand what is being said. If build-up exercises are provided for dialogue memorization, then learners can deal with natural speed. Natural speed also allows learners to get accustomed to the way the language is actually used

185

in the target environment, and it helps preserve natural pronunciation and intonation patterns.

CONCLUSION

Teachers have their students for a short time, so it is imperative that they make the best possible use of that time. Selecting and developing good materials that reflect an emphasis on performance ultimately save a great deal of time. The less teachers need to manipulate and adapt existing materials, the more time they have for creating efficient and effective classroom activities. It is unlikely that teachers will find "ideal" materials because circumstances and needs differ with local conditions, but the recommendations in this chapter will help teachers to look critically at materials to determine whether they are worth adopting, even if some adaptation is required. Generally speaking, materials that are based on communicative approaches will be readily adaptable to the performance-oriented approach that we describe in this book. Materials that emphasize meaning (and contextualized authentic language) provide a good base from which to adopt a performed culture approach in the classroom; on the other hand, materials that place emphasis on structure (i.e., vocabulary and grammar) tend to provide only a partial picture of the language-learning task and usually require substantial supplementing in order to be successful in a performance-oriented approach. Ultimately, this wastes time that could be used in more productive ways. Good, carefully selected and created materials save time, which fosters more efficient and effective classrooms.

Chapter Seven

CONCLUSION AND RECOMMENDATIONS

SUMMARY

This book presents foreign language learning and teaching as more than a linguistic endeavor: It is a holistic view of language learning as cultural behavior. Having a knowledge of the structural parts— grammar and vocabulary—does not guarantee successful communication or the establishment of lasting relationships with members of the target culture. It is only by understanding *how* the Chinese, Japanese, and Koreans communicate that learners will be successful in their overseas endeavors. Success in learning a foreign language is not measured by the number of words memorized, or by the ability to talk about discrete points of grammar. On the contrary, success is measured by the ability to communicate in such a way that the native interlocutors are at ease and mutually comfortable relationships are established and maintained over time. This success requires knowing much more about the people than merely the things they say or write; the keen learner must also understand the social and cultural behavior that always accompanies the living language and that is never divorced from any utterance, anywhere, at any time.

In this final chapter, we discuss two issues. First, we offer recommendations on how to apply the research and information we have discussed in each chapter to the actual foreign language classroom. Thus, this chapter not only serves as a succinct overview of the contents of each chapter, but also offers concrete suggestions on how to apply that information in the classroom or in course design. And second, we address the need for and importance of formal teacher training.

RECOMMENDATIONS

Chapter One: *Performed Culture*

1. Learning should be meaning based and contextualized; teachers should include nonlinguistic and cultural elements to support and give meaning to linguistic information.
2. All material should be introduced and practiced in an appropriate social and cultural context.
3. Learners should be introduced to nonlinguistic elements of cultural communication.
4. In-class performance provides an ideal platform for integrating cultural and linguistic information.
5. Learners should be introduced to and understand the five elements of each performance: time, place, roles, script, audience.
6. Teachers should familiarize learners with a variety of language genres and styles.

Chapter Two: *Performing Culture: Performance-Based Curriculum*

1. The spoken language is primary and as such should be the focus of beginning-level language classes.
2. Teachers should draw attention to the distinction between spoken and written language conventions and styles.
3. The four skills should not be mixed prematurely.
4. The written language should be introduced only after a foundation in the spoken language has been established.
5. Romanization (*pinyin*) is an important tool in the learning process as a representation of the spoken language.
6. FACT sessions focus on knowledge about the language and culture and should be kept to a minimum—in general, approximately one session for every four ACT sessions.
7. ACT sessions conducted in the target language, where students perform in the language, should be the focus of instruction.
8. Daily performance evaluation enhances student performance and gives a clear indication of what learners can actually do in the target language.

Chapter Three : *Speaking and Listening in Culture*

1.   Activities should always be contextualized, and they should explicitly identify the five elements of the given performance.

2.   ACT classes, should be conducted exclusively in the target language.

3.   Teachers should speak at normal conversational speed.

4.   Learners need evaluative feedback on all areas of language use, including pronunciation, intonation, vocabulary, grammatical structures, discourse markers, body language, and social appropriateness.

5.   Learners should have opportunities to participate in a number of genres, with variations on each to help them develop a sense for culturally appropriate performance in different situations.

6.   Both speaking and listening comprehension activities (always contextualized) should be part of the formal evaluation of learners on quizzes and tests. Conversational skills cannot be adequately tested on paper-and-pencil tests.

Chapter Four: *Reading and Writing*

1.   Reading should be treated as an active skill by focusing on the social roles and outcomes of reading texts.

2.   Reading and writing should begin only after learners have a foundation in oral and aural skills.

3.   Authentic texts and tasks should be used in the classroom as much as possible.

4.   At the beginning level, learners' focus should be on literacy skills (i.e., learning to read and write what they can say and understand); at upper levels, instruction can focus on strategies for dealing with nonpedagogical, authentic artifacts.

5.   Learners need opportunities to participate in a number of reading and writing genres, with variations on each that help them develop a sense for culturally appropriate uses in different contexts.

6.   Using a Romanization system will help learners develop the connection between reading and the phonological system.

7.   Characters should be taught in context.

8.   Learners need to understand the graphemic, phonemic, and semantic components of characters.

9.   For Chinese, traditional characters should be introduced first, followed by simplified characters at the upper levels.

10.   Classroom time should focus on prereading and postreading exercises when teaching reading skills.

11.   Teachers should make use of a variety of reading strategies, such as skimming exercises, scanning exercises, and reading for detail.

12.   Learners need training in the writing process—especially prewriting, drafting, and revising—and should receive feedback in each of these areas.

Chapter Five: *A Performative Approach to Grammar, Vocabulary, and Discourse*

1.   FACT sessions are the place to discuss grammar, vocabulary, and the social and cultural implications of the language, and to answer questions.

2.   Prescriptive grammar explanations should be contrasted with descriptive examples from authentic language texts.

3.   Grammar explanations and examples should be presented in authentic contexts.

4.   One-word definitions of vocabulary items are generally insufficient; learners require thorough explanations of vocabulary items that show how they are used in a variety of contexts.

5.   Learners need ample opportunities to observe, understand, and practice using important discourse strategies (i.e., grammar items that function beyond the sentence level).

6.   Teachers should focus on tasks when introducing grammar patterns.

Chapter Six: *Evaluating and Developing Materials for East Asian Languages*

1.   New material should be presented in a systematic and comprehensive manner.

- Presentation: familiarize learners with the material they will be learning.

- Performance: provide opportunities for learners to perform in the target language.
- Practice: provide opportunities for and coach learners in practicing using the material in a variety of contexts.
- Review: regularly review and assess the understanding of material that has been presented, performed, and practiced.

2. There should be a specific purpose or objective for using video in the classroom.

- For intensive video viewing, short, manageable excerpts are best.
- For extensive viewing, learners can identify many nonlinguistic behaviors that are portrayed in video.
- Using video can help learners make the connection between linguistics and the social and cultural implications of the language used.

3. When selecting materials for classroom use, teachers should consider the following issues:

- Is the language introduced natural and authentic?
- Is there a significant cultural component to the material?
- Are the skills treated separately?
- Are a variety of communicative situations represented in the materials?
- Are vocabulary items presented in contexts that show proper usage?
- Are learners exposed to a variety of reading skills?
- Are video and audio materials presented in natural contexts?

TEACHER TRAINING

Reading and studying a text like this one are certainly an important, even essential part of improving teaching skills. It is important to be aware of the research that exists in the field of East Asian language pedagogy and to be introduced to effective ways to teach Chinese, Japanese, and Korean to learners. However, we do acknowledge that lasting changes in the classroom are more likely to take place if teachers have access to a teacher-training program where they not only learn about research and effective methodologies, but also have the opportunity to observe, tutor, practice teach, and receive immediate feedback. O'Malley and Chamot (1990, 155–156) suggest that an effective way to present a theory of teaching has three steps: 1) presentation of the theory, 2) demonstration of the new approach, and 3) immediate practice and feedback. In this book, we have presented a theory, but in this format we cannot demonstrate this approach or provide an opportunity for practice or feedback. These components are accomplished through a formal teacher-training program. (For a more complete discussion of teacher training for East Asian languages, see Christensen and Noda 2002.)

For teacher training to be effective and worthwhile, theory, research, and practice (with feedback) must be integrated. To facilitate this, it is highly desirable to hold a teacher-training program in conjunction with a language program. Such an arrangement provides invaluable opportunities for close interaction between teacher trainees, master teachers, and language students at various levels. If trainees have the opportunity to observe and teach real classes, permanent changes in their own classrooms are more likely to take place. This kind of program offers the following benefits:

1. Trainees observe the *learning* process firsthand.
2. Trainees can tutor individual students to gain a better understanding of how learners prepare for class, what strategies they use, how technology is used, and so on.
3. Trainees observe the *teaching* process firsthand.
4. Trainees can develop their own lesson plans and practice teaching (and receive feedback) in real classrooms with real students.

5.   Trainees can produce and implement assessment measures and evaluate learner performance.
6.   Trainees are exposed to syllabi, overall course design, and program development issues.

FINAL COMMENTS

The performed culture approach to teaching East Asian Languages described in this book calls for a more holistic and comprehensive approach to teaching and learning. It requires us to look beyond linguistics and address the many other aspects of performing in a foreign culture, whether it be asking directions as target natives expect people to ask directions or reading a literary text and doing with it what a native would.

The performed culture approach admittedly is not easy to incorporate in the classroom. In fact, it requires a great deal of effort for teachers to fully implement these ideas into regular classroom practice. However, we believe the rewards, in terms of the learners' skill development, are well worth the effort. If this approach is drastically different from what you are currently doing, we recommend that you implement it in stages. We owe it to our students to teach in the most efficient and effective way possible. By so doing, our students will be prepared to study, work, and live comfortably in the Chinese-, Japanese-, or Korean-speaking world.

Bibliography

WORKS CITED

Agar, Michael. 1994. *Language Shock: Understanding the Culture of Conversation*. New York: William Morrow and Company.

Bar-Lev, Zev. 1991. "Two Innovations for Teaching Tones." *Journal of the Chinese Language Teachers Association* 26, no. 3:1–24.

Bauman, Richard. 1977. *Verbal Art as Performance*. Prospect Heights, IL: Waveland Press.

Bennett, Andrew. 1995. "Introduction." In *Readers and Reading*, ed. Andrew Bennett. New York: Longman.

Bernhardt, Elizabeth B. 1986. "Reading in the Foreign Language." In *Listening, Reading, Writing: Analysis and Application*, ed. Barbara H. Wing. Middlebury, VT: Northeast Conference on the Teaching of Foreign Languages, 93–115.

Bourgerie, Dana Scott. 1996. "Acquisition of Modal Particles in Chinese Second Language Learners." In *Chinese Pedagogy: An Emerging Field*, ed. Scott McGinnis. Columbus: The Ohio State University Foreign Language Publications, 107–134.

Bransford, John D., and Marcia K. Johnson. 1972. "Contextual Prerequisites for Understanding: Some Investigations of Comprehension and Recall." *Journal of Verbal Learning and Verbal Behavior* 11, no. 6:717–726.

Brod, Richard, and Elizabeth B. Welles. 2000. "Foreign Language Enrollments in United States Institutions of Higher Education, Fall 1998." *ADFL Bulletin* 31, no. 2:22–29.

Brooks, Nelson. 1997. "Teaching Culture in the Foreign Language Classroom." In *Pathways to Culture*, ed. Paula R. Heusinkveld. Yarmouth, ME: Intercultural Press, 11–37.

Brown, H. Douglas. 1994a. *Principles of Language Learning and Teaching*. 3rd ed. Upper Saddle River, NJ: Prentice Hall Regents.

———. 1994b. *Teaching by Principles: An Interactive Approach to Language Pedagogy*. Upper Saddle River, NJ: Prentice Hall Regents.

Bruner, Jerome. 1986. *Actual Minds, Possible Worlds*. Cambridge, MA: Harvard University Press.

———. 1996. *The Culture of Education*. Cambridge, MA: Harvard University Press.

Bryant, Daniel. 1992. "The Why and Why Not of Pinyin—A Response to DeFrancis." *Journal of the Chinese Language Teachers Association* 17, no. 12:111–114.

Burke, Kenneth. 1969. *A Grammar of Motives*. Berkeley: University of California Press.

Carlson, Marvin. 1996. *Performance: A Critical Introduction*. London and New York: Routledge.

Carrell, Patricia L., Joanne Devine, and David E. Eskey. 1988. *Interactive Approaches to Second Language Reading*. Cambridge: Cambridge University Press.

Chafe, Wallace. 1994. *Discourse, Consciousness, and Time: The Flow and Displacement of Conscious Experience in*

Speaking and Writing. Chicago: University of Chicago Press.

Chan, Marjorie K. M. 1980. "Temporal Reference in Mandarin Chinese: An Analytical-Semantic Approach to the Study of the Morphemes Le, Zai, Zhe, and Ne." *Journal of the Chinese Language Teachers Association* 15, no. 3:33–79.

Chin, Yin-lien C. 1972. "How to Teach Mandarin Retroflex and Palatal Sounds." *Journal of the Chinese Language Teachers Association* 7, no. 2:77–81.

Choo, Miho, and William O'Grady. 2003. *The Sounds of Korean: A Pronunciation Guide.* Honolulu: University of Hawai'i Press.

Christensen, Matthew B. 1994. "Variation in Spoken and Written Mandarin Narrative Discourse." Ph.D. Dissertation. The Ohio State University.

_____. 1996. *Spoken Cantonese: Presentation and Context.* Columbus: The Ohio State University Foreign Language Publications.

————. 1997. "The Acquisition of Temporal Reference Marking among Learners of Chinese." Paper presented at the Chinese Language Teachers Association Annual Conference. Nashville, Tennessee.

————. 1998. "The Acquisition of Anaphoric Reference Markers among Learners of Mandarin Chinese." Paper presented at the American Association of Applied Linguistics Annual Conference. Seattle, Washington.

_____, and Roxana Sukyee Fung. 1995. *Spoken Cantonese: Acquisition and Presentation.* Columbus: The Ohio State University Foreign Language Publications.

_____, and Xiaobin Jian. 1995. *Spoken Cantonese: Performance and Acquisition.* Columbus: The Ohio State University Foreign Language Publications.

_____, and Mari Noda. 2002. *A Performance-Based Pedagogy for Communicating in Cultures: Training Teachers for East Asian Languages.* Columbus: The Ohio State University Foreign Language Publications.

Chu, Chauncey, C. 1990. "Semantics and Discourse in Chinese Language Instruction." *Journal of the Chinese Language Teachers Association* 25, no. 3:15–29.

Coady, James M. 1979. "Psycholinguistic Model of the ESL Reader." In *Reading in a Second Language*, ed. Ronald Mackay, Bruce Barkman, and R. R. Jordan. Rowley, MA: Newbury House, 5–12.

Crystal, David. 1987. *The Cambridge Encyclopedia of Language.* Cambridge: Cambridge University Press.

Davis, James N., and Linda Bistodeau. 1993. "How Do L1 and L2 Reading Differ? Evidence from Think Aloud Protocols." *Modern Language Journal* 77, no. 4:459–472.

DeFrancis, John. 1976. *Beginning Chinese.* New Haven and London: Yale University Press.

———. 1984. "Phonetic vs. Semantic Predictability in Chinese Characters." *Journal of the Chinese Language Teachers Association* 19, no. 1:1–21.

———. 1986. "Graphic Representation of Chinese Tones." *Journal of the Chinese Language Teachers Association* 21, no. 2:27–42.

De Mente, Boye Lafayette. 1996. *NTC's Dictionary of China's Cultural Code Words.* Lincolnwood, IL: NTC Publishing Group.

Eco, Umberto. 1979. *The Role of the Reader.* Bloomington: Indiana University Press.

Erbaugh, Mary. 1990. "Mandarin Oral Narratives Compared with English: The Pear/Guava Stories." *Journal of the Chinese Language Teachers Association* 25, no. 2:21–42.

————, ed. 2002. *Difficult Characters: Interdisciplinary Studies of Chinese and Japanese Writing.* Columbus: Ohio State University, National East Asian Languages Resource Center.

Eskey, David E. 1986. "Theoretical Foundations." In *Teaching Second Language Reading for Academic Purposes,* ed. Fraida Dubin, David E. Eskey, and William Grabe. Reading, MA: Addison-Wesley, 3–23.

Everson, Michael E. 1988. "Speed and Comprehension in Reading Chinese: Romanization vs. Characters Revisited." *Journal of the Chinese Language Teachers Association* 23, no. 2:1–15.

————, and Yasumi Kuriya. 1998. "An Exploratory Study into the Reading Strategies of Learners of Japanese as a Foreign Language." *Journal of the Association of Teachers of Japanese* 32, no. 1:1–21.

Fasold, Ralph. 1990. *Sociolinguistics of Language.* Oxford: Blackwell.

Fish, Stanley. 1980. *Is There a Text in This Class?* Cambridge, MA: Harvard University Press.

Fromkin, Victoria, and Robert Rodman. 1998. *An Introduction to Language.* 6th ed. Fort Worth, TX: Harcourt Brace College Publishers.

Garcia, Elvira. 1998. "Spanish, French, and German: An Edwardian Pattern for a Postmodern World." *ADFL Bulletin* 30, no. 1:9–11.

Goodman, Kenneth S. 1970. "Reading: A Psycholinguistic Guessing Game." In *Theoretical Models and Processes of Reading*, ed. Harry Singer and Robert B. Ruddell. Newark, DE: International Reading Association, 259–272.

Gough, Philip B. 1972. "One Second of Reading." In *Language by Ear and by Eye*, ed. James F. Kavanagh and Ignatius G. Mattingly. Cambridge, MA: MIT Press, 331–358.

Grabe, William. 1988. "Reassessing the Term 'Interactive.'" In *Interactive Approaches to Second Language Reading*, ed. Patricia L. Carrell, Joanne Devine, and David E. Eskey. Cambridge: Cambridge University Press, 56–70.

Hall, Edward T. 1959. *The Silent Language*. New York: Anchor Books.

———. 1966. *The Hidden Dimension*. New York: Anchor Books.

———. 1976. *Beyond Culture*. New York: Anchor Books.

Hammerly, Hector. 1985. *An Integrated Theory of Language Teaching and Its Practical Consequences*. Blaine, WA: Second Language Publications.

Heusinkveld, Paula R. 1997. *Pathways to Culture*. Yarmouth, ME: Intercultural Press.

Hinds, John. 1983."Contrastive Rhetoric: Japanese and English." *Text* 3, no. 2:183–195.

———. 1986. *Situation vs. Person Focus*. Tokyo: Kuroshio.

Hopper, Paul J. 1979. "Aspect and Foregrounding in Discourse." In *Syntax and Semantics, Volume 12: Discourse and Syntax*, ed. T. Givon. New York: Academic Press, 213–241.

Horodeck, Richard Alan. 1987. "The Role of Sound in Reading and Writing Kanji." Ph.D. Dissertation. Cornell University.

Hu, Wenzhong, and Cornelius L. Grove. 1991. *Encountering the Chinese: A Guide for Americans*. Yarmouth, ME: Intercultural Press.

Hudson, Thom. 1982. "The Effects of Induced Schemata on the 'Short Circuit' in L2 Reading: Non-Decoding Factors in L2 Reading Performance." *Language Learning* 32:1–31.

Hymes, Dell. 1974. *Foundations in Sociolinguistics*. Philadelphia: University of Pennsylvania Press.

Iser, Wolfgang. 1978. *The Act of Reading*. Baltimore: The Johns Hopkins University Press.

Jannedy, Stefanie, Robert Poletto, and Tracey L. Weldon, ed. 1994. *Language Files*. Columbus: The Ohio State University Press.

Jian, Xiaobin, and Matthew B. Christensen. 1995. *Spoken Cantonese: Context and Performance*. Columbus: The Ohio State University Foreign Language Publications. 1994.

Johnson, Dale. 1985. "Tonal Spelling—An Idea Whose Time Is Overdue." *Journal of the Chinese Language Teachers Association* 20, no. 1:67–68.

Johnson, Keith, and Helen Johnson, ed. 1998. *Encyclopedic Dictionary of Applied Linguistics*. Oxford: Blackwell.

Jorden, Eleanor. 1986. "On Teaching Nihongo." *Japan Quarterly* 33, no. 2:139–147.

———. 1992. "Broadening Our Boundaries: The Less Commonly Taught and the Truly Foreign Languages." In *Teaching Languages in College*, ed. Wilga M. Rivers. Lincolnwood, IL: National Textbook Company, 141–155.

————, and A. Ronald Walton. 1987. "Truly Foreign Languages: Instructional Challenges." *Annals of the American Academy of Political and Social Science* 496 (March 1987):110–124.

Just, Marcel Adam, and Patricia A. Carpenter. 1980. "A Theory of Reading: From Eye Fixations to Comprehension." *Psychological Review* 87, no. 4:329–354.

Kamil, Michael L. 1986. "Reading in the Native Language." In *Listening, Reading, Writing: Analysis and Application*, ed. Barbara H. Wing. Middlebury, VT: Northeast Conference on the Teaching of Foreign Languages, 71–91.

Ke, Chuanren. 1996. "An Empirical Study on the Relationship between Chinese Character Recognition and Production." *Modern Language Journal* 80, no. 3:340–349.

Knowles, Elizabeth, ed. 1999. *The Oxford Dictionary of Quotations*. Oxford: Oxford University Press.

Konomi, Emiko. 1997. "Curriculum Design: Teaching Japanese in the Humanities." In *Shaping the Next Generation*, ed. J. Marshall Unger. Columbus: The Ohio State University Foreign Language Publications, 37–45.

Krashen, Stephen D. 1997. *Foreign Language Education the Easy Way*. Culver City, CA: Language Education Associates.

Kubler, Cornelius C., et al. 1997. *NFLC Guide for Basic Chinese Language Programs*. Washington D.C.: National Foreign Language Center and The Ohio State University Foreign Language Publications.

Lee, Iksop, and S. Robert Ramsey. 2000. *The Korean Language*. Albany: State University of New York Press.

Lee, James F., and Bill Vanpatten. 1995. *Making Communicative Language Teaching Happen*. New York: McGraw-Hill.

Li, Charles N., and Sandra A. Thompson. 1981. *Mandarin Chinese: A Functional Reference Grammar.* Berkeley: University of California Press.

Light, Timothy. 1976. "Comparative Reading Speeds with Romanized and Character Texts." *Journal of the Chinese Language Teachers Association* 11, no. 1:1–10.

Lundelius, Jay Osborn.1992. "Pinyin vs. Tonal Spelling." *Journal of the Chinese Language Teachers Association* 27, no. 3:93–108.

Makino, Seiichi, Yukiko Abe Hatasa, and Kazumi Hatasa. 1998. *Nakama 1.* Boston: Houghton Mifflin.

Martin, Samuel E. 1975. *A Reference Grammar of Japanese.* New Haven, CT: Yale University Press.

Matsunaga, Sachiko 1994. *The Role of Phonological Coding in Reading Kanji: A Research Report and Some Pedagogical Implications.* Technical Report 6. Honolulu: University of Hawai'i, Second Language Teaching & Curriculum Center.

————. 1995. *Role of Phonological Coding in Reading Kanji.* Honolulu: University of Hawai'i, Second Language Teaching & Curriculum Center.

McClelland, James L. 1986. "The Programmable Blackboard Model of Reading." In *Parallel Distributed Processing: Explorations in the Microstructure of Cognition, Volume 2.* ed. James L. McClelland, David E. Rumelhart, and The PDP Research Group. Cambridge, MA: Bradford Books, 122–169.

McGinnis, Scott. 1997a. "Tonal Distinction Errors by Beginning Chinese Language Students: A Comparative Study of American and Japanese Native Speakers." In *Chinese Pedagogy: An Emerging Field*, ed. Scott McGinnis.

Columbus: The Ohio State University Foreign Language Publications, 81–92.

————. 1997b. "Tonal Spelling versus Diacritics for Teaching Pronunciation of Mandarin Chinese." *Modern Language Journal* 81, no. 2:228–236.

Mickel, Stanley L. 1980. "Teaching the Chinese Writing System." *Journal of the Chinese Language Teachers Association* 15, no. 1:91–98.

Miller, Carolyn R. 1984. "Genre as Social Action." *Quarterly Journal of Speech* 70:151–167.

Miracle, W. Charles. 1989. "Tone Production of American Students of Chinese: A Preliminary Acoustic Study." *Journal of the Chinese Language Teachers Association* 24, no. 3:49–65.

Morain, Genelle. 1986. "Kinesics and Cross-Cultural Understanding." In *Culture Bound: Bridging the Cultural Gap in Language Teaching*, ed. Joyce Merrill Valdes. Cambridge: Cambridge University Press, 64–76.

Mori, Masako. 1995. "Reading Bilingually: Crosslinguistic Study of Reading Comprehension in English and Japanese by Intermediate and Advanced Level Japanese Speakers of English as a Second Language (ESL) and English Speakers of Japanese as a Foreign Language (JFL)." Ph.D. Dissertation. University of Minnesota.

Mueller, Gunter A. 1980. "Visual Contextual Cues and Listening Comprehension: An Experiment." *Modern Language Journal* 64, no. 3:335–340.

National Foreign Language Center. 1993. *A Framework for Introductory Japanese Language Curricula in American High Schools and Colleges*. Washington, D.C.: National Foreign Language Center.

Noda, Mari. 1994. "'Authentic' Materials and Authenticity in the Instruction of Japanese as a Foreign Language." In *Proceedings of the Sixth Annual Lake Erie Teachers of Japanese Conference*, ed. Yukiko Abe Hatasa and Kazumi Hatasa. West Lafayette, IN: Purdue University, 159–171.

Nunan, David. 1989. *Designing Tasks for the Communicative Classroom*. Cambridge: Cambridge University Press.

Ochs, Elinor. 1990. "Indexicality and Socialization." In *Cultural Psychology: Essays on Comparative Human Development*, ed. James W. Stigler, Richard A. Shweder, and Gilbert Herdt. Cambridge: Cambridge University Press, 287–308.

Omaggio Hadley, Alice. 2001. *Teaching Language in Context*. 3rd ed. Boston: Heinle and Heinle.

O'Malley, J. Michael, and Anna Uhl Chamot. 1990. *Learning Strategies in Second Language Acquisition*. Cambridge: Cambridge University Press.

Packard, Jerome L. 1990. "Effects of Time Lag in the Introduction of Characters into the Chinese Language Curriculum." *The Modern Language Journal* 74, no. 2:167–175.

Quackenbush, Hiroko C. 1977. "English Loanwords in Japanese: Why Are They Difficult for English-Speaking Students?" *Journal of the Association of Teachers of Japanese* 12, no. 2–3:149–173.

Rayner, Keith, and Alexander Pollatsek. 1989. *The Psychology of Reading*. Englewood Cliffs, NJ: Prentice Hall.

Richards, Jack C. and Theodore S. Rodgers. 1986. *Approaches and Methods in Language Teaching*. Cambridge: Cambridge University Press.

Ruddell, Robert B., Martha Rapp Ruddell, and Harry Singer. 1994. *Theoretical Models and Processes of Reading*. 4th ed. Newark, DE: International Reading Association.

Rumelhart, David E. 1977. "Toward an Interactive Model of Reading." In *Attention and Performance VI*, ed. Stanislav Dornic. Hillsdale, NJ: Lawrence Erlbaum, 573–606.

Samuels, S. Jay, and Michael L. Kamil. 1984. "Models of the Reading Process." In *Handbook of Reading Research*, ed. P. David Pearson. New York: Longman, 185–224.

―――. 1988. "Models of the Reading Process." In *Interactive Approaches to Second Language Reading*, ed. Patricia L. Carrell, Joanne Devine, and David E. Eskey. Cambridge: Cambridge University Press, 22–36.

Schank, Roger C. 1976. "The Role of Memory in Language Processing." In *The Structure of Human Memory*, ed. Charles N. Cofer. San Francisco: W. H. Freeman and Company, 162–189.

―――. 1982. *Dynamic Memory*. Cambridge: Cambridge University Press. [cited]

―――. 1990. *Tell Me a Story: A New Look at Real and Artificial Memory*. New York: Scribner.

Schechner, Richard. 1987. "General Introduction to the Performance Studies Series." In *The Anthropology of Performance*, by Victor Turner. New York: PAJ Publications.

Schiffrin, Deborah. 1994. *Approaches to Discourse*. Oxford: Blackwell.

Scholes, Robert. 1982. *Semiotics and Interpretation*. New Haven, CT: Yale University Press.

Schumann, John H. 1976. "Social Distance as a Factor in Second Language Acquisition." *Language Learning* 26, no. 1:135–143.

Shen, Susan Xiaonan. 1989. "Toward a Register Approach in Teaching Mandarin Tones." *Journal of the Chinese Language Teachers Association* 24, no. 3:27–47.

Shibatani, Masayoshi. 1990. *The Languages of Japan*. Cambridge: Cambridge University Press.

Shore, Bradd. 1996. *Culture in Mind: Cognition, Culture, and the Problem of Meaning*. Oxford: Oxford University Press.

Smith, Frank. 1971. *Understanding Reading: A Psycholinguistic Analysis of Reading and Learning to Read*. New York: Holt, Rinehart and Winston.

Spinelli, Emily. 1997. "Increasing the Functional Culture Content of the Foreign Language Class." In *Pathways to Culture*, ed. Paula R. Heusinkveld. Yarmouth, ME: Intercultural Press, 213–224.

Stanovich, Keith E. 1980. "Toward an Interactive-Compensatory Model of Individual Differences in the Development of Reading Fluency." *Reading Research Quarterly* 16, no. 1:32–71.

Stewart, Edward C., and Milton J. Bennett. 1991. *American Cultural Patterns: A Cross-Cultural Approach*. Yarmouth, ME: Intercultural Press.

Swales, John M. 1990. *Genre Analysis*. Cambridge: Cambridge University Press.

Tai, James H-Y. 1985. "Temporal Sequence and Chinese Word Order." In *Iconicity in Syntax*, ed. John Haiman. Amsterdam: John Benjamins 49–72.

Tang, Yanfang. 1996. "Linguistically Accurate and Culturally Appropriate: The Use of Video in Chinese Language Instruction." In *Chinese Pedagogy: An Emerging Field*, ed. Scott McGinnis. Columbus: The Ohio State University Foreign Language Publications, 285–314.

Tsujimura, Natsuko. 1996. *An Introduction to Japanese Linguistics*. Oxford: Blackwell.

Turner, Victor. 1987. *The Anthropology of Performance*. New York: PAJ Publications.

Unger, J. Marshall. 2004. *Ideogram: Chinese Characters and the Myth of Disembodied Meaning*. Honolulu: University of Hawai'i Press.

Walker, Galal. 1984. "Literacy and Reading in a Chinese Language Program." *Journal of the Chinese Language Teachers Association* 19, no. 1:67–84.

———. 1989. "Intensive Chinese Curriculum: The EASLI Model." *Journal of the Chinese Language Teachers Association* 24, no. 2:43–83.

———. 1991. "Gaining Place: The Less Commonly Taught Languages in American Schools." *Foreign Language Annals* 24, no. 2:131–150.

———. 2000. "Performed Culture: Learning to Participate in Another Culture." In *Language Policy and Pedagogy: Essays in Honor of A. Ronald Walton*. eds. Richard D. Lambert and Elana Shohamy. Amsterdam: John Benjamins. 221-236.

———, and Mari Noda. 2000. "Remembering the Future: Compiling Knowledge of Another Culture." In *Reflecting on the Past to Shape the Future*, ed. Diane W. Birckbichler. Lincolnwood, IL: National Textbook Company, 187–212.

Wardhaugh, Ronald. 1992. *An Introduction to Sociolinguistics.* 2nd ed. Oxford: Blackwell.

Warnick, J. Paul. 1996. "A Phenomenology of Reading Performances: Reading Japanese as a Foreign Language." Ph.D. Dissertation. The Ohio State University.

————. 1999. "Reading, Rereading, and Reading Comprehension." Paper presented at the Association of Teachers of Japanese Annual Conference. Boston.

Watabe, Masakazu. 1996. "The Uses and Abuses of Romanization." Paper presented at the American Council on the Teaching of Foreign Languages Annual Conference. Philadelphia.

————. 1997. "Japanese Language Teaching without Teaching Context." In *Shaping the Next Generation*, ed. J. Marshall Unger. Columbus: The Ohio State University Foreign Language Publications, 93–103.

Welles, Elizabeth B. 2004. "Foreign Language Enrollments in United States Institutions of Higher Education, Fall 2002." *ADFL Bulletin* 35, no. 2-3:7–26.

White, Caryn M. 1981. "Tonal Production and Interference from English Intonation." *Journal of the Chinese Language Teachers Association* 16, no. 2:27–56.

Whitlock, Margaret Susan. 1993. *Toward a Cross-Cultural Comparison of Chinese and American Narrative.* The Ohio State University: unpublished thesis.

Wierzbicka, Anna. 1992. *Semantics, Culture, and Cognition: Universal Human Concepts in Culture-Specific Configurations.* Oxford: Oxford University Press.

————. 1997. *Understanding Cultures through Their Key Words.* Oxford: Oxford University Press.

Woo, William. 1976. "A Musical Approach to Tone Teaching in Mandarin." *Journal of the Chinese Language Teachers Association* 11, no. 2:96–102.

Xie, Tianwei. 1992. "Topic Controlled Deletion in Topic Chains in Chinese: A Comparison between Native Speakers and Foreign Language Learners." *Journal of the Chinese Language Teachers Association* 27, no. 3:21–31.

OTHER REFERENCES
The following references were consulted during the course of writing this book.

Alderson, J. Charles. 1984. "Reading in a Foreign Language: A Reading Problem or a Language Problem?" In *Reading in a Foreign Language*, ed. J. Charles Alderson and A. H. Urquhart. New York: Longman, 1–27.

Allen, Joseph Roe. 1984. "Chinese Script and Lexicography for the Uninitiated: Pedagogical Notes." *Journal of the Chinese Language Teacher's Association* 19, no. 3:35–86.

Anderson, Neil J. 1991. "Individual Differences in Strategy Use in Second Language Reading and Testing." *Modern Language Journal* 75, no. 4:460–472.

Atchison, Jean. 1991. *Language Change: Progress or Decay?* 2nd ed. Cambridge: Cambridge University Press.

Bachnik, Jane M., and Charles J. Quinn, Jr. 1994. *Situated Meaning: Inside and Outside in Japanese Self, Society, and Language.* Princeton, NJ: Princeton University Press.

Bakhtin, Mikhail M. 1986. "The Problem of Speech Genres." In *Speech Genres and Other Late Essays*, ed. Caryl Emerson and Michael Holquist, trans. Vern W. McGee. Austin: University of Texas Press, 60–102.

Bar-Lev, Becky. 1995. "Does the Home Make a Difference? A Comparison of Home-Exposure and Non-Home Exposure Students of Mandarin." *Journal of the Chinese Language Teachers Association* 30, no. 3: 55–68.

Barnett, Marva A. 1988. "Reading through Context: How Real and Perceived Strategy Use Affects L2 Comprehension." *Modern Language Journal* 72, no. 2:150–162.

———. 1989. *More Than Meets the Eye: Foreign Language Reading: Theory and Practice.* Englewood Cliffs: NJ: Prentice Hall Regents.

Benedict, Ruth. 1989. *The Chrysanthemum and the Sword: Patterns of Japanese Culture.* Boston: Houghton Mifflin. First published 1946.

Bialystok, Ellen. 1981. "The Role of Conscious Strategies in Second Language Proficiency." *Modern Language Journal* 65, no. 1:24–35.

Block, Ellen. 1986. "The Comprehension Strategies of Second Language Readers." *TESOL Quarterly* 20, no. 3:463–494.

Bonin, Therese M. 1982. "Teaching Culture in Beginning Language Classes." *Journal of the Chinese Language Teachers Association* 17, no. 3:33–48.

Botoman, Rodica C. 1982. "Creating a Cultural Context for Beginning Language Students: The Romanian Experience." *Journal of the Chinese Language Teachers Association* 17, no. 3:49–62.

Brown, Gillian, and George Yule. 1983. *Discourse Analysis.* Cambridge: Cambridge University Press.

Buck, David D. 1974. "The Use of Broadcast Television Programs as a Means of Advanced Conversational Instruction." *Journal of the Chinese Language Teachers Association* 9, no. 2:93–97.

Bybee, Joan L. 1985. *Morphology.* Philadelphia: John Benjamins.

Carrell, Patricia L. 1991. "Second Language Reading: Reading Ability or Language Proficiency?" *Applied Linguistics* 12, no. 2:159–179.

————, Becky G. Pharis, and Joseph C. Liberto. 1989. "Metacognitive Strategy Training for ESL Reading." *TESOL Quarterly* 23, no. 4:647–678.

Chamot, Anna Uhl, and Lisa Kupper. 1989. "Learning Strategies in Foreign Language Instruction." *Foreign Language Annals* 22, no. 1:13–24.

Chen, Qiao Jeremy. 1997. "Learning Chinese Characters through Self-Study: An Experiment with the Diglot Reader Method." Master's Thesis. Brigham Young University

Cheyney, Arnold B. 1992. *Teaching Reading Skills through the Newspaper*. 3rd ed. Newark, DE: International Reading Association.

Chi, T. Richard. 1989. "Observations of the Past, Present, and Future of Teaching Mandarin Chinese as a Foreign Language." *Journal of the Chinese Language Teachers Association* 24, no. 2:109–122.

————. 1996. "Toward a Communicative Model for Teaching and Learning Chinese as a Foreign Language: Exploring Some New Possibilities." In *Chinese Pedagogy: An Emerging Field*, ed. Scott McGinnis. Columbus: The Ohio State University Foreign Language Publications, 1–28.

Chi, Yin L. 1989. "The Role of Listening Comprehension in Classroom Instruction." *Journal of the Chinese Language Teachers Association* 24, no. 1:63–69.

Chiba, Hiroko. 1995. "Processing Kanji Characters in Reading Japanese as a Foreign Language." Ph.D. Dissertation. University of Illinois at Urbana-Champaign.

Chikamatsu, Nobuko. 1995. "The Effects of L1 Orthography on L2 Japanese Word Recognition." Paper presented at the American Association for Applied Linguistics Conference. Long Beach, California.

Chin, Tsung. 1973. "Is It Necessary to Require Writing in Learning Characters?" *Journal of the Chinese Language Teachers Association* 8, no. 3:167–170.

Ching, Nora, and Eugene Ching. 1975. "Teaching the Writing of Chinese Characters." *Journal of the Chinese Language Teachers Association* 10, no. 1:20–24.

Christensen, Matthew, and Xiaoqi Wu. 1993. "An Individualized Approach for Teaching False Beginners." *Journal of the Chinese Language Teachers Association* 28, no. 2:91–100.

————. 2000. "Anaphoric Reference in Spoken and Written Chinese Narrative Discourse." *Journal of Chinese Linguistics* 28, no. 2:303–336.

Christopherson, Steven L., Charles B. Schultz, and Yvonne Waern. 1981. "The Effect of Two Contextual Conditions on Recall of a Reading Passage and on Thought Processes in Reading." *Journal of Reading* 24, no. 7:573–578.

Chu, Yu-kuang. 1974. "Perception of Chinese Characters: An Experimental Study." *Journal of the Chinese Language Teachers Association* 9, no. 2:57–65.

Clark, L. H. 1972. *The Eye-Voice Span in Reading Japanese.* Unpublished paper.

Claudi, Ulrike, and Bernd Heine. 1986. "On the Metaphorical Base of Grammar." *Studies in Language* 10, no. 2:297–335.

Cole, Michael. 1996. *Cultural Psychology: A Once and Future Discipline.* Cambridge, MA: The Belknap Press of Harvard University Press.

Crowder, Robert G., and Richard K. Wagner. 1992. *The Psychology of Reading.* 2nd ed. New York: Oxford University Press.

D'Andrade, Roy. 1990. "Some Propositions about the Relations between Culture and Cognition." In *Cultural Psychology: Essays on Comparative Human Development*, ed. James W. Stigler, Richard A. Shweder, and Gilbert Herdt. Cambridge, MA: Cambridge University Press, 65–129.

Dewey, Dan P. 1997. "Kanji Coding Strategies of Native Readers and of Non-Native Readers with Various Backgrounds." Master's Thesis. Brigham Young University.

Dien, Albert.1985. "Survey of Chinese Language Teaching 1983–84." *Journal of the Chinese Language Teachers Association* 20, no. 1:99–108.

Douglas, Masako O. 1992. "Development of Orthography-Related Reading/Writing Strategies by Learners of Japanese as a Foreign Language." Ph.D. Dissertation. University of Southern California.

Dresser, Norine. 1996. *Multicultural Manners*. New York: Wiley.

Duranti, Alessandro. 1997. *Linguistic Anthropology*. Cambridge: Cambridge University Press.

Eddy, Peter A., James J. Wrenn, and Sophia A. Behrenn. 1980. *Chinese Language Study in American Higher Education: State of the Art*. Language in Education: Theory and Practice vol. 30. Washington, D.C.: Center for Applied Linguistics.

Evans, Grant, ed. 1993. *Asia's Cultural Mosaic: An Anthropological Introduction*. New York: Prentice Hall.

Everson, Michael E. 1993. "Research in the Less Commonly Taught Languages." In *Research in Language Learning: Principles, Processes, and Prospects*, ed. Alice Omaggio Hadley. Lincolnwood, IL: National Textbook Company, 198–228.

———. 1996. "Exploiting Background Knowledge in the Development of Chinese Pedagogical Reading Materials." In

Chinese Pedagogy: An Emerging Field, ed. Scott McGinnis. Columbus: The Ohio State University Foreign Language Publications, 93–106.

Falsgraf, Carl, and Diane Majors. 1995. "Implicit Culture in Japanese Immersion Classroom Discourse." *Journal of the Association of Teachers of Japanese* 29, no. 2:1–21.

Ferrara, Kathleen. 1993. "Pragmatic Transfer in American's Use of Japanese Thanking Routines." Paper presented at the American Association for Applied Linguistics Conference. Atlanta, Georgia.

Fukada, Atsushi. 1994. "Senmon Nihongo Dokkai Kyooiku No Hoohoo." *Nihongo Kyooiku*, 82:13–22.

Fukao, Yuriko. 1994. "Koogakukei No Senmon Dokkai Kyooiku Ni Okeru Nihongo Kyooiku No Yakuwari." *Nihongo Kyooiku*, 82:1–12.

Goffman, Erving. 1981. *Forms of Talk*. Philadelphia: University of Pennsylvania Press.

Golinkoff, Roberta Michnick. 1975–76. "A Comparison of Reading Comprehension Processes in Good and Poor Comprehenders." *Reading Research Quarterly* 11, no. 4: 623–659.

Goodnow, Jacqueline J. 1990. "The Socialization of Cognition." In *Cultural Psychology: Essays on Comparative Human Development*, ed. James W. Stigler, Richard A. Shweder, and Gilbert Herdt. Cambridge: Cambridge University Press, 259–286.

Grabe, William. 1991. "Current Developments in Second Language Reading Research." *TESOL Quarterly* 25, no. 3:375–406.

Groebel, Lillian. 1981. "Reading: The Students' Approach as Compared to Their Teachers' Recommended Method." *English Language Teaching Journal* 35, no. 3:282–287.

Gumperz, John J., and Stephen C. Levinson, ed. 1996. *Rethinking Linguistic Relativity*. Cambridge: Cambridge University Press.

Hall, Edward T. 1987. *Hidden Differences: Doing Business with the Japanese*. New York: Anchor Books.

Harada, Fumiko Kamiya. 1988. "The Effect of Three Different Orthographical Presentations of a Text upon the Reading Behaviors of Native and Non-Native Readers of Japanese: An Eye-Tracking Study." Ph.D. Dissertation. The Ohio State University.

Hatasa, Kazumi. 1989. "A Study of Learning and Teaching of Kanji for Non-Native Learners of Japanese." Ph.D. Dissertation. University of Illinois at Urbana-Champaign.

Hatasa, Yukiko A. 1995. "Effects of Time Lag in the Introduction of Japanese Scripts into the Japanese Language Curriculum." In *Proceedings of the Third Princeton Japanese Pedagogy Workshop*, ed. Seiichi Makino. Princeton, NJ: Princeton University Press, 172–223.

Hatch, Evelyn. 1992. *Discourse and Language Education*. Cambridge: Cambridge University Press.

Hayes, Edmund B. 1987. "The Relationship between Chinese Character Complexity and Character Recognition." *Journal of the Chinese Language Teachers Association* 22, no. 2:45–57.

Hendry, Joy. 1993. *Wrapping Culture*. Oxford: Clarendon Press.

Hinds, John. 1982. "Japanese Conversational Structures." *Lingua* 57:301–326.

Hintikka, Merrill B., and Jaakko Hintikka. 1986. *Investigating Wittgenstein*. Oxford: Blackwell.

Ho, Shang H. 1976. "Comments on Teaching Chinese Reading." *Journal of the Chinese Language Teachers Association* 11, no. 1:52–57.

Hopper, Paul, and Elizabeth Closs Traugott. 1993. *Grammaticalization*. Cambridge: Cambridge University Press.

Horiba, Yukie. 1990a. "The Role of Language Competence and Causal Thinking in Second Language Narrative Comprehension: A Comparative Study of Non-Native Intermediate, Non-Native Advanced and Native Readers of Japanese." Ph.D. Dissertation. University of Minnesota.

———. 1990b. "Narrative Comprehension Processes: A Study of Native and Non-Native Readers of Japanese." *Modern Language Journal* 74, no. 2:188–202.

———. 1993a. "The Role of Causal Reasoning and Language Competence in Narrative Comprehension." *Studies in Second Language Acquisition* 15, no. 1:49–81.

———. 1993b. "Narrative Comprehension Processes: A Study of Native and Non-Native Readers of Japanese." In *Methods That Work II: Ideas for Literacy and Language Teachers*, ed. John W. Oller and Patricia Richard-Amato. Boston: Heinle and Heinle, 230–246.

———. 1994. "The Role of Elaborations in L2 Discourse Comprehension: The Effect of Encoding Task on Recall." Paper presented at the Second Language Research Forum. Montreal, Canada.

———. 1996. "The Role of Elaboration in L2 Text Memory: The Effect of Encoding Task on Recall of Causally Related

Sentences." *The Modern Language Journal* 80, no. 2: 151–164.

————, Paul W. van den Broek, and Charles R. Fletcher. 1993. "Second Language Readers Memory for Narrative Texts: Evidence for Structure-Preserving Top-Down Processing." *Language Learning* 43:345–372.

Hosenfeld, Carol. 1984. "Case Studies of Ninth Grade Readers." In *Reading in a Foreign Language*, ed. J. Charles Alderson and A. H. Urquhart. New York: Longman, 231–244.

Hoskin, Kathryn Barton. 1997. "Motivation, Self-Esteem, Self-Confidence, and Anxiety in Beginning Mandarin Chinese Learners." Master's Thesis. Brigham Young University.

Hsu, Francis L. K. 1981. *Americans and Chinese: Passages to Differences*. 3rd ed. Honolulu: University of Hawai'i Press.

Huey, Edmund Burke. 1908/1916. *The Psychology and Pedagogy of Reading*. New York: Macmillan.

Ikeda, Kazuko. 1992. "Implicit Curriculum in Japanese Language Teaching: Case Studies of Two High School Teachers of Japanese." Ph.D. Dissertation. University of Oregon.

Ikegami, Yoshihiko. 1991. *The Empire of Signs*. Amsterdam: John Benjamins.

Joiner, Elizabeth G. 1990. "Choosing and Using Videotexts." *Foreign Language Annals* 23, no. 1:53–64.

Jorden, Eleanor Harz, and Mari Noda. 1987. *Japanese: The Spoken Language, Part 1*. New Haven, CT: Yale University Press.

Kamada, Osamu. 1986. "Discourse Analysis and Second Language Pedagogy: A Study of Reported Speech in Japanese as a First and a Second Language." Ed.D. Dissertation. University of Massachusetts.

————, and Wesley M. Jacobsen, ed. 1990. *On Japanese and How to Teach It.* Tokyo: The Japan Times.

Kamil, Michael L. 1984. "Current Traditions of Reading Research." In *Handbook of Reading Research I*, ed. P. David Pearson. New York: Longman, 39–62.

Kawaguchi, Yoshikazu. 1993. "Komyunikat(e)ibu. Apuroochi No Kanji Shidoo." *Nihongo Kyooiku* 80:15–27.

Kellerman, Marcelle. 1980. *The Forgotten Third Skill.* Oxford: Pergamon Press.

Knight, Stephanie L., Yolanda N. Padron, and Hersholt C. Waxman. 1985. "The Cognitive Reading Strategies of ESL Students." *TESOL Quarterly* 19, no. 4:789–792.

Koda, Keiko. 1986. "Cognitive Processes in Second Language Reading." Ph.D. Dissertation. University of Illinois at Urbana-Champaign.

————. 1988. "Cognitive Processes in Second Language Reading: Transfer of L1 Reading Skills and Strategies." *Second Language Research* 4, no. 2:133–156.

————. 1989a. "Effects of L1 Orthographic Representation on L2 Phonological Coding Strategies." *Journal of Psycholinguistic Research* 18, no. 2:201–222.

————. 1989b. "The Effects of Transferred Vocabulary Knowledge on the Development of L2 Reading Proficiency." *Foreign Language Annals* 22, no. 6:529–540.

————. 1990a. "Factors Affecting Second Language Text Comprehension." In *Literacy Theory and Research: Analyses from Multiple Paradigms*, ed. Jerry Zutell and Sandra McCormick. Chicago: National Reading Conference, 419–427.

————. 1990b. "The Use of L1 Reading Strategies in L2 Reading: Effects of L1 Orthographic Structures in L2 Phonological Structure." *Studies in Second Language Acquisition* 12, no. 4:393–410.

————. 1992. "The Effects of Lower-Level Processing Skills on FL Reading Performance: Implications for Instruction." *Modern Language Journal* 76, no. 4:502–512.

————. 1993a. "Task-Induced Variability in FL Composition: Language-Specific Perspectives." *Foreign Language Annals* 26, no. 3:332–346.

————. 1993b. "Transferred L1 Strategies and L2 Syntactic Structure in L2 Sentence Comprehension." *Modern Language Journal* 77, no. 4:490–500.

————. 1994. "Second Language Reading Research: Problems and Possibilities." *Applied Psycholinguistics* 15:1–28.

Kubler, Cornelius C. 1979. "Some Differences between Taiwan Mandarin and Textbook Mandarin." *Journal of the Chinese Language Teachers Association* 14, no. 3:27–39.

————. 1993. "Teaching Advanced Conversation and Comprehension through *Xiangsheng.*" *Journal of the Chinese Language Teachers Association* 28, no. 1:1–11.

Labov, William. 1988. *Sociolinguistic Patterns.* Philadelphia: University of Pennsylvania Press.

Lakoff, George, and Mark Johnson. 1980. *Metaphors We Live By.* Chicago: University of Chicago Press.

Lave, Jean. 1990. "The Culture of Acquisition and the Practice of Understanding." In *Cultural Psychology: Essays on Comparative Human Development*, ed. James W. Stigler,

Richard A. Shweder, and Gilbert Herdt. Cambridge: Cambridge University Press, 309–327.

Lee, David. 1992. *Competing Discourses: Perspective and Ideology in Language.* New York: Longman.

Lee, Frances Yufen. 1994. "The Effect on Listening Comprehension of Using Television Commercials in a Chinese as a Second Language Class." Master's Thesis. Brigham Young University.

Lee, James F. 1986. "Background Knowledge and L2 Reading." *Modern Language Journal* 70:350–354.

Lehmann, Winfred P. 1992. *Historical Linguistics.* London: Routledge.

Leitch, Vincent B. 1995. "Reader-Response Criticism." In *Readers and Reading,* ed. Andrew Bennett. New York: Longman, 32–65.

Levinson, Stephen C. 1992. "Activity Types and Language." In *Talk at Work: Interaction in Institutional Settings,* ed. Paul Drew and John Heritage. Cambridge: Cambridge University Press, 66–100.

Light, Timothy, and Galal Walker. 1982. "Individualizing Chinese Instruction: A Preliminary Report to the Field." *Journal of the Chinese Language Teachers Association* 16, no. 2:123–132.

Liu, Irene. 1983. "The Learning of Characters: A Conceptual Approach." *Journal of the Chinese Language Teachers Association* 18, no. 2:65–76.

Loew, Helene Z. 1984. "Developing Strategic Reading Skills." *Foreign Language Annals* 17, no. 4:301–303.

Loschky, Lester, and Robert Bley-Vroman. 1993. "Grammar and Task-Based Methodology." In *Tasks and Language Learning: Integrating Theory and Practice*, ed. Graham Crookes and Susan M. Gass. Clevedon, UK: Multilingual Matters, 123–167.

Luke, Kenneth C. 1983. "The Zero Pronoun in Mandarin Chinese." *Journal of the Chinese Language Teachers Association* 18, no. 3:1–15.

Lund, Randall J. 1990. "A Taxonomy for Teaching Second Language Listening." *Foreign Language Annals* 23, no. 2:105–115.

Makino, Seiichi. 1990. "Structuralism with Contextualization." *Journal of the Association of Teachers of Japanese* 25, no. 2:218–223.

Mandelbaum, David G., ed. 1949. *Edward Sapir: Selected Writings in Language, Culture, and Personality*. Berkeley: University of California Press.

Manguel, Alberto. 1996. *A History of Reading*. New York: Penguin Books.

McGinnis, Scott, and Chuanren Ke. 1992. "Using Authentic Cultural Materials to Teach Reading in Chinese." *Foreign Language Annals* 25, no. 4:233–238.

Miller, Carol R. 1984. "Genre as Social Action." *Quarterly Journal of Speech* 70, no. 2: 151–167.

Miyazaki, Satoshi. 1991. "The Teaching of Japanese and Japanese Honorifics: The Point of View of Honorific Avoidance." *Japanese Language Education around the Globe*. Vol. 1. Tokyo: The Japan Foundation Japanese Language Institute, 91–103.

Morimoto, Takiko. 1994. "The Effects of a Reading Strategy and Reciprocal Peer Tutoring on Intermediate Japanese Reading Comprehension." *Japanese Language Education around the Globe*. Vol. 4. Tokyo: The Japan Foundation Japanese Language Institute, 75–83.

Nagata, Noriko. 1993. "Intelligent Computer Feedback for Second Language Instruction." *The Modern Language Journal* 77, no. 3:330–339.

———. 1995. "An Effective Application of Natural Language Processing in Second Language Instruction." *CALICO* 13, no. 1:47–67.

———. 1997. "The Effectiveness of Computer-Assisted Metalinguistic Instruction: A Case Study in Japanese." *Foreign Language Annals* 30, no. 2:187–200.

———, and M. Virginia Swisher. 1995. "A Study of Consciousness-Raising by Computer: The Effect of Metalinguistic Feedback on Second Language Learning." *Foreign Language Annals* 28, no. 3:337–347.

Nara, Hiroshi. 1990. "Developing CAI Material for Improving Reading Skills in Japanese." *Literary and Linguistic Computing* 5, no. 2:139–144.

———, and Mari Noda. 2003. *Acts of Reading: Exploring Connections in Pedagogy of Japanese*. Honolulu: University of Hawai'i Press.

Noda, Mari. 1998a. *Faculty Guide to Japanese: The Spoken Language Interactive CD-ROM. Program*. New Haven, CT: Yale University Press.

———. 1998b. *User's Guide to Japanese: The Spoken Language Interactive CD-ROM Program*. New Haven, CT: Yale University Press.

Noguchi, Mary. 1995. "Component Analysis of Kanji for Learners from Non-Kanji Using Countries." *The Language Teacher* 19, no. 10:11–14.

Ogawa, Takashi. 1991. "Yomi No Sutoratejii, Purosesu to Jookyuu No Dokkai Shidoo." *Nihongo Kyooiku* 75, no. 82:78–86.

———. 1993. "Yomi Ni Okeru Komyunikat(e)ibu Apuroochi Ni Tsuite." *Nihongo Kyooiku* 80:136–145.

Ohta, Amy Snyder. 1990. "The Secrets of Our Success: A Study of Five Successful Learners of Japanese." Master's Thesis. University of California at Los Angeles.

———. 1995. "Applying Sociocultural Theory to an Analysis of Learner Discourse: Learner-Learner Collaborative Interaction in the ZPD." *Issues in Applied Linguistics* 6, no. 2:93–112.

Okurowski, Mary Ellen. 1987. "Teaching Chinese at the Text Level through Textual Cohesion." *Journal of the Chinese Language Teachers Association* 22, no. 2:59–80.

Olshavsky, Jill Edwards. 1976–1977. "Reading as Problem Solving: An Investigation of Strategies." *Reading Research Quarterly* 12, no. 4:654–674.

Omaggio, Alice C. 1984. "Making Reading Comprehensible." *Foreign Language Annals* 17, no. 4:305–308.

Padron, Yolanda N., and Hersholt C. Waxman. 1988. "The Effect of ESL Students' Perceptions of Their Cognitive Strategies on Reading Achievement." *TESOL Quarterly* 22, no. 1:146–150.

Paris, Scott G., and Meyer Myers II. 1981. "Comprehension Monitoring, Memory, and Study Strategies of Good and Poor Readers." *Journal of Reading Behavior* 13, no. 1:5–22.

Phillips, June K. 1984. "Practical Implications of Recent Research in Reading." *Foreign Language Annals* 17, no. 4:285–299.

Pritchard, Robert. 1990. "The Effects of Cultural Schemata on Reading Processing Strategies." *Reading Research Quarterly* 25, no. 3:273–295.

Quinn, Charles J. 1991. "Giving Spoken Language Its Due." *Journal of the Association of Teachers of Japanese* 25, no. 2:224–267.

————. 1995. "Language-Games and Rhetorical Skills: Growing Genres Spoken and Written." Unpublished manuscript, The Ohio State University.

Rivers, Wilga, ed. 1992. *Teaching Languages in College: Curriculum and Content.* Lincolnwood, IL: National Textbook Company.

Robeck, Mildred C., and Randall R. Wallace. 1990. *The Psychology of Reading.* 2nd ed. Hillsdale, NJ: Lawrence Erlbaum.

Rogers, Carmen Villegas, and Frank W. Medley. 1988. "Language with a Purpose: Using Authentic Materials in the Foreign Language Classroom." *Foreign Language Annals* 21, no. 5:467–478.

Rubin, Joan, and Irene Thompson. 1982. *How to Be a More Successful Language Learner.* Boston: Heinle and Heinle.

Salzman, Mark. 1986. *Iron & Silk.* New York: Vintage Books.

Sandsbury, Lynne. 1980. "Giving Students the Opportunity to Read." *Journal of the Chinese Language Teachers Association* 15, no. 2:95–110.

Sayeg, Yuki. 1996. "The Role of Sound in Reading Kanji and Kana: A Review." *Australian Review of Applied Linguistics* 19, no. 2:139–151.

Schieffelin, Bambi B., and Elinor Ochs, ed. 1986. *Language Socialization across Cultures.* Vol. 3, Studies in the Social and Cultural Foundations of Language. Cambridge: Cambridge University Press.

Schulz, Renate A. 1984. "Second Language Reading Research: From Theory to Practice." *Foreign Language Annals* 17, no. 4:309–312.

Scollon, Ron, and Suzanne Wong Scollon. 1995. *Intercultural Communication: A Discourse Approach.* Oxford: Blackwell.

Sergent, Wallace K., and Michael E. Everson. 1992. "The Effects of Frequency and Density on Character Recognition Speed and Accuracy by Elementary and Advanced L2 Readers of Chinese." *Journal of the Chinese Language Teachers Association* 27, no. 1:29–44.

Sperber, Dan. 1996. *Explaining Culture: A Naturalistic Approach.* Oxford: Blackwell.

Stempleski, Susan, and Barry Tomalin. 1990. *Video in Action.* New York: Prentice Hall.

Swaffar, Janet. 1985. "Reading Authentic Texts in a Foreign Language: A Cognitive Model." *Modern Language Journal* 69:15–34.

———, and Susan Bacon. 1993. "Reading and Listening Comprehension: Perspectives on Research and Implications for Practice." In *Research in Language Learning: Principles, Processes, and Prospects*, ed. Alice Omaggio Hadley. Lincolnwood, IL: National Textbook Company, 124–155.

Tai, James H-Y. 1978. "Anaphoric Restraints in Mandarin Chinese Narrative Discourse." In *Anaphora in Discourse*, ed. John Hinds. Edmonton, Alberta: Linguistic Research, 279–338.

————. 1989. "Toward a Cognition-Based Functional Grammar of Chinese." In *Functionalism and Chinese Grammar*, ed. James H-Y. Tai and Frank F. S. Hsueh. South Orange, NJ: Chinese Language Teachers Association, 187–226.

Tamamura, Fumio. 1993. "Nihongo Ni Okeru Kanji: Sono Tokushitsu to Kyooiku." *Nihongo Kyooiku* 80:1–14.

Tan-Choy, Chun S., and Huei-ling C. Worthy. 1985. "Description and Determination of ACTFL Chinese Language Speaking Proficiency Levels." *Journal of the Chinese Language Teachers Association* 20, no. 1:85–93.

Taniguchi, Sumiko. 1991. "Shikoo Katei o Dashiau Dokkai Juugyoo: Gakushuusha Sutoratejii No Kansatsu." *Nihongo Kyooiku* 75:37–50.

Tatematsu, Kikuko. 1990. "Jookyuu Gakushuusha Ni Taisuru Dokkai Shidoo." *Nihongo Kyooiku* 72:136–144.

Tateoka, Yoko. 1996. "Bunshoo Koozoo No Chigai Ga Dokkai Ni Oyobosu Eikyoo." *Nihongo Kyooiku* 88:74–90.

Taylor, Insup, and M. Martin Taylor. 1995. *Writing and Literacy in Chinese, Korean and Japanese*. Amsterdam: John Benjamins.

Taylor, John. 1989. *Linguistic Categorization*. Oxford: Clarendon Press.

Tetrault, Emery W. 1984. "In Support of a Natural Order in Second Language Reading." *Foreign Language Annals* 17, no. 4:313–315.

Tohsaku, Yasu-Hiko. 1994. *Yookoso! An Invitation to Contemporary Japanese*. New York: McGraw-Hill.

Tollini, Aldo. "The Importance of Form in the Teaching of Kanji." In *Japanese Language Education around the Globe*. Vol. 4.

Tokyo: The Japan Foundation Japanese Language Institute, 107–116.

Toma, Chikako, and Tamotsu Toshima. 1989. "Developmental Change in Cognitive Organization Underlying Stroop Tasks of Japanese Orthographies." *International Journal of Psychology* 24, no. 5:547–559.

Toyoda, Etsuko. 1995. "Kanji Gakushuu Ni Taisuru Gakushusha No Ishiki." *Nihongo Kyooiku* 85:101–113.

Turner, Frederick. 1985. *Natural Classicism: Essays on Literature and Science.* New York: Paragon House.

Umino, Tae. 1993. "The Role of Nonlinguistic Clues in Inferencing in L2 Listening Comprehension." In *Japanese Language Education around the Globe.* Vol. 3. Tokyo: The Japan Foundation Japanese Language Institute, 31–48.

Unger, J. Marshall, ed. 1997. *Shaping the Next Generation.* Columbus: The Ohio State University Foreign Language Publications.

Walker, Galal. 1982. "Videotext: A Course in Intermediate to Advanced Chinese." *Journal of the Chinese Language Teachers Association* 17, no. 2:109–122.

———. 1985. "Designing Effective Language Training for Professionals." *ADFL Bulletin* 17, no. 1:35–38.

Walton, A. Ronald. 1989. "Chinese Language Instruction in the United States: Some Reflections on the State of the Art." *Journal of the Chinese Language Teachers Association* 24, no. 2:1–42.

———. 1991. "Expanding the Vision of Foreign Language Education: Enter the Less Commonly Taught Languages." In *Critical Issues in Foreign Language Instruction,* ed. Ellen Silber. New York: Garland, 160–185.

————. 1996. "Reinventing Language Fields: The Chinese Case." In *Chinese Pedagogy: An Emerging Field*, ed. Scott McGinnis. Columbus, OH: The Ohio State University Foreign Language Publications, 29–79.

Wang, Alvin Y., and Margaret H. Thomas. 1992. "The Effect of Imagery-Based Mnemonics on the Long-Term Retention of Chinese Characters." *Language Learning* 42, no. 3:359–376.

Wang, Fred Fangyu. 1972. "Problems in Reading Chinese." *Journal of the Chinese Language Teachers Association* 7, no. 3:116–123.

Warnick, J. Paul. 2001. "Reading as Socio-Cultural Performance." In *Advances in Japanese Language Pedagogy*, ed. Hiroshi Nara. Columbus, OH: National East Asian Languages Resource Center, 137–180.

Wenden, Anita, and Joan Rubin, ed. 1987. *Learner Strategies in Language Learning*. Englewood Cliffs, NJ: Prentice Hall International.

Wong, Timothy C. 1990. "On a Core of Agreement in Chinese Language Instruction." *Journal of the Chinese Language Teachers Association* 25, no. 1:85–92.

————. 1994. "The Government Language Paradigm in the Academy: Some Observations." *Journal of the Chinese Language Teachers Association* 29, no. 2:13–22.

Yamada, Jun, Hiroyuki Imai, and Yuji Ikebe. 1990. "The Use of the Orthographic Lexicon in Reading Kana Words." *The Journal of General Psychology* 117:311–323.

Yamada, Minako. 1995. "Dokkai Katei Ni Mirareru Kiyuu Chishiki No Eikyoo to Bunpoo Nooryoku No Kankei Ni Tsuite." *Nihongo Kyooiku* 86:26–38.

Yamamoto, Hirofumi. 1995. "Senmon Nihongo Dokkai Shien Shisutemu No Hyooka to Hoohoo." *Nihongo Kyooiku* 85:90–100.

Yamashita, Sayoko. 1994. "Is the Reading Comprehension Performance of Learners of Japanese as a Second Language the Same as That of Japanese Children? An Analysis Using a Cloze Test." *Japanese Language Education around the Globe.* Vol. 4. Tokyo: The Japan Foundation Japanese Language Institute, 133–146.

Yanagimachi, Tomoharu. 1996a. "The Acquisition of Referential Devices in Japanese by English-Speaking Learners: A Case of First and Second Person Reference." Paper presented at the Second Language Research Forum. Tucson, Arizona.

———. 1996b. "Referential Form Choice in the Oral Narrative Discourse of Native and Non-Native Speakers of Japanese." *The 7th Conference on Second Language Research in Japan.* Niigata, Japan: The Language Programs of the International University of Japan, 59–79.

Yang, Jane Parish. 1993a. "Chinese Children's Stories: Teaching Discourse Strategies for Beginning Chinese." *Journal of the Chinese Language Teachers Association* 28, no. 3:35–47.

———. 1993b. "Kissinger Went to China to Drink Tea— Collaborative Storytelling in Beginning Chinese." *Journal of the Chinese Language Teachers Association* 28, no. 1: 13–24.

———. 1995. "Integrating Authentic Materials into the Intermediate Classroom with Taiwan TV Ads." *Journal of the Chinese Language Teachers Association* 30, no. 1:65–73.

Yang, Ranchang. 1981. "Tonal Pronunciation Errors and Interference from English Intonation." *Journal of the Chinese Language Teachers Association* 16, no. 2:27–56.

Zhang, Dao-yi. 1981. "An Overview of Chinese Language Teaching at the Beijing Language Institute." *Journal of the Chinese Language Teachers Association* 16, no. 2:91–106.

Zvetina, Marina. 1987. "From Research to Pedagogy: What Do L2 Reading Studies Suggest?" *Foreign Language Annals* 20, no. 3:233–238.

Appendices

APPENDIX 1: THE RESTAURANT SCRIPT

We acknowledge that no cultural script is complete without target language dialogue. Because this book is not a language book, we defer the language-specific dialogue of this script to individual teachers as they see appropriate. In the scripts that follow, we focus exclusively on behavioral culture.

Knowing how to behave in a dining situation is extremely important. It will put one's hosts at ease and will enable the participant to feel comfortable knowing what to expect. Knowing what to say in these kinds of situations gives confidence and the ability to participate fully with one's dining associates.

American Cultural Script
The following discussion describes an American cultural script for an average sit-down restaurant in urban American culture, which can range from a Denny's to a very good, expensive restaurant. Though protocols may differ among restaurants, there is a general procedure that is followed. Significant differences are pointed out in the text.

Entering the Restaurant and Getting a Table
Upon entering an American restaurant, one finds oneself in a waiting area, sometimes with chairs or benches. Between the waiting area and the entrance to the restaurant seating area is usually a podium or a small table or counter where a host or hostess greets customers, and asks them how many are in the party and whether they have a reservation. If the restaurant is currently full, the hostess will ask for the name of a person in the party and will write it down on a waiting list. The customers will then sit and wait. Customers who call in advance to make a reservation for a particular time will usually be seated very close to that time. At many restaurants, there is a bar where people can buy a drink and congregate until a table is ready

for them. When a table is ready, the hostess will usually call out the customer's name and the number of people in the party.

Being Seated

The hostess leads the diners to a table. Usually diners do not have a choice about where they sit, though occasionally, the hostess will ask customers whether they have a preference. Sometimes the choice may be offered between a booth and a regular table. If customers are led to a table that they really dislike, it is acceptable to ask the hostess for a different table; however, if the restaurant is very busy and crowded, this type of request is frowned upon. The hostess stays at the table until everyone is seated. She then passes out a menu to each person in the party and explains that a server will come by shortly to take the diners' order.

There are usually two types of tables in American restaurants. Booths consist of a table with fixed padded benches on two sides and a wall or divider on the third, far side. Diners enter from the open end that faces the inner part of the restaurant. There also are standard square, rectangular, or round tables and chairs situated throughout the restaurant. Each table often has a small caddie that holds salt and pepper shakers, little packets of sugar and sugar substitutes (for flavoring coffee), and sometimes a small pitcher of cream, a bottle of ketchup, or other types of condiments, depending on the type of restaurant.

The Server

After the diners have been seated, they will look at the menu for a few minutes (anywhere from five to twenty minutes, depending on the restaurant and how busy it is). Usually diners at more expensive restaurants will be given more time to order. The server will arrive to take the orders. Beverages are also solicited at this time. In the United States, it is common to have a drink before dinner.

The server (male or female) will come to the table and will greet the diners and introduce him- or herself. The way a server treats customers will often determine the amount of the tip left at the end of the meal; therefore, it is in the server's best interest to treat the customers very well. Some servers will be very congenial, chatting and even joking with the customers. After the introduction and some small talk, the server will often describe any specials the restaurant has for that day and ask if the diners are ready to order or if they have any questions about the menu items. If one has not yet decided what to order, it is acceptable to tell the server that a few more minutes are needed. The server will leave and then return in a few minutes to take the order.

Nicer restaurants generally serve complimentary bread with butter, or tortilla chips in Mexican restaurants, which gives diners something to eat while they wait for their meal. Servers may float around the restaurant to refill water glasses, bring more bread or chips, or clear plates and silverware away when diners are finished eating.

The Menu

Menus are typically arranged in the following categories: appetizers, salads, soups, main dishes, chef's specials (an optional category), side dishes, drinks, and desserts.

Appetizers often are ordered first, and are eaten before the main dishes are brought. It is also common in American restaurants to order soup or salad at the beginning of the meal; these also are eaten before the main course arrives. It is customary for each person to order his or her own entree, though the group may decide on some appetizers to share. However, some people also prefer to order and eat their own appetizer themselves. After diners have ordered their meals, the server will collect all the menus and leave. As already mentioned, appetizers will be brought first, followed by soup and/or salad if that was ordered. Many restaurants include a soup or salad (but usually not both) with the main entree.

During the Meal

The server will usually bring all the meals for the party at the same time, or at least within a few minutes of each other. After diners have been eating for a few minutes (maybe five to ten minutes), the server will usually return to ask if everything is okay with the meal. Usually diners will agree that everything is fine, even if they are not completely satisfied with the meal. Reasons for not being satisfied, and that may warrant notifying the server, include receiving something one did not order, receiving food that is under- or overcooked, or finding a foreign object in the food. The server will come back to the table periodically to see if there is anything the diners need—such as something more to drink, or a condiment.

As each diner finishes eating, a server will ask if he or she is finished and will offer to take the plates. Good service requires that plates be removed soon after diners finish eating. When most of the group has finished, the server will ask if anyone is interested in dessert, coffee, or an after-dinner drink (usually an alcoholic beverage). Sometimes there is a separate dessert menu, it may be on the regular menu, or examples of each dessert may be displayed on a cart that is brought to the table to inspect. Whether dessert or drinks are ordered or not, near the end or after everyone has finished eating, the check is brought by the server. In more informal, less expensive restaurants, the check is sometimes brought shortly after the food is served.

Dining Etiquette

In the United States, it is considered rude to burp, slurp, or make any other bodily noise during the meal. It is considered polite to keep elbows off the table and not talk with one's mouth full. For most people, it is acceptable to talk freely during dinner, and business may be conducted over a meal in a restaurant. All food and any other scraps of food, such as bones, shells, and so on, are kept on one's individual plate. It is not acceptable to put these items directly on the table. If a diner needs something on the table that is not within reach, it is appropriate to ask politely for a companion to pass it around. A diner could say something like "John, please pass the pepper" or "Could you pass the pepper please?"

After the Meal/Paying the Check

In most American restaurants, a meal is paid in two ways: either from the table, or directly to a cashier near the entrance to the restaurant. It is not difficult to figure out which procedure should be followed: If the server brings the bill in a folder or on a small plastic tray, the money for the bill (or a charge card) and the bill are generally put in the folder or on the tray, and then the server will come by and pick it up. The change will be brought back a few minutes later. If the bill is presented alone, the standard procedure is to leave a tip on the table and then take the bill to the cashier and pay directly. At nicer, more expensive restaurants, the bill is paid from the table. Less expensive restaurants will require that customers go to the cashier to pay the bill.

Leftover food is often taken home to eat later. This is particularly true of more expensive restaurants. If there is food remaining, it is appropriate to ask the server for a "doggie bag" or a box. He or she will then return with a paper or styrofoam box. Sometimes the diner will put the food in the container, or the server may take the plates and return with the leftover food in the take-out box.

Tipping

Tips for servers are expected at sit-down restaurants in the United States. Standard tipping practices recommend leaving at least 15% of the total cost of the meal. If there is a large number of people in the party, usually eight or more, the tip will automatically be included in the bill. Exceptionally good service may be rewarded with a 20% or more tip. The tip can be added to the bill if you are paying with a credit card, or left on the table when paying with cash. It is considered rude and unacceptable not to leave a tip or to leave a very small tip, unless the service was truly terrible.

Leaving the Restaurant

When diners are ready to leave, the server will typically thank them for coming, again asking if everything was to their satisfaction. Before they leave the restaurant, the host/hostess also will ask the diners if everything was okay and thank them for coming to the restaurant, and then wish them a nice day or evening or other such pleasantries.

Chinese Cultural Script

Next we describe the script for a typical sit-down, casual restaurant in China; in more expensive formal restaurants, service and eating etiquette will differ slightly.

When invited out by a Chinese friend or associate, it is important to wear nice clothes. Appearances are very important to the Chinese. Dressing up for friends or associates tells them that the relationship is valued and that one feels honored to be their guest.

Entering the Restaurant and Getting a Table

In China, restaurants may or may not have a reception area to wait in for a table. Often upon entering a restaurant, one will be in the middle of the dining room. There typically is not a host/hostess to greet diners or to seat them. In a Chinese restaurant, diners are expected to find their own place to sit.

Tables

In most Chinese restaurants, (not including very small, informal restaurants), tables are large and round and seat anywhere from eight to ten diners. Smaller groups share a table. Chinese restaurants tend to be quite busy, thus the space between tables may only be wide enough for a single person to walk through. Round tables almost always have a lazy Susan in the middle, which facilitates the Chinese style of family dining. There are usually no condiments on a Chinese table, though there may be small bottles of soy sauce and/or hot sauce. One will find small ceramic teacups and chopsticks at each place (or they are brought shortly after the group is seated).

After the diners are seated, tea is often served while they are deciding what to order. Like water automatically served in American restaurants, there is no charge for tea in a Chinese restaurant.

The Server

The server's role in a Chinese restaurant is simply to bring the food to the diners. After diners have seated themselves (the time will depend on the restaurant and how busy it is), the server will arrive with a few menus. It is not customary to give each person a menu; for a party of six or eight, usually one or two menus will be passed out. Often one person, or perhaps two, is designated to order the meal. Often the person of honor, perhaps the guest, is selected by the host to order the dishes, although there may be a bit of friendly bantering about who should order. It is considered somewhat of an honor to order the dishes for a meal. After the party agrees what to order, the server will take the order and collect the menus. If diners have questions for the server or if they need anything, they must call out to the server or motion for him or her to come help out. Normally the server does not check regularly on the table as in a Western restaurant, except in very nice restaurants.

If appetizers are available, they are ordered separately so they can be eaten while diners are waiting for the main meal to come. It is more common for Chinese to drink alcoholic beverages during a meal rather than before and after as is common in the United States.

Chinese Dining

Eating in a Chinese restaurant is a group experience. Unlike in American restaurants, diners order several different dishes and everyone shares them. This is the reason for the lazy Susan—easy access for everyone to all the ordered dishes.

Chinese dishes are brought out as they are prepared. It is not uncommon for some dishes to be completely consumed before others are brought out. In many parts of China, particularly in the South, plain steamed white rice is eaten with a meal. Rice is usually not brought automatically; one must order it when ordering the other dishes. Usually one's rice bowl will be refilled without any extra charge. Each diner will have his or her own individual rice bowl. Plates are typically not supplied unless one is at a Chinese fast-food establishment, where food is often served heaped on a large plate and eaten by one person with a spoon or sometimes with a spoon in conjunction with chopsticks.

Everyone eats off the plates in the center of the table. Sometimes a serving spoon is supplied with each dish. If so, it is appropriate to dish food directly into your rice bowl. Usually one dish at a time is eaten in this way, and each person usually takes only a small amount. Sometimes diners will use their chopsticks to transfer food from the platter to their rice bowl.

The host of the party may serve guests from the dishes in the center of the table. For example, if someone is visiting a friend in China, or a friend takes a guest out to eat at a restaurant, the friend might select especially good pieces of meat or vegetables and put them in the guest's bowl with his or her chopsticks. In situations like this, it is polite to express gratitude to the person who has done the serving.

From small, private restaurants to large, state-owned ones, many restaurants have private dining rooms with large tables, open spaces, and karaoke facilities for diners. Large groups use these rooms for social occasions.

A Chinese Menu

A typical Chinese menu is arranged by the category of dish. It may begin with chef's specials, then the following categories are usually found, though not necessarily in this order: appetizers, seafood, poultry, pork, beef, vegetable and vegetarian dishes (sometimes bean curd dishes are listed in their own category), fried rice, noodle dishes (sometimes separated by fried noodles and soft noodles in broth), soup, beverages. Menus can be very challenging to understand for the first-time visitor to China. The names of Chinese dishes often are quite fancy, even beautiful, but they are not necessarily understandable by each word in the name. You may get a general idea about what the dish is by looking at the name, but you may not be able to tell what the ingredients are.

Chinese Eating Etiquette

When eating a Chinese meal, whether in a restaurant or at someone's home, there are several rules of etiquette that should be followed.

• The lazy Susan in the middle of the table is designed for a group eating experience. Diners should not reach across the table to serve themselves food. It is polite to eat those dishes that are close to oneself, within easy reach. When the food is rotated, then one may select dishes within easy reach.

• If one is eating meat that is on the bone or shellfish, it is appropriate to pile the bones, shells, or other nonedible items neatly at the top of the table or to the side of one's rice bowl. Often at home, the Chinese will spread newspaper on the table before a meal. Cleaning up then involves simply rolling up the newspaper (with the bones, shells, and other scraps) and throwing it away. It is not appropriate to put bones in one's rice bowl.

• Fish is usually served whole—with the head, tail, and fins intact. When one side of the fish has been consumed, the complete fish is turned over with chopsticks to gain access to the other side. Diners should not dig through the bones to get to the meat on the other side of the fish.

• It is important that individual chopsticks are free of grains of rice or other bits of food before taking food from the dishes in the center of the table. The reasons for this are obvious.

•   It is considered impolite to place chopsticks in one's rice perpendicular to the table. This action is associated with Buddhist funeral rites.

•   It is acceptable to burp, slurp, or make other sounds of satisfaction with one's mouth while at the Chinese dining table. It is also acceptable to place one's elbows on the table.

•   The individual rice bowl should be held in the diner's hand and brought close to the mouth when eating rice. Often, the bowl is brought to the lips and the rice is "shoveled" in; this prevents grains of rice from falling on the table. One must avoid the temptation to lift the rice from the bowl on the table—doing so will most likely make a mess.

•   It is not polite to take the last thing on a plate. It is best to first offer the remaining food to someone else, even picking up the plate or the food item with one's chopsticks and physically offering it to another diner. That person will almost always refuse and suggest that another diner eat it. If one is truly not hungry, it may be offered to someone else. If someone offers the last of a dish, one should politely decline several times, perhaps suggesting that someone else eat it. If the offers are persistent, one should politely accept after refusing it several times.

•   When serving soup with a large serving spoon, it is polite to dip the spoon into the pot from the back—that is, dip the spoon into the soup from the back edge of the spoon to the front. When drinking soup with one's own spoon, it is considered polite to sip from the side of the spoon, and not put the whole spoon in one's mouth.

•   Often no drinks (other than hot tea) are offered at a Chinese meal. The Chinese generally believe that drinking during a meal is not good for digestion. They will drink tea before and after a meal, but it is not a common practice to drink cold beverages during a meal, even in the heat of the summer. Water is typically not served at Chinese restaurants, unless one does not drink tea and specifically requests "boiled water."

•   It is polite to accept whatever a Chinese host or friend offers. It does not mean that one has to eat a lot of it, but declining an offer of food or drink may hurt the host's feelings. It is better to accept something, rather than nothing. For example, if a diner who does not drink tea for some reason (perhaps religious reasons) is offered tea, it is best to simply indicate that he or she does not drink tea but would like some "boiled water" or other readily available beverage.

• Diners should always be very appreciative and offer thanks to those who have hosted the dinner. They should mention that the hosts shouldn't have gone to so much trouble, that they have really been inconvenienced, and so on.

• When a meal is over, diners typically clean their teeth with toothpicks provided at the table. One should be careful cover the mouth with a hand while cleaning teeth; it is considered rude to clean teeth without obstructing the view with a hand.

• A meal will often be concluded with fresh fruit, such as watermelon or oranges. Dessert generally is not served in Chinese restaurants or even after a meal at a Chinese home.

Concluding the Meal and Paying the Check

At the end of a meal, one must ask the server to bring the bill; it most likely will not be brought automatically. To the Chinese, eating is a very social affair sometimes lasting for hours. Therefore, when the party is ready to leave, they are expected to request the bill. Paying the bill at a Chinese restaurant is a memorable experience. Because of the Chinese group orientation, it is considered an honor to be able to pay the bill for a group of friends. It is very common for an argument to erupt over who will pay the bill. Typically, several in the party will offer and will banter with each other for this privilege. Paying the bill brings some prestige and honor to a person. Sometimes the arguing can get fairly vigorous, with money pushed into another's hands, then thrown back, and so forth. In the end, one person will pay the bill. It is not customary, even among a group of friends, for everyone to pitch in and split the bill. Chinese friends will play this game of offering to pay the bill even if they know they will not, in the end, do so. There is an informal order that says the person who pays the bill this time will not be expected to pay the next time. Everyone usually takes turns paying the bill. Nevertheless, it is still important to offer to pay, and to banter with the others who will also be offering to pay. After the bill has been paid, sincere thanks are offered to the person who eventually paid. When visiting a friend in China, he or she will almost certainly pay for the meals, even if it is a financial burden. The Chinese view this as their responsibility to take care of their guest while they are visiting.

Tipping is not required or expected at Chinese restaurants. The insistence on leaving a tip will usually make the Chinese uncomfortable. In other service industries such as hotels, service charges are usually automatically added to the price.

Japanese Cultural Script
Appropriate behavior in a Japanese restaurant will depend on the kind of restaurant that is being visited. More expensive, Western-style restaurants will be more like Western restaurants than traditional Japanese restaurants. Likewise, fast-food establishments will also be slightly different than typical traditional Japanese restaurants.

Reservations
In typical Japanese restaurants, it is ordinarily a good idea to make reservations, even though it is not required for small groups. When customers make reservations, the restaurant will ask for the name, the number in the party, and a telephone number. If it is a set menu, the order can be given in advance. If a restaurant has tables and chairs as well as *tatami* mats (woven bamboo mats as a floor covering), customers may request their preference. One may also request private rooms, if they are available. There is usually no additional charge for a private room.

Being Seated
One may not proceed to the table unescorted. The server will escort diners to the room; thus diners wait near the entrance area until that time. When it is crowded, the customers state their name, the number in the party, and smoking preference and then wait on the seats in the entry area.

Rooms are divided by sliding doors. Most rooms have an alcove in which a flower arrangement and a seasonal hanging scroll are displayed. The scrolls, which are changed seasonally, are intended as a means to appreciate the season; they show scenery, calligraphy, or floral depictions.

Some restaurants require customers to remove their shoes and thus have slippers available for them. In this case, customers are given an exchange receipt and a number ticket.

Western-style tables and chairs at fast-food restaurants are arranged in the same way as in Western restaurants. Diners at a very expensive Japanese restaurant called *ryootei* usually sit on *tatami* mats with *zabuton* (cushions) and armrests. Most Japanese restaurants have *tatami* mats, but in *hori-gotatsu*–style restaurants, diners sit on the floor at a low, Japanese-style table with a hole cut into the floor below the table for diners' legs to drop into rather than sitting on one's feet in traditional style; the hole in the floor prevents diners' feet from going to sleep.

At the Table
After seating the group, the server will take orders for (alcoholic) drinks. Diners may look at beverage menus in ordering. At the same time, dining menus are distributed. Depending on the time period, the menus may also include special menus such as the lunch menu or seasonal menus. Water or tea is almost always served. These may be served when the menus are received, while diners are looking at the menus, or immediately after ordering, depending on the restaurant. The tables are provided with chopsticks, a chopstick rest, glasses and *sake* (rice wine) cups, and a steamed hand towel. It is appropriate to wipe your face as well as your hands with the towel. The towel is not usually taken away until a diner has finished eating. Diners usually receive a hot towel before they eat, and at better restaurants, either a hot or cold one after they eat.

The Menu
Hors d'oeuvres are served together with the *sake*. These items generally are not listed on the menu because they usually consist of vegetables or fish in season and thus depend on what is available at market that day. Following the hors d'oeuvres, each course is brought in order. The timing of each course depends on the restaurant, but there usually is not a long wait in between. After each person is served, the server may explain the dish briefly. With dishes that are difficult to eat, there is also an explanation about how to proceed. Diners generally use the same pair of chopsticks for the entire meal. However, the chopsticks are not placed on the plate; instead, they are placed on the chopstick rest.

Menus are usually given to all the diners, but in most cases, the host orders the various dishes. For a very expensive restaurant, the order must be placed when the reservation is made. The menu will be known by the type of restaurant it is. In this case, entrée menus are not provided, but a menu of alcoholic beverages is usually brought to the table. When a boss or another person invites a guest to a restaurant and it is expected that he or she will pay for the meal, it is important for that person to order first; then the guest must *never* order anything more expensive. To do so would be very impolite.

In Japanese restaurants, each diner usually has his or her own dish(es), unlike in Chinese restaurants where the food is served and eaten family style. Japanese food is served in various kinds and shapes of serving dishes. It is said that the Japanese eat with their eyes, so the dishes used to serve the food and how the food is arranged in them are very important. Food preparation and arrangement approach an art form in Japan.

Rice is generally served toward the end of the meal, together with hot tea and a new steamed hand towel. Following this, seasonal fruit is served as dessert.

Servers
Most servers are dressed in traditional Japanese clothing. There is usually at least one server per room. Servers are typically very polite. Casual chit-chat is not common between the server and the diners, though a server may ask questions such as, "What's the occasion?" or "Is this a company gathering?" Tips are not expected; the tax and service fee are included in the price.

Table Manners
• Burping is considered rude in Japanese culture, though slurping is accepted in some cases. Noodles in Japan such as *udon*, *soba*, or *raamen* are supposed to be eaten
in soups, and slurping is appropriate. When Japanese eat soup without noodles, it is considered rude to slurp.
• If there happen to be bones in a meat dish (there usually are not), diners can cover their mouths with a napkin while taking bones out with their other hand.

• Japanese usually do not eat the shells of shellfish. Normally the meat is taken out of the shell with chopsticks. Holding the shell with your hand while doing so is common.

Paying the Check

The bill is usually brought to the table after all the dishes have been served. The customer then carries the bill to the payment counter near the entrance to pay. At some restaurants, diners do not receive a bill but instead are expected to go to the cashier directly and pay there when finished eating. Some restaurants have a display near the payment counter with items customers can take home, such as homemade pickles, dressing, and specialty foods. If shoes were checked, the number ticket and receipt are returned and the shoes are received. After payment is made, both the customers and the restaurant personnel express thanks, and the customers leave.

APPENDIX 2: COMPARATIVE CHART OF PERFORMED CULTURE, AUDIOLINGUALISM AND COMMUNICATIVE LANGUAGE LEARNING

Comparison between the audiolingual approach, the communicative approach, and the performed culture approach. The audiolingual and communicative portions are adapted from Richards and Rodgers (1986, 67–68).

Audiolingual	Communicative	Performed Culture
Focus on structure and form	Focus on meaning	Focus on contextualized meaning within cultural context
Memorization of structure-based dialogues	Dialogues not memorized; centered on communicative functions	Memorized dialogues based on authentic cultural situations
Language items not necessarily contextualized	Contextualization is primary	Contextualization within authentic cultural scripts
Language learning means learning sounds, words, or structures	Language learning means learning to communicate	Language learning means learning to behave appropriately in the target culture
Mastery or overlearning is the goal	Effective communication is the goal	Effective, authentic, and accurate linguistic and social behavior is the goal
Drilling is a central technique	Drilling may occur, but peripherally	Drilling is used as a build-up to more authentic communicative exercises
Native speaker–like pronunciation is the	Comprehensible pronunciation is the	Accurate, nativelike pronunciation is the

goal	goal	goal
Grammar explanations are avoided	Any device that helps the learner is accepted—varying according to age, interest, etc.	Grammar explanations are useful with an appropriate balance between ACT and FACT classes
Communicative activities come only after a long process of rigid drills and exercises	Attempts to communicate may be encouraged from the very beginning	Authentic communication is encouraged from the very beginning within structured models
Use of the student's native language is prohibited	Judicious use of native language is accepted where feasible	Use of native language is acceptable only during FACT sessions
Translation is forbidden at early levels	Translation may be used where students need or benefit from it	Translation may be used peripherally
Reading and writing are deferred until speech is mastered	Reading and writing can start from the first day, if desired	Reading and writing is deferred until a foundation in oral and aural skills has been attained
The target linguistic system is learned through the overt teaching of patterns of the system	The target linguistic system is learned best through the process of struggling to communicate	The target linguistic systems and cultural behavior is learned through an appropriate balance of performance (ACT) and lecture (FACT)
Linguistic competence is the desired goal	Communicative competence is the desired goal (i.e., the ability to use the	Authentic cultural behavior, both linguistic and nonlinguistic, is the

	linguistic system effectively and appropriately)	desired goal
Varieties of language are recognized, but not emphasized	Linguistic variation is a central concept in materials and methodology	Linguistic variation is important as it relates to authentic cultural behavior
The sequence of units is determined solely by principles of linguistic complexity	Sequencing is determined by any consideration of content, function, or meaning that maintains interest in learners	Sequencing is determined by both linguistic complexity and important social and cultural scripts
The teacher controls the learners and prevents them from doing anything that conflicts with the theory	Teachers help learners in any way that motivates them to work with the language	The teacher functions like a theatical director, guiding, coaching, and correcting in culturally authentic performances
"Language is habit," so errors must be prevented at all costs	Language is created by the individual learner, often through trial and error	Language is created by modeling, coaching, and correcting in cultural performances
Accuracy, in terms of correct use of form, is a primary goal	Fluency and acceptable language are the primary goals; accuracy is judged not in the abstract but based on the context	Authentic cultural accuracy is the primary goal: nativelike performances and comfort for the native interlocutor, not mere acceptable language, are strived for
Students are expected to interact with the language	Students are expected to interact with other people, either in the	Students are expected to take advantage of language models

system, embodied in the forms that students are to use	flesh through pair and group work, or in their writings	provided through video and audio, as well as have regular interaction with the teacher and other students
The teacher is expected to specify the language that students are to use	The teacher cannot know exactly what language the students will use	In early instruction, the teacher specifies what language to use based on authentic models; as learners progress, more and more freedom is allowed to personalize the communicative performances
Intrinsic motivation will spring from an interest in the structure of the language	Intrinsic motivation will spring from an interest in what is being communicated by the language	Intrinsic motivation will spring from an interest in the culture and native behavior in the target environment and the desire to communicate with natives in that environment

Index

Pronunciation, 8, 24-5, 37-8, 43, 47,
49-54, 57, 63, 65, 78-85, 88-92,
94-6, 99, 102, 104, 107, 109,
112-4, 117, 119, 124, 128, 152,
178, 186, 189

R

Reading, 8, 11, 26, 35-7, 41-3,
45-55, 60-1, 63-6, 69-70, 73,
104, 107-8, 112-31, 167-8,
170-2, 183-5, 189-91, 193

Realia, 119-20

Restaurant script, 26-8, 59,

Role of student, 69, 70

Role play, 154, 178-9

Roles, 17, 19, 25-7, 33-4, 42, 59, 61,
69, 74, 77, 144, 166, 171, 174,178,
183, 188-9

Romanization, 33, 48-53, 56-7, 113,
119, 169, 188-9

S

Scaffolding, 62-3, 101, 156, 161

Script, 9, 19, 21, 24-34, 47, 49-51,
53-6, 59, 73, 77, 102, 144, 153,
161, 174, 188

Second language, 5, 15, 47, 58, 86,
112, 122, 134, 136

shūmiànyǔ, 40, 46, 185

Skill mix, 42, 44, 109

Speech, 6, 20, 36-43, 46, 66, 68, 86,
88-9, 93, 95-8, 101-2, 104-5,
108, 134-5, 181

Spoken language, 8, 33, 36-8, 40-3,
45-7, 49, 53-5, 73, 97, 107, 109,
114, 119, 171, 185, 188

Strategy, 34, 43, 46, 108, 117,127-8,
135-6, 140, 147, 150, 152-3, 177,
185

Syllabus, 25

T

Target culture, 10, 15, 20-5, 27, 31,
41, 44-6, 59, 62, 66, 68, 71, 73, 79,
82, 85, 90, 92-3, 95-6, 98, 100,
118-9, 121, 123, 125-9, 140, 176,
178, 180, 187

Target language, 5, 7, 18, 20, 32,
36, 43, 45, 48-9, 55, 58-9, 61, 64,
66, 69, 74, 79, 83, 91, 94, 98, 103,
108, 117, 128-9, 134-7, 140-1,
144, 150, 153, 155, 160, 164, 169,
174, 179, 188-9, 191

Task-based instruction, 160

Teacher, 13, 17-8, 33, 60-1, 63,
65-70, 69, 74, 77-8, 88, 91, 95, 97,
100-1, 103-4, 115, 118, 123-4,
126,128-9, 141, 150, 155, 157,
159, 163-4, 167-70, 176-8, 181-4,
186-93

Teacher training, 187, 192

Text, 28, 34-7, 40-1, 44-7, 50, 52,
54, 69, 75-6, 104-5, 109, 111-3,
115-30, 139, 157, 159, 163-7, 170,
180, 182-5, 189-90, 193

Tones, 47, 80, 85-92

為我
餵我

糕點
高點